# JOHN XXIII AND AMERICAN
PROTESTANTS

# John XXIII and American Protestants

BY

## EUGENE C. BIANCHI

*with a foreword by*

ALBERT C. OUTLER

CORPUS BOOKS
*Washington—Cleveland*

*To my Mother and Father*

*with Filial Affection*

Corpus Instrumentorum, Inc.
1330 Massachusetts Ave., N.W.
Washington, D.C. 20005

First Printing 1968

# *Foreword*

After every turning point in history, men need to have it put in just perspective, lest its meaning be blurred and the opportunities it has created be lost or forfeited. No one any longer doubts that the pontificate of John XXIII was such a turning point in modern church history or that the ecumenical council he summoned and launched has opened a new chapter in the life of the Christian community.

But already it is difficult to see it all steadily and whole. We have begun to forget how unexpected the half-decade between 1958 and 1963 really was. We have begun already to lose sight of the improbable fact that a peasant-pope would succeed a Roman nobleman and launch the Roman Catholic Church upon an uncharted venture in renewal whose repercussions have only just begun to be felt. Now that Vatican II has achieved so much, it is easy to forget how little we expected of it. We have begun to take the new ecumenical situation for granted, without reminding ourselves of how much we owe to a man whose goodness was so guileless and whose love so effortless. Thus we are in danger of underestimating the shock it gave to Protestants who had for so long assumed that their relations with Rome had been *fixed* forever, by the anathemas of Trent, by the papal dogmas, by the Canon Laws against fraternizing with "schismatics, heretics, and apostates," by the strictures of *Mortalium Animos*, and more. But if we forget all this, we shall fail to appreciate the full effect and import of the Johannine revolution and thus misconstrue the issues and opportunities that press on us now in the post-conciliar period.

For generations, Protestants had been taught on good authority that the Roman position was invariable and non-negotiable, that the teachings of papal encyclicals were beyond appeal or revision, that another general council after Vatican I would be redundant. Then came Pope John and his calling of what promised to be just such a council. It was, therefore, not surprising that we could scarcely comprehend the series of unlikely events that followed or that we were unsettled by the shattering of our anti-Roman stereotypes and the spoiling of our anti-Roman prejudices. We have scarcely begun to respond to the challenges of Vatican II. The post-conciliar ferment among Catholics has not been contained within the limits of the Catholic Church; its feedback continues to affect every aspect of church life in America and elsewhere.

In such a time of flux and transition, it is important to repair our memories of how it all began—how the situation actually was before Pope John and his Council, how the ecumenical prospects seemed then, how the new vision of the future of the Christian community emerged and took shape. It is this refreshment of memory that Father Bianchi has provided for us in this interesting and important book. In it we have a vivid recapturing of a significant aspect of American church history in one of its most decisive short spans, with special attention paid to the various ways American Protestants reacted to the strange new events in Rome—and at home! At just the right moment, Professor Bianchi has caught and recorded the motifs and shifts in this syndrome of relations and has set it down for all to see. The result is a historical account of uncommon current interest and one that will continue to be a useful resource for future historians in their efforts to understand the epoch of which Pope John is both symbol and agent.

There are two obvious audiences for such a survey. One, of course, consists of Catholics who are interested in seeing themselves as they appeared to Protestant eyes before the new situation had been fully realized. On the other side are Protestants who may have forgotten, or suppressed, their preconciliar biases and their original astigmatisms. Both groups are well served by Bianchi's narrative. Those who will read it with some care will be better prepared for the ongoing ecumenical dialogue—partly because it shows how far we have moved in six years, partly because it suggests how much further we have yet to go.

The most important service I can offer here is a Protestant's testimony that Father Bianchi's study is a reliable one, balanced and fair. It checks out, not only with my memories of those days, but also with my diaries and notes at the time. Our author has waded through a huge file of church periodicals (and books) from which he has culled, patiently and carefully, a substantial and well-ordered summary of Protestant editorial opinion, "conservative" and "liberal," on most of the obvious issues as these were seen and judged in the period from 1958 to 1963—their estimates of Pope John and his concern for *aggiornamento* (updating the Church), his unexpected offers of friendship to non-Catholics, the curious overlap of the Johannine papacy and the Kennedy campaign and election, the generally belated changes in Protestant attitudes and moods as the Council progressed, the perplexities and challenges of the resulting situation in the light of the debates about ecumenism and religious liberty. Everyone knows that religious journalism has a high ratio of straw to grain and that the threshing of the grain is a tedious business. But tedious labor sometimes pays off, and it has done so handsomely in this book. Through the merits of Bianchi's drudgery, we now can come to terms with at least a part of our ecumenical past in preparation for our future in the ecumenical dialogue.

A fair sample of the anti-Catholic biases of American Protestants is here laid out without partisan accusation or apology. The citations are accurate and broadly representative, and are not marshaled in defense of a special editorial thesis. What is missing, however—though everywhere assumed—is the tragic prehistory of Protestant-Catholic relations before Pope John and the psychological grounds for Protestant reactions toward Rome. And yet it is this prehistory that we must recover and transvalue if we are to transcend it. We need to remember how the old wounds were first opened and then cicatrized and how their scar tissues came to be sanctified. We need to be aware of how deeply the defense mechanisms of the wars of religion had come to be second nature on both sides. The "new-breed" Catholic needs the exercise of trying to understand how stanch and assured the Protestant stereotypes about Rome were in 1958—how certain we were that she still stood by the maxim of Constance that good faith need not be kept with heretics (viz., *us!*), that the anathemas of Trent and the strictures of Canon Law remained unmitigated, that Rome's unswerving goal was temporal dominance and papal absolutism, that she was un-reformed in fact and irreformable in principle. Beneath it all was the residue of doubt, inherited from the reformers them-selves, that Rome understood the gospel or really cared to be obedient to it: God's utter sovereignty, the sheer gratuity of his mercy and pardon, the all-sufficiency of Christ's mediation and grace, the primacy of faith, the untrammeled authority of holy Scripture.

During the past half-century, this Catholic-Protestant alienation had come to be relatively polite, but it was still virtually absolute on both sides, governed by conditioned reflexes and caricatures. Few on either side were disposed to expose themselves to the others, and there was no reasonable hope of real reconciliation in the foreseeable future. I still remember being startled by Pope Paul VI's first allocution—at the opening of Session Two—when he spoke of his concern for mutual repentance and forgiveness for the wrongs of this bitter past:

> We speak now to the representatives of the Christian denomi-nations separated from the Catholic church, who have never-theless been invited to take part as observers in this solemn

assembly. We greet them from our heart. We thank them for
their participation. We transmit through them our message as
father and brother to the venerable Christian communities they
represent.

Our voice trembles and our heart beats the faster both
because of the inexpressible consolation and reasonable hope
their presence stirs up within us as well as because of the deep
sadness we feel at their prolonged separation.

If we are in any way to blame for that separation, we humbly
beg God's forgiveness and ask pardon, too, of our brethren who
feel themselves to have been injured by us. For our part, we
willingly forgive the injuries which the Catholic church has suffered and forget the grief endured through the long series of dis-
sensions and separations. May the heavenly Father deign to hear
our prayers and grant us true brotherly peace.

The point is that, as I listened, *spontaneous* examples leapt to my
mind of Catholic crimes against Protestants—after which it took
a full moment of *conscious recall* to match *that* tally with a
comparable one of Protestant crimes against Catholics. For
example, it was as "instinctive" for me to dredge up the stereotype of "Bloody Mary" as it must have been for the English
monsignor at my elbow (who lived in the Venerable English
College on the Via Montserrato) to remember the forty alumni
of his college who had been done to death by "Good Queen
Bess."

It is not, therefore, surprising that when Pope John opened
his heart and arms to his separated brethren and summoned a
general council concerned with Christian unity, the professional
guardians of the Protestant tradition reacted warily. Professor
Bianchi traces the fever chart of their reactions, itemizing their
suspicions one by one and marking off the slow changes that followed, as the generality of Protestant editors swung round to
recognize and welcome the new day dawning in Catholic-Protestant relations. The analysis of this complex response to the
unexpected is the most edifying and valuable contribution of
this book.

It begins with the impact of the personality of Pope John

on American public opinion, moves quickly to a review of the remarkable coincidence of the Kennedy campaign and election, and then comes to a climax with a summary of Protestant responses to the emerging prospects of a "progressive" victory at Vatican II. The story closes with the Council half concluded and with the Protestant reactions still unfolding, but it does take us past the point of no return in the Council's history, past the conscious closure of "the Counter-Reformation era" in the Roman Catholic Church, into the first pages of the new chapter in church history that Vatican II began to write, in which the thrust toward the recovery of Christian unity was clearly a dominant factor.

Looking backward now, many may be as intrigued as I was by Professor Bianchi's evidence that, in the beginning at least, the gap between the anti-Catholic biases of Protestant "conservatives" and "liberals" was not nearly as wide on this as on other issues. The "liberals" responded heartily to Pope John's friendliness, but there was a sizable company of them who continued to sound their warnings that the Roman reality remained unchanged and that neither pope nor Council could change *that*. It is a phenomenon worth noticing that men who had outgrown their ethnic and racial prejudices, who could be counted on to support most good causes for civil rights and human brotherhood, should still have retained without embarrassment a lively residue of their old-fashioned anti-Roman prejudice. It is good to have on record Bianchi's quotations from such well-known "liberals" as H. P. Van Dusen, Harold Bosley, J. H. Nichols, and others and to notice how curiously similar they sound to the statements of stanch fundamentalists like E. S. James or militant anti-Romans like Glenn Archer.

On the one hand, this wariness reflected the depth and fervor of Protestant fears of Rome. On the other hand, it reflected the anxieties of men who had been severely shaken by the unexpected renewal in the Roman Catholic Church and its import for Protestantism. Even yet, we are in the preliminary stages of the Protestant effort to match the achievements of Vatican II with something like equivalent ventures in self-understanding and reform. The stereotypes that served us so long are not easily discarded even by men of reason and good will. Thus, for example, last June, a Lutheran professor suggested that since Vatican II had altered Rome's ecumenical stance, it was at least reasonable that Protestants should reconsider their relations with Rome and recanvass the possibility of reunion (not by "return" but "convergence"). It was a liberal "ecumenical weekly," *Christian Century*, that brusquely dismissed any such notion with a tart editorial entitled "Protestant Hara-kiri!"

It is, of course, a commonplace that Vatican II made poor prophets of us all, in either camp. This was inevitable, as we can see now, for the Council was the dynamic focus of a quite unprecedented constellation of momentous events that "made history" faster than anyone could grasp it: the "man sent from God whose name was John," the election of a Roman Catholic to the American presidency and the subsequent proof that he was not a clerical puppet, the entrance of the Orthodox churches into the World Council of Churches (at New Delhi in 1961), the dramatic reversals in Session One of Vatican II, the election of Giovanni-Battista Montini and his decisive leadership in guiding the Council to a successful climax—and all of this in the midst of a world-wide revolution that was, and still is, making a mockery of merely nominal Christianity. The lasting value of Bianchi's project is that he recognized this as the "fullness of time" it was and that he found a significant prism through which to view and measure it. Thus he has turned a mountainous pile of research notes into a readable, reliable narrative with focus, depth, and insight. The result is a slice of good history— a tale of immediate interest to those who wish to rehearse their own recent pasts, and yet also a permanent resource for those who will come hereafter with questions about the texture and feel of a great event that shaped their destiny as well as ours.

I confess a mild frustration that the story is here concluded *before* all the returns were in (i.e., at the end of Session Two). What this suggests, obviously, is that we need something like a sequel that would continue the survey through the conclusion of the Council and into the initial stages of the post-conciliar epoch. Here we have the story of Protestant reactions *before* the Council was an assured success. Even so, as Father Bianchi shows, there was a significant change in temper and insight among Protestants as they became aware of the miracle of Vatican II. But what happened to the American Protestant mind during Sessions Three and Four and in the early stages of the post-conciliar epoch, as the ecumenical dialogue began to spread and stir in Catholic seminaries, parishes, and chanceries? How are Protestants facing up, or failing to face up, to the challenges and opportunities for ecumenical cooperation and self-renewal in the light of the post-conciliar developments? It is, perhaps, greedy to ask for more than Professor Bianchi has given us here, but since he has done the first half of the job with such skill and sensitivity, it is clear that he could carry the same story forward toward a more decisive terminus. This greatly needs doing—and no one could do it better.

As Pope Paul said in his farewell address to the observers, the *ecumenical* victory of Vatican II was its prompting of separated Christian brethren to new ventures of love for one another, a renewed belief in the possibility of Christian unity as an actual prospect in some real future. There are, of course, grave issues that remain at loggerheads; there are ancient negations that still have to be revoked without compromise; there are old problems that will yield only to creatively new solutions not yet proposed. It was given to Pope John to be the agent of the first miracle that reopened the dialogue. But other miracles are still required before its fruition is assured. The veterans of the old era can rejoice in its passing, but they are not likely to see and occupy "the promised land" themselves. It will take another generation or so to reap the full harvest of the Johannine revolution, and even they will find themselves in urgent need of the wisdom and hope that come from sound history. They, and we, need to distinguish between conviction and bias, between immutable truth and the possibility of its transformed manifestation. Professor Bianchi's story of "how it was" can serve as a guide to *how it may be*. It is, therefore, triply useful: as a mirror of the past, as a warning to all over-zealous defenders of the past now outmoded, and as a stimulus to those who have come to realize that the gracious Providence that has brought us so much further than we ever dreamed surely means to lead us on toward that unity God wills for us and that He will one day provide.

> Professor Albert C. Outler
> *Perkins School of Theology*
> *Southern Methodist University*
> *Dallas, Texas*

# Acknowledgements

I am deeply grateful to Professor Robert T. Handy of New York Union Theological Seminary for his invaluable guidance and encouragement in the preparation of this book. The completed work owes much to Professor Handy's wisdom and critical suggestions. I also wish to thank Professor Thomas F. O'Dea of the University of California, Santa Barbara and Professor Joseph L. Blau of Columbia University for their assistance in this project. In addition to the librarians at Union Theological, I am indebted to the helpful California librarians of San Francisco Theological Seminary, Golden Gate Baptist Theological Seminary, Berkeley Baptist Divinity School, Pacific School of Religion, Church Divinity School of the Pacific, and Pacific Lutheran Theological Seminary.

Finally, I wish to acknowledge my gratitude to the many publishers whose books and magazines are cited in this book, and to thank the following for permission to quote copyrighted matter:

Geddes MacGregor for a passage from his *The Vatican Revolution*; *The Journal of Church and State* for a passage from "Roman Catholic Clericalism" by W. Stanley Rycroft; *Missions* for Paul Blanshard's "Are Protestants Asleep at the Switch?"; Morehouse-Barlow Co. for *The Second Vatican Council* by Presbyter Anglicanus; *Presbyterian Life* for "Pope John XXIII" by Robert McAfee Brown; Association Press for *A Short Primer for Protestants* by James H. Nichols and *The Ecumenical Scandal on Main Street* by

Eugene C. Bianchi, S.J.
*University of Santa Clara*

# Contents

# Introduction

It has become a commonplace to speak of the Johannine revolution in the Roman Catholic Church. Nearly everyone senses that something momentous happened when the supposed *papa di passaggio* opened the windows of the Church and let the winds of conciliar renewal blow through the halls of the Vatican. Those open windows also revealed a unique image of the papacy in the person of Angelo Roncalli. Both the man and the Council made the brief pontificate of John XXIII a turning point in church history—the "interim pope" not only challenged the imagination of his own coreligionists, but also stirred hopes for a better world in others, believers and nonbelievers alike. Among separated Christians especially, the age-old longings for church unity were revitalized.

This study purposes to examine the impact of Pope John on the Protestant community in the United States. It hopes to throw some light on the questions: What influence did John XXIII and his Council have on the attitudes of Protestant Americans toward the Catholic Church? If there were changes of outlook among Protestants, how may they be best described and analyzed? What were the key issues on which the Johannine revolution pivoted? And finally, what does the Protestant reaction to Pope John indicate about the structures and activities of contemporary Roman Catholicism? From a close look at Protestant views concerning Catholicism when the Roman Church was in a period of intense self-appraisal, a modest assessment of the future of Protestant-Catholic dialogue in the United States can be attempted.

Although this study is limited mainly to the years 1958 to 1963, it should be briefly placed in a wider historical context. The reactions of various Protestant communions to the Catholic Church derive in part from the European heritage whence they originated. The intellectual and religious tradition handed down from one generation of Protestants to another has openly or covertly influenced their attitudes toward the Catholic Church. Those from Puritan English traditions, with their repugnance for prelacy and princedom, have seen Catholicism as a threat to democratic forms of congregational life in both church and state. The forefathers of these Protestants, in union with leading Enlightenment rationalists, structured the nascent American society. Thus, the successors of the Puritans long tended to identify the American way with the Protestant ethos. A significant part of the Protestant stance in America depended on a protest against an "alien" Catholicism. The immigrant and disadvantaged social status of the majority of Catholics during the nineteenth and early twentieth centuries presented little immediate intellectual threat. But the political and religious cohesiveness of the Catholic community, especially in large urban centers, was a mounting cause of concern to those in the Puritan-American tradition. Catholic political power was feared as an instrument of a highly centralized hierarchy.

Protestant orthodoxy and Protestant liberalism alike viewed the papal church as a serious danger to evangelical faith and national freedom. The more conservative-evangelical churches continued the classical Reformation polemic against Catholic doctrine and polity. They also feared the growth of Catholic political power in the cities. American Catholics, for their part, formed their own groupings in education, hospitalization, and voluntary societies to protect their identity and heritage against a growing secularization of life and against the attractive lure of the Protestant "establishment." Since Catholics were generally gathered in cities, they had less contact with the more rural, evangelical-conservative Protestants. This very isolation tended to widen the gap of understanding. The more conservative Lutheran churches, located mainly in the Midwest, also perpetuated the classic Reformation challenges to Catholic teaching. These Lutherans, though somewhat out of the main stream of Calvinist-American tradition,[1] were nevertheless conscious of the Catholic threat to congregational and political democracy, for despite their lack of much social and political involvement, many American Lutherans were influenced by pietist traditions, which in Europe had struggled against state-church unions.

The more liberal wings of the Protestant churches in America presented a special challenge to the Catholic community. Protestant liberalism had scrutinized its orthodoxies in the light of modern philosophies, higher biblical criticism, scientific and evolutionary progress. In the nineteenth century, an individualistic and emotional evangelicalism in American Protestantism made it all the more difficult for these churches to meet the challenge of the new learning with adequate theological sophistication. Much Reformation doctrine tended to be watered down or discarded; the risk of amalgamating liberal Protestantism and American democracy grew. This development made Catholics even more fearful of what was seen as Modernist contagion. Most American Catholic church leaders were poorly schooled for interpreting the new currents of thought. Their education had, for the most part, been confined to the rather formalistic and static concepts of post-Tridentine seminaries; they were no match for the Enlightenment. These Catholic leaders were also greatly preoccupied with preserving the faith of the poor and uneducated immigrants. Immediate pastoral and administrative tasks kept them in a closed Catholic world.

The more sophisticated Protestant liberal found it hard not to classify Catholic communities as dangerous pockets of intellectual obscurantism and clerical domination. When, during the 1930's, Protestant liberalism began to be doctrinally strengthened and refined, the American Catholic Church, still reeling from the intellectual backlash of Modernism, was too defensive and closed in on itself to take much notice. The Depression of 1929–41 and World War II taught both Catholics and Protestants some vital lessons in Christian social realism, but it was not until after the war that a substantial Catholic intellectualism began to flower. The seed of the Johannine renewal and the new dialogue with Protestant Christianity was silently growing. But on the surface of American life, there were still in the Catholic community many traces of legalistic rigidity, unthinking militancy, and ideological oversimplification.

Such ideologies have in more or less subtle ways shackled the understandings of both Protestants and Catholics in America. It is important to reflect briefly on the implications of these ideologies for this treatment of Protestant reactions to Pope John and Vatican II. In 1959, the sociologist and religious thinker Thomas F. O'Dea discussed the tension-creating ideologies that separate Protestants and Catholics in America.[2] He described the inner tensions of Catholic "hyper-integralists," whose personal and group security depended on their polemical reaction to the secularizing aspects of Protestant liberalism. These deep-rooted feelings were further embittered by the traditional Counter-Reformation hostilities and also by the Irish memory of oppression at the hands of a Protestant ruling class. Although the Catholic "hyper-integralists" rejected the American intellectual establishment, steeped in liberal Protestant and Enlightenment concepts, they fervently embraced American business values and patriotic sentiments.

Protestant forms of such integralism, especially in more rural, evangelical quarters, manifested the often unexamined ideologies of hostility to Catholicism. This study will reveal the easy stereotypes, the intellectual rigidity, and the crusading militancy of this kind of Protestantism. But Protestant liberalism has also cherished its favorite ideologies in opposition to the Catholic Church. O'Dea called these liberals the "hyper-reformationists," who protected their personal and social security by defending America from Catholicism. The growing

Catholic community presented a threat to the Protestant hegemony in American life, and Catholics also provided a foil against which the weapons of the Reformation polemic could be tested. Such jousting also helped these Protestants fend off the creeping dangers of secularization.

Although the typical Catholic or Protestant could not be so easily categorized by 1959, an important residue of hard-line ideologies remained on the American scene. Chapter 1 will give abundant evidence of this. Furthermore, it must not be supposed that within these ideological positions honest and profound theological and moral problems were nonexistent. Yet these Protestant and Catholic ideologies tended to create their own fantasy-world of dubious security. They supplied the rigid framework in which the exchange of ideas all too frequently took place. Many Protestants and Catholics are still hampered by subtle forms of these ideologies in thinking about mutual problems. A confusion of secular nationalism and religion results from these attitudes, and the fantasy-world on which the ideologies are often enough based is not tested by the reality of developments in religious theory and practice. "Only dialogue will deliver us from the spell of the ideologists,"[3] O'Dea concluded. The advent of Pope John and his Council helped to relax some of these rigid ideologies, and made possible a new and unexpected dialogue between Protestants and Catholics.

A word on method is in order. This study of Protestant attitudes in the United States is limited mainly to the years 1958 to 1963, which span the pontificate of John XXIII. The documentation is drawn from Protestant literature published, for the most part, in the United States. In addition to books by Protestant authors closely related to the five-year period, this study relies heavily on a broad cross-section of denominational and nondenominational journals. The more than thirty periodicals researched represent the mainline churches of American Protestantism and cover various ecclesiastical traditions from Southern Baptist to Episcopal.

The method of research was historical and descriptive. In the documents studied, nearly all the material dealing with the Roman Catolic Church was examined and correlated. This abundant documentation, by the very topics emphasized within it, provided both the structure of the chapters and the basis for interpretative analysis. It should be clearly recognized, however, that the very selection and correlation of materials already implies interpretation on the part of the author. It serves no purpose to deny this element of subjectivity in an attempt to achieve a quite impossible sort of objectivity. All that can legitimately be hoped for is that the author's presentation and interpretation do not distort the reality under consideration. Thus, this study makes no pretension of being a scientific sociological analysis, based on the accepted norms of statistical probability in that discipline. Such sociological controls have not been applied to the content analysis in this work.

The most important books by American Protestants written within the period studied and relevant to the topic were consulted. The periodicals were selected to provide a broad and reliable spectrum of Protestant opinion. One should, of course, question just how representative the articles and editorials were of Protestant sentiments about the Catholic Church, for journalists are to some degree expected to reflect the attitudes of their editors or their ecclesiastical superiors. Moreover, only the more educated and articulate write articles and editorials. The difference between their views and those of the less cultivated among their readership cannot be lightly dismissed. And yet, these very difficulties provide important clues for determining the reliability and the wide acceptance of the opinions expressed in these periodicals. Editors and church officials cannot for long simply impose their ideas on a dissenting constituency; they must write within an accepted range of widely received opinions and beliefs. Furthermore, although a gap always exists between the intelligentsia and the less cultivated, widely distributed journals tend to form and direct the opinions of their readership. Further, periodicals have the educative advantage of weekly or monthly repetition of ideas. Thus, they form and are formed by the views that gain wide currency among their constituents.

It might well be argued that a study of a longer period of time, covering years both preceding and following the immediate pontificate of Pope John, would provide a wider perspective. In one sense, this is true, for broader historical perspective usually adds new dimensions to the understanding of any human development. But three reasons prompted the restricted time chosen for this study. First, such limitation of subject matter permits more intense focus on the issues involved. Second, a particular value would seem to accrue from an examination of attitudes and reactions in close proximity to the events studied. It helps to know what people spontaneously thought or said as Catholic developments unfolded. It also can reveal more truly what changed or did not change *during* the five years under investigation. Moreover, periodical literature tends to manifest and reiterate responses to important events as they happen. Third, since the Vatican Council ended only in 1965, the vantage point for hindsight is not yet securely established. Thus, it seems wiser to follow the more modest course of trying to interpret the changes in Protestant outlook as they came about, rather than to sketch a more extensive frame of reference.

Another important aspect of method was to determine the criteria for choosing the various periodicals. An attempt was made to consult the broad spectrum of U.S. Protestantism from the theologically liberal to the fundamentalist communions, from the socially progressive and involved groups to bodies that look dimly on social action and foster individual conversion of heart and a somewhat negative morality. In the realm of ecumenism, the periodical literature used in the study portrays both the communities committed to church-unity movements and those opposed to organizational ecumenism. The latter are, in the main, the more fundamentalist and evangelical bodies. Their "spiritual ecumenicity" means a rejection of large, bureaucratic structures of church unity such as the National Council of Churches and the World Council of Churches. These interdenominational agencies are viewed as super-churches which might infringe on the freedom of individual denominations in matters of doctrine, polity, finance, and social involvement. The idea of spiritual ecumenism, as understood by many evangelicals, borders on a Docetic vision of the true church as an invisible communion removed from harsh and visible earthly realities.

These distinctions focus on two terms used repeatedly in the study: "liberal" and "conservative." It is of utmost importance to clarify how these ambiguous words are employed in this work. "Liberal" will refer to those groups, reviews, or persons who maintained a more irenic and open stance toward the Catholic Church. "Conservative" will denote those bodies, periodicals, or individuals who reacted in a more closed and polemical fashion to the Roman Church. Although general attitudes toward Catholicism will constitute the main criteria for applying the terms "liberal" or "conservative," other nuances of interpretation must be introduced. First, to avoid any rigid stratification of a particular journal or church, the spectrum of liberal to conservative as described above should be seen as a continuum of opinions. Second, persons and groups generally liberal toward the Catholic Church in matters of doctrinal reformulation will at times be as stanchly opposed to Catholicism in matters of church-state relationships and religious liberty as the conservative groups usually are. Third, it is worth noting that, if other spectra of interpretation had been chosen, groups that in this study are referred to as conservative would be classified as liberals. In questions of the relation between church and state, for example, a number of groups classified in this work as "conservative" because of their polemical approach to Catholicism would be thought of as "liberal" from the standpoint of American political democracy. Fourth, the term "liberal" will often enough fit those groups more open to change in doctrinal formulation and pastoral experimentation. And, conversely, "conservative" will frequently be attached to bodies upholding more literalistic orthodoxies and generally resisting change. But this is not the main understanding of the two terms as employed in the following chapters. To repeat, the main distinction between "liberal" and "conservative" as used in this study relates to more open and friendly attitudes toward Catholicism on the one hand and more polemical and closed attitudes on the other.

The periodicals were carefully chosen to reflect a wide variety of opinions toward Catholicism. The following is a brief introduction to the principal journals used in the study. Their characteristics will become clearer as the work unfolds. On the conservative side of the spectrum, *United Evangelical Action* is an interdenominational review and the official organ of the National Association of Evangelicals. *Eternity* is a similar magazine, but probably less influential in terms of representation and diffusion. A far more important evangelical, nondenominational review is *Christianity Today*, a serious journal of opinion of conservative bent. It is widely distributed, and must be classified as an especially intelligent attempt to confront the issues of the day from an evangelical viewpoint. *Christian Herald* is a nondenominational, family-oriented monthly of evangelical persuasion.

Southern Baptists constitute the largest Protestant denomination in the United States. Their literature would fall mainly into the conservative category. Perhaps the most influential single journal of opinion in the southwestern region of the Southern Baptist Convention has been the Texas *Baptist Standard*. A representative review from the southeastern area is *Biblical Recorder* in North Carolina. *Journal of Church and State* is a learned periodical published at Baylor University. Although it comes from a Southern Baptist environment, its attitudes toward Catholic political involvement have been quite liberal. *Watchman-Examiner*, published by northern Baptists, has consistently taken a polemical stance toward Catholicism, especially its relation to American democracy. *Missions* is a monthly of the American Baptist Convention; foreign missions are its principal concern, but it has generally followed a line somewhat similar to that of *Watchman-Examiner* toward the Roman Church.

*Lutheran Witness* is an organ of the Missouri Synod Lutherans. Of the three main Lutheran reviews researched, *Lutheran Witness* has been the most critical of the Catholic

Church. The American Lutheran Church is represented by *Lutheran Standard*, while the position of the Lutheran Church in America is reflected in *Lutheran*. The latter journal would have to be classified as generally liberal, in the sense defined above. All the Lutheran periodicals cited show a special interest in doctrinal issues, and frequently criticize Catholicism on this level. *Dialog*, a newer Lutheran intellectual journal, has provided some particularly significant articles on Catholic-Protestant relations.

The moderate and often ecumenically open opinions of the Disciples of Christ are found in the citations from *World Call* and *Christian*. Also of liberal tendency is the journal of the United Presbyterian Church in the U.S., *Presbyterian Life*. A southern Presbyterian counterpart is *Presbyterian Outlook*. The important Congregationalist tradition in America is echoed in *United Church Herald*, the organ of the United Church of Christ. This review is, for the most part, quite liberal, as is also the well-known Methodist magazine *Christian Advocate*. Among Episcopal publications, *Living Church* manifests a high-church tendency, and during the period studied, consistently maintained an openness toward ecumenical relations with Rome. *Witness* and *Churchman*, on the other hand, criticized Catholicism more frequently.

The most important single review in this study is *Christian Century*, a nondenominational weekly journal of opinion published in Chicago. Perhaps this periodical more than any other represents a middle ground of intelligent and critical Protestant opinion. It is difficult to characterize its attitude toward the Catholic Church in the period under study. Suffice it to say that *Christian Century*'s direction in the period of Pope John became increasingly liberal. *Christianity and Crisis* also played a very important role in understanding Protestant liberal reactions toward Catholicism and toward the Johannine renewal in particular. Finally, various scholarly reviews such as *Religion in Life, Theology Today*, and *Lutheran Quarterly* are also cited.

The thesis of this work might be stated thus: a significant

change in American Protestant thought about the Roman
Catholic Church took place during the pontificate of John XXIII.
The following chapters document, describe, and, to some extent,
interpret this theme in its various manifestations. An important
sub-thesis is that the significant change in American Protestant
attitudes toward Rome was not widely revealed in the written
sources until after the first session of Vatican II. A further sub-
thesis is that the presidency of John F. Kennedy contributed
importantly to this change of attitude toward the Roman Church.
The impact of the Johannine revolution as here presented must
include, therefore, not only pope and Council, but also the
legacy of that other John, who helped to shatter hoary stereotypes from the Catholic and Protestant past.

The division of material in the following chapters seemed
to flow naturally from close inquiry into a broad selection of
Protestant journals on the question: What were they really saying
from week to week about Roman Catholicism? The first chapter
provides a background against which the subsequent change can
be observed. This chapter underscores the Protestant image of
the Catholic Church when Angelo Roncalli became Bishop of
Rome and during a considerable time thereafter. It was generally
the image of an authoritarian monolith bent on world domination.
Rigid hierarchical control was complemented by passive and
fearful obedience. Authoritarian dominance was the keynote;
the goal of Catholicism was to serve materially and spiritually
the purposes of hierarchy and institution. This goal, as described
in much Protestant literature, was thought to be achieved largely
by antidemocratic political tactics. The Roman Catholic spirit
was depicted as alien to, and basically destructive of, the
cherished institutions of pluralistic American democracy with
its separation of church and state.

It was felt that the Catholic ethos especially undermined
a core doctrine of U.S. Protestantism—religious liberty. Major
examples of this danger to the rights of conscience were persecutions in Catholic countries abroad and coercive strategies on
birth control at home. On the theological level, Catholicism was
seen as caught in the trammels of unscriptural and inalterable

doctrines. Roman intransigence and haughty aloofness only confounded the problem. Also inimical to any meaningful theological development were the Roman methods of thought-control through the Index of Forbidden Books and censorship. Yet, despite these seemingly incorrigible shortcomings, Catholicism, in the eyes of some more liberal and ecumenical Protestants, showed hopeful signs of fruitful development.

The second chapter deals with Pope John's announcement of an ecumenical council and with various characteristics of the pontiff himself. In more conservative-evangelical quarters the response to the proposed council was one of suspicion. In liberal circles, the tone was generally cautious and occasionally hopeful. But even here, there were deep misgivings about the possibility of a genuine ecumenical openness on the part of Rome. The visits of non-Catholic religious leaders to the pope received favorable and unfavorable comments. Although notes of muted optimism could be heard concerning the personal traits of John himself, no significant change in Protestant reactions manifested itself.

Chapter 3 centers on the American contribution to the Johannine revolution in the rise of Senator Kennedy to the presidency. The election campaign was an occasion for copious and heartfelt outbursts of Protestant feeling about the specter of a Catholic in the White House. Latent fears came to the surface, and some were hysterically exaggerated. But in early years of his administration President Kennedy helped to allay these apprehensions by his firm stands on separation of church and state. The most important test case of his integrity, in Protestant eyes, was his position on federal aid to education. The President's forthrightness, even in face of hierarchical opposition, seemed to confirm the thesis of liberal American Catholics about separation of church and state. Kennedy's influence in changing Protestant attitudes was most evident in Free-Church communities.

Pope John's concern for the great social and political problems confronting humanity found a ready echo among American Protestants. Chapter 4 chronicles and interprets these Protestant responses to the papal encyclicals *Mater et Magistra* and *Pacem in Terris*. Although favorable comment predominated in the Protestant press, serious criticisms of these encyclicals were also raised. The weaknesses pointed out by Protestant commentators related closely to criticisms of Catholic positions and attitudes in other parts of the study. On the whole, however, the Johannine openness and flexibility in social, political, and economic matters constituted an important factor in altering Protestant views on Catholicism.

As the first session of Vatican II approached, the volume of copy devoted to the Council increased noticeably in Protestant publications. Much of it, especially in more conservative journals, was still wary and pessimistic. But an appreciable amount of the comment on the forthcoming session appeared cautiously optimistic. In either case, the Protestant viewpoint on doctrinal and pastoral issues came to the fore as a challenge proffered to Vatican II. The Ecumenical Council gave new impetus to the Catholic-Protestant dialogue.

The events of the first session, especially as reported by Protestant delegate-observers, constituted a meaningful turning point in Protestant attitudes toward Roman Catholicism in the United States. Even the more conservative journals presented the happenings of the fall of 1962 as a new and vital episode in the history of ecumenicity. The events in Rome were viewed as important for all Christian churches. Periodicals that had previously given little or no space to Catholic doings, except to object to them, carried full and positive accounts of the Council; indeed, nearly all the more important reviews commissioned the service of a special Rome correspondent. Protestants were impressed to see the Catholic hierarchy adopt attitudes and affirm tenets that had long been thought to be of Protestant vintage. The dialogue that might have occurred at Trent resumed with old and new issues confronting separated Christians. All this is the material of Chapter 5.

A short chapter deals next with Protestant reactions at the death of John XXIII. When compared with the generally respectful and correct responses from Protestants at Pius XII's death in 1958, the universal paean of sincere sorrow and high praise indicated a significant change of attitude. John's death was not received routinely; it was the death, to cite one writer at the time, of the best pope the Protestants ever had. It is particularly interesting to note the reactions of conservative Protestant periodicals, some of which had hardly mentioned the death of Pius XII. Although it is customary to praise the dead, there was much more than mere formality in these testimonials.

The final chapter elaborates continuing problems and new openings in Protestant-Catholic exchanges on the American scene. A number of the friction-causing issues described in the first chapter are still present. It would be naive to suppose that pope, President, and Council could wipe out the long heritage of controversial doctrines and opposing stances. But by 1963 there was a new hope abroad that the ancient and modern obstacles to Protestant-Catholic relations could be approached from both sides in a very new climate of opinion. This new atmosphere, based on an open willingness to listen and learn from separated brothers, is one of the marvels of recent centuries. It is the contention of this study that the Johannine renewal in the Catholic Church was the major factor in producing a changed outlook toward Catholicism among American Protestants.

# 1

## The Catholic Image in Protestant Eyes

### AUTHORITARIAN MONOLITH

From a broad survey of Protestant literature preceding and immediately following the elevation of Pope John XXIII, the dominant image of the Roman Catholic Church that emerges is that of an authoritarian monolith. This monolith frame of reference was more than an extrinsic label; it was thought of as describing the very essence of the Roman Church—a highly centralized dictatorial power bent on domination. This Catholic power was viewed as a manipulator of souls from cradle to grave by demanding absolute obedience to Roman mandates as representative of the will of God. Manipulation for power aggrandizement extended from the high reaches of the hierarchy to the lower clergy and to the laity. Catholicism was also thought to control national and international governments for its own purposes.

In his book *The Unfinished Reformation*, Charles C. Morrison, a former editor of *Christian Century*, echoed a widespread evangelical view of Catholicism as a system of medieval control over a docile multitude. He felt that the sacramental worship and absolutist hierarchy of the church depersonalized the individual, reducing him to a status of passive obedience. The soul of man was not his own, but was in the keeping of hierarchs. For Protestants this amounted to a "radical perversion" of the gospel, the abject surrender to "authoritarian sacerdotalism and its pretensions."[1] Another evangelical Protestant, Stanley I. Stuber, raised the same specter of Vatican world power. He saw Protestantism firmly set against the apparent attempt of the Vatican to grasp world domination, for Protestants feared the control of moral and spiritual affairs by a pope at Rome.[2] Stuber's whole book is an interesting description of a kind of legalistic and closed Catholicism that might be derived from the typical Catholic handbook then prevalent.

Among the Protestant weeklies, *Watchman-Examiner*, a northern Baptist publication, pointed to religious authoritarianism as manifested in Pope John's creation of twenty-three new cardinals. The editorial noted their promise of obedience to his "pontifical majesty." After describing the ceremony with its courtly and subservient forms, the writer concluded: "There is not a vestige of any of this in the New Testament's revelation of the church."[3] Later, the same weekly reflected on the dictum that all power corrupts, and applied it to the power structure of Catholicism. Such Roman power inspired fear, and there could be no commerce with a church that instilled fear.[4] Still later in the pontificate of Pope John, this review urged its readers to pray for the success of a Billy Graham crusade in Latin America, on the grounds that South America was the citadel of Roman Catholic clericalism and political power, dedicated to keeping people in "spiritual darkness and ecclesiastical bondage."[5]

Another magazine, *Baptist Standard*, which is influential among many Southern Baptists, carried the forthright views of E. S. James concerning the Catholic monolith. He editorialized on a statement by Christopher Dawson that Catholics in the United States were not "pulling their weight." Referring to Dawson's chair of Roman Catholic studies at Harvard University, James counseled his readers not to hold their breath until Notre Dame University set up a chair of Protestant studies. James found the Roman hierarchy exerting far too much weight in all areas of American life.[6] He was unhappy about the weight exerted by the Catholic power structure within the American press, as evidenced by the broad coverage given to the death of Pius XII. Alleged Roman pressure in political and diplomatic affairs was of paramount concern to James, and even when he approved some Catholic purpose, he could find fault in the manner in which it was carried out. In New Mexico, for example, Catholic authorities forbade the faithful to participate in a beauty contest, as a protest against nudity. *Baptist Standard* approved, but regretted that one church could wield so much power in such a coercive way.[7]

*Baptist Standard* constantly warned its readers to beware of a hierarchy that had set its sights on controlling American life, just as it manipulated millions of Catholic souls from cradle to grave.[8] In a similar vein, an important evangelical magazine ran a long article in 1959 about the "religious Goliath" of completely autocratic Rome. The author described the Catholic Church as a "multi-billion dollar organization ... looked upon with suspicion and resentment by millions of enlightened Americans." He viewed the splendor of papal celebrations as attempts to impress people with the power of the Vatican monolith. Then he asked: "How would Jesus look in the midst of all that earthly hypocrisy?"[9]

In such conservative reviews,[10] it was customary to compare Catholic authority structures to totalitarian regimes. This theme was strongly emphasized by Paul Blanshard in the tenth-anniversary republication of his controversial book *American Freedom and Catholic Power*. Far from seeing any need to alter his charges of the previous decade, Blanshard reaffirmed that the "central power structure of the Catholic dictatorship has not changed."[11] He found evidence for this in the facts that neither the Catholic bishops nor the people of the United States had been allowed to hold a plenary council during the intervening decade, and that Pius XII had moved even more to the right with his definition (1950) of the dogma of the Assumption of the Blessed Virgin.

The allegation that the Catholic Church is dictatorial was

a familiar note in Southern Baptist circles. With a note of desperation, the *Baptist Standard* editorialist wondered how American Catholics could be submissive to such "despotism in the name of religion." These same Catholics would die to defend democracy, the editor asserted, but they were nonetheless willing to knuckle under to a totalitarianism as severe as that of Russia or China.[12] Again, the same review could find little sympathy for the complaints of a Cuban bishop who decried the government take-over of church property. It seemed strange to hear such plaints from one who was part of a clerical hierarchy that ruled half a billion persons with an iron hand. Catholic totalitarianism decided when a man should be forgiven, whom he should marry, where he could worship, how many children he might have, and where he could be buried.[13]

The same note was rung by Charles C. Morrison, who described Catholicism as the "prototype upon which the systems of modern totalitarianism have been fashioned."[14] With characteristically doctrinal interests, a Lutheran organ made the same point. The Communist Party and the Roman Catholic Church were similar in that they both thought themselves totally right and everyone else wrong. According to both systems, all outsiders had been led astray and were called to return to one or the other infallible cult.[15] Even more progressive journals viewed Catholicism as a form of totalitarianism. In *Christianity and Crisis*, John C. Bennett, a professor at Union Theological Seminary in New York, editorialized on the erroneous image of Communism which had appeared in a statement issued by the American bishops. He criticized the bishops' black-and-white view of Communism, and their tendency to place all the blame on their adversary. It seemed that the totally ideological Catholic view of Communism ignored the realities of historical conditioning. Thus Dr. Bennett concluded that both Catholicism and Communism found it very difficult to adjust an absolute system to changing historical reality. An outsider, he felt, readily assumed that it could not be done.[16]

Also among the more ecumenically-minded Protestant thinkers, Robert McAfee Brown stressed the problem of authority as a basic issue in understanding Roman Catholicism. Although he noted areas of growing Catholic-Protestant rapprochement in this country, he believed that the Catholic Church, with its rigid authoritarian stance, had seriously to ask itself whether the gospel could in any significant way reform the church.[17] Similarly, Winthrop S. Hudson, a Protestant church historian, saw little hope for dialogue with a church that insisted so strongly on obedience to its every dictate. Such obedience, extending into every aspect of life, seemed to Hudson to be the central trait of Catholicism. He thought it futile to hope for harmony with a communion whose view of its own authority precluded the possibility of seeing the church standing under the judgment of God.[18] And yet, any crack detected in the monolithic structure of the church was noted with interest in more sympathetic Protestant quarters. When Father Hugh J. Halton, O.P., was replaced as Catholic student counselor at Princeton University because of his narrow views, *Christian Century* scored those views, but it also indicated the positive Protestant hope for Catholicism "in every new evidence of strain within the supposedly monolithic Rome."[19]

## POLITICAL POWER ALIEN TO DEMOCRACY

The authoritarian Catholic monolith was especially feared by American Protestants in relation to democratic institutions. Official Catholic documents, such as the *Syllabus of Errors* and other papal pronouncements of the nineteenth century, and Roman actions were cited to underline the antidemocratic threat of Catholicism. Protestants feared for the American system of democracy if ever the Catholic hierarchy gained control over the destinies of the nation. The spirit of this hierarchy was seen as absolutist, and its activities were considered plots for domination. Catholics with more liberal, democratic ideas appeared as a relatively unimportant group on the periphery of the Catholic Church. During the years under consideration in this study, the antidemocratic character of the Roman Church was

exemplified in Protestant literature by the Prato incident (see
pp. 42–43), the papal election, new appeals for an American
ambassador to the Vatican, and attempts to control education by
demanding public funds for Catholic schools and opposing
public schools.

The strongest fears of Catholic threats to political and
social freedom were expressed among conservative-evangelical
publications, and most stridently by leaders of POAU (Protestants and Other Americans United for the Separation of Church
and State). Paul Blanshard represented the latter point of view
succinctly:

> The Catholic problem, as I see it, is not primarily a religious
> problem. It is a matter of the use and abuse of power by an orga-
> nization that is not only a church but a state within a state, a state
> above a state, and a foreign-controlled society within American
> society.[20]

Catholicism was thus seen as a conspiracy to take over the United
States and strangle its freedoms. The editors of the Baptist
magazine *Missions* concluded that the conflict between American
freedom and Catholic power was as crucial as ever in such areas
as censorship, education, mixed marriage, medicine, and
science.

Another official of POAU, C. Stanley Lowell, mused about
what would happen if the United States were to become 51 per
cent Catholic. Catholic political theory, as propounded in the
often cited *Catholic Principles of Politics* by John A. Ryan and
Francis J. Boland, would make a shambles of the great American
tradition separating church and state. Surely, the views of Leo
XIII, the *Civiltà Cattolica*, and Francis J. Connell, a conservative moralist at the Catholic University of America, Washington,
D.C., would prevail over the weak voices of a few liberal
Catholics. The position of John Courtney Murray, S.J., on church
and state would crumble before that of Cardinal Alfredo Otta-
viani, director of the Vatican's Holy Office. Americans would
win federal aid to Catholic schools, obtain stipends from the
government to priests, achieve a Washington-Vatican concordat,

and see disadvantaged Protestants treated with snide amusement and official contempt.[21]

*United Evangelical Action*, the "Voice of Evangelical Christianity in America," pinpointed the Catholic political threat by seeing it centered in the hierarchy. Catholics must hold, argued Clyde W. Taylor, that the church is always superior to the state, which, therefore, is bound to submit to the hierarchy. This means that in the United States the hierarchy would be duty-bound to change the fundamental laws of the land. He cited in evidence a statement of the American bishops in 1948 claiming that "church-state separation is a mere shibboleth of doctrinaire secularism." Thus, citizens could expect continued efforts on the part of the hierarchy to gain tax support and financial aid, to infiltrate the best Catholic students into government, and build their political lobby (the National Catholic Welfare Conference) in Washington.[22] This hierarchical plot, in the estimation of E. S. James, was not lacking in subtlety. Christopher Dawson had recently remarked that Protestant-Catholic tensions in the United States were in the grave. James maintained that the bishops would like Protestants to think precisely this, and so be off their guard. The hierarchy would then find it much easier to put men under the "iron hand of the papacy." This editor hoped that there would be a mighty resurrection from the grave dug by Dawson, before it was too late for America.[23]

Even in what may be called a more middle range of American Protestant opinion, the same menace of Catholic political power alien to democratic forms was intensely felt. The church historian James H. Nichols graphically delineated Catholicism as the "new leviathan squatting in the Puritan heritage."[24] Through the organization Catholic Action, the Roman political force had applied systematic and destructive pressure on the American cultural ganglia. The antidemocratic thrust of Catholicism had been exerted pragmatically through the urban poor. It had been felt in campaigns of book-banning and school boycotts. At home and abroad, Catholicism represented for Nichols an irrepressible effort to conquer liberal democracies.

A Protestant seminary professor, Ilion T. Jones, marshaled

Pius IX's *Syllabus of Errors* and Leo XIII's *Immortale Dei* as evidence of Catholic antidemocratic attitudes. He saw these documents suppressing the freedom of individuals, so necessary for a democratic nation, and advocating the union of church and state. The Catholic "double citizenship" was a blatant contradiction of American tradition. It made the welfare of the citizen as a human person subservient to the well-being of the church. Consequently, Jones charged, in Catholic thought Canon Law was always superior to civil law, and the weal of the church was the end that justified any means.[25] Like many other Protestants only a few years earlier, Jones foresaw little hope for the liberal views of John Courtney Murray, whose tenets of church-state did not reflect authentic Catholic teaching nor did they represent, as far as could be deduced, the opinions of the hierarchy. In a minority situation, expediency continued to be the deceitful hallmark of the Catholic political machine.[26]

The church's claim to have power to bind under sin was also looked upon by Protestant writers as a Catholic tactic to coerce the faithful for political ends. In general, Protestant and Jewish groups could not exert the extreme pressures of Roman clericalism in imputing sin and brandishing excommunications. Such was the theme of an article by Charles L. Sewrey, who deplored Catholic pressure on people to vote according to the dictates of the hierarchy. As an example, he cited the drive of Roman officials in New Orleans to organize votes against compulsory racial segregation. "Are they not," Sewrey questioned, ". . . so under the domination of their religious overlords as to constitute a major threat of political bossism in the name of faith and morals?"[27]

In *Christianity and Crisis*, John C. Bennett echoed in more nuanced terms the continuing tension between an authoritarian, centralized hierarchical church and an open, pluralistic, democratic society.[28] Bennett was quite willing to respect Catholic dogmatic intolerance, but he was alarmed when it took the form of a natural-law policy affecting such areas as birth-control legislation, medical ethics, and mixed marriages. Bennett had the perspicacity, however, to point out that much of Catholic polity was a matter of faith and, as such, demanded respect from those who advocated religious liberty. It is interesting to note how absolute—even to being seen as matters of faith—various Catholic structures and operations appeared before Vatican II. Bennett described the Protestant fear of Catholic political power when it affected vital realms of national life. This power seemed bent on controlling the public school by dominating boards of education and imposing disabilities on non-Catholic educators. The Catholic political thrust opposed school bond issues, and thus hurt the necessary development of the public school. Catholic boycotts of publishers, merchants, and newspapers were interpreted as trampling on the rights of non-Catholic citizens. Persecutions of Protestants in Spain and Latin America (to be discussed in more detail later) were viewed as a foretaste of what would happen if the Roman political machine ever came to power in America. Thus, the propaganda in the Catholic press for diplomatic representation at the Vatican was understood as a move to secure a favored position for Catholicism on the American political scene.

Bennett was not alone among Protestant liberals who seriously questioned the Catholic stand on political power in America. Martin E. Marty also thought that it was impossible to argue for present Catholic-Protestant peace from the fact that papal and U.S. interests had not clashed in the past. Marty maintained that as the Roman Catholic Church had recently become stronger in the United States, tensions with other Christian groups had increased.[29] For the Catholic Church was so well organized that, even as a minority group in America, its hopes for political power could be realized. An adaptation of Roman Catholicism to democratic ways could not point with any security to past precedents. Al Smith's stand on democratic principles of government seemed to be refuted on all sides in the Catholic press. And more recently the position of John Courtney Murray had been subjected to criticism from influential quarters on the basis of the supposedly traditional Catholic concept of church-state relations.

Three incidents in the early years of the Johannine pontificate serve especially to illustrate the fear of Catholic political
power as reflected in the Protestant press. The first was the
widely reported case of Bishop Pietro Fiordelli of Prato, Italy,
who was brought into civil court on charges of defaming a
divorced couple who married outside the Catholic Church. A
lower-court decision went against the bishop. *Baptist Standard*
rejoiced that non-Catholics in Italy were supported by law, and
that even in Italy a priest was not immune from prosecution.[30]
It was alleged that because Catholic privileges had thus been
adversely affected, Pius XII had canceled the celebration of
the anniversary of his coronation. *Baptist Standard* did not
advert to the particularly intense friction between Catholics
and Communists in this part of Italy. But the review saw the
whole episode as a vivid example of what was expected when
one church became a state religion. Because of the Lateran
Pact, heavier penalties were exacted for an offense against the
established or favored Roman Church.[31] And when the Italian
Supreme Court reversed the decision of the lower court against
the bishop on the basis of the Pact, *Watchman-Examiner* termed
it deplorable,[32] for the decision meant that Italian citizens were
to be abandoned to the mercy of Canon Law with no guarantees
of protection from civil legislation.

Even among more liberal journals, opinions on the Prato
case were about the same. *World Call*, the international missionary magazine of the Disciples of Christ, editorialized that the
bishop did not uphold the sacredness of marriage by calling
two people immoral for following the laws of the land. It
was not good for any church to have special privileges before
the law, because this would tend to separate its faithful from
the legalized church and lower their esteem for it.[33] The Methodist review *New Christian Advocate* used the incident to contrast
the Lateran Pact, which was the source of the special treatment
for the Catholic Church, with the Italian civil constitution. The
former was called a fascist and totalitarian document, while the
latter was termed democratic and, therefore, Protestant.[34] The
bishop's condemnation, said the *Advocate*, would have been

acknowledged as libelous in any civilized country. Reflecting on the danger to separation of church and state, *Christian Century* held that the will of the bishop must not be allowed to invalidate Italian law. And the cries of "persecution" emanating from Pius XII and other Catholic leaders manifested the Catholic rejection of church-state separation. This church continued to cling to the outmoded supremacy of ecclesiastical law over civil law.[35] Thus, the Prato incident served to confirm American Protestants in their conviction that Catholicism was an ominous political power.

A second reaction to the Catholic Church as a political force was the protest, raised mainly by POAU, over American Catholic cardinals voting in the election of the new pope. This was seen as an exercise of citizenship in a foreign nation. For the pope is the ruler of a state; he has an army of Swiss Guards; he is enthroned as an autocrat, and elevates cardinals to churchly princedom. POAU, therefore, asked the secretary of State, John Foster Dulles, whether the three American cardinals participating in the papal conclave did not forfeit their U.S. citizenship under American naturalization and immigration laws. If a Protestant minister voted in an Italian election, he would forfeit his citizenship—were Cardinals exempt from U.S. law?[36] Paul Blanshard summarized the underlying thrust of this protest by stating that the "Vatican is a pluperfect negation of the American principle of separation of church and state," because it is centered in a politico-religious individual.[37] For Blanshard, this was more than a quibble; double citizenship symbolized foreign control of many American minds.

A third incident revived the old controversy about U.S. diplomatic representation at the Vatican. Representative Victor L. Anfuso, a Roman Catholic from New York, introduced into Congress a petition for an ambassador to the Vatican. Again the American Protestant interpretation of separation of church and state was at stake. The Vatican, warned *Watchman-Examiner*, with all its thrones, princes, and medieval pomp, was still the headquarters of the Roman Church. It should not be recognized as a state, lest the issue of voting cardinals be raised again.[38] Another more influential review called the attention of Protestants to the fact that the Roman Church, as the country's largest denomination, required close watching, for the principle of separation was in greater danger than ever.[39]

Under many different guises, Americans were cautioned to beware of the antidemocratic threat of Catholicism. They were told to look behind the Catholic protestations of loyalty to American traditions, for the hierarchy was not accountable to either the people or the civil government. It was accountable only to the pope, who spoke absolutely on social, economic, and political questions. Since he claimed supreme jurisdiction in interpreting natural law, the economic and social orders were subject to him. Clearly, such Romanism was hard to reconcile with Americanism.[40]

In the same vein, E. S. James revealed the four fronts on which the Roman Catholic clergy was attacking the wall of separation of church and state.[41] By "controlled immigration and uncontrolled multiplication," Catholic population growth was placing an ever more potent weapon in the hands of the hierarchy. The second front of the conspiracy was in the realm of mass communications, in which the Catholic political giant was said to be preparing journalists and diplomats. The last two fronts were stepped-up lobbying in Washington and a massive assault on the schools. Rome considered the latter top priority, and was marshaling all its forces for a financial breaching of the wall of separation.

A recurrent charge against the Catholic Church in America was that it sought by devious means to finance sectarian interests with public funds. Protestants were not to be called bigots because they objected to paying Roman Catholic bills. Protestants, too, wanted a Christian nation, but no church had the right to live off the state, *Watchman-Examiner* stated.[42] The same periodical strongly criticized the sale of land in New York's Lincoln Center to Fordham University. This was interpreted as a collusion of municipal and ecclesiastical politics.[43] A similar charge was hurled against St. Louis University for acquiring twenty-two acres of land without public consultation. For the Jesuits, it was said, separation of church and state meant that their church should be supported by the state.[44] Whether it was a question of a TV station in New Orleans or of land for expansion in Chicago, the Jesuits were described as committed to a policy of raiding the public coffers. It was hoped that wiser Catholic leaders would manage to keep the Jesuits within bounds.[45] But the prospects for such containment were minimal when the bishops themselves were bent on a Roman-style union of church and state. Seeking special privileges for Catholic institutions seemed to be of the essence of the Roman Church. It was in this context that the tax-exemption dispute over the Christian Brothers' winery in California was cast. *World Call* agreed with Glenn L. Archer and POAU that if church-related institutions went into business, they should pay taxes. Furthermore, the church should refrain from entering into such ventures, and thus " let the church be the church."[46]

The Catholic political power structure was viewed not only as grasping public funds for its own uses, but also as dedicated to the destruction of the public school. In keeping with article 1374 of Canon Law, Catholics were to boycott public schools. One way to harm the public school system was to refuse to support bond issues for the development of these schools. *Christian Century* urged Catholic politicians to separate themselves from such tactics.[47] Closely linked with this strategy was the divisiveness fostered by the hierarchy, which demanded that contacts with non-Catholics be minimized. This was achieved not only by constructing parochial schools, but also by duplicating many community societies. Catholics, it was claimed, were creating a ghetto within the larger American society, and thus weakening that society to abet the political purposes of Catholicism.[48] The same note was struck by a Baptist periodical when Catholic students were warned against fraternizing with Protestants at graduation celebrations. The editorialist, commenting on the overabundance of prejudice already in vogue, declared that "a conscripting church is an anomaly in a free land."[49]

News from abroad also helped to consolidate the opinion among Protestants in this country that political machinations were the lifeblood of Catholicism. The Italian situation was cited as an example of Catholic pressure at the ballot box. *Osservatore Romano* had urged Catholics to vote in a united front against the menace from the left. But *Watchman-Examiner* accused Catholic leaders of corrupting Christianity by political involvement, and also of giving an aura of false sanctity to the evil practices that plague the political affairs of state.[50] The Free-Church tradition, although somewhat oblivious of its own shortcomings, had lost none of its uneasiness about mixing religion and politics. In France, too, political Catholicism was seen as paying the price for the St. Bartholomew's Day Massacre. Although the Roman Church had lost its grip on the populace and was but a relic of a past tyranny, the clericals still wanted to place the state under the church.[51] The history of modern Europe proliferated with examples of the Roman Catholic Church striving whenever it could for political preferment and patronage. Reflecting on this charge, Glenn L. Archer of POAU exclaimed: "The destiny of America is either Rome or Independence Hall."[52] In a similar mood, an editorialist advanced a curious argument for a Protestant ecumenism of sorts. He offered two reasons why "Protestant and Free-Churches [sic] should band together, while maintaining their denominational statuses." The first reason was the growing political power of the Catholic Church with its centralized authority structure and its lust for temporal power. The second reason for Protestant unity was the Communist threat in America.[53] Not only were religious foundations for ecumenism overlooked, but the last argument revealed an interesting inconsistency in reference to the Catholic-Communist struggle in other lands.

The above examples pointed to a widespread apprehension among American Protestants over the political intentions of Catholicism. The extent and reiteration of the fear of Roman political power established a dominant image of Catholicism in Protestant eyes in the early years of Pope John's reign. And yet, as will be shown at the end of this chapter, more perceptive

Protestant thinkers saw signs of hope for a less political, more democratically oriented Catholicism. Most Protestants, however, were not yet aware of the new chords ready to be sounded in Catholicism. It took a Pope John to play them loudly enough to be heard.

## CATHOLICISM DENIES RIGHTS OF CONSCIENCE

In addition to being characterized by its monolithic authority structure and its political antidemocratic bias, the Catholic Church was suspect on the question of religious liberty. At home and abroad, Roman Catholicism appeared to work to impose its faith and morals on all others, without regard for their freedom of conscience. Charges were leveled of Catholic oppression of religious freedom in Latin America, Spain, and Italy. Civil, religious, and social limitations were imposed on non-Catholics, and were justified by the old conceptualistic doctrine that "error has no rights." This view had generally prevailed in Catholic thought from the time of the Reformation until quite recently. The experiences of Catholics living in the new democracies, and especially in America, gradually brought Catholic teaching to a more personalist and existential view—not about the abstract "rights of error," but about persons with inalienable rights of conscience. Further, newer historical, developmental, and existentialist thought forms helped the Catholic Church eventually to reformulate its attitude toward religious liberty. But this has been a recent development as far as official doctrine and "Catholic" lands are concerned. Yet even in the United States, the birth-control controversies in the late 1950's were seen as the imposition of Catholic views on the free consciences of others.

The Vatican was presented in Protestant periodicals as a force of clever opportunism. Where it could extirpate heretics by fire and sword, it would do so. But in a minority situation, the "Roman Babylon" would bide its time until it had won enough power to impose Catholic views. The constant theme was: Rome has not changed, only its tactics have altered. It was "in minority, a lamb. On equality, a fox. In the majority, a tiger."[54] This topic was of great concern for all American Protestant bodies, as will be shown, but especially for evangelicals, who traditionally were intensely missionary-minded. *Watchman-Examiner* noted that where the Roman Catholic Church dominated, religious freedom for other Christians was gradually reduced under systematic oppression. It was hoped that the World Council of Churches would press this point home on the Vatican,[55] so that Rome would no longer be able to avoid the issue of persecution, which was a grave concern for evangelicals. Even when A. F. Carrillo de Albornoz explained more liberal Roman Catholic views on religious liberty in his *Roman Catholicism and Religious Liberty* his exposition could hardly be believed. To many Protestants, his book represented the views of a few liberal Catholic theologians, but not the official voice of the church. *Missions* commented that only the papal voice counted in Catholicism. The periodical then interpreted the views of Leo XIII in the light of expediency.[56]

Colombia was a focal point of Protestant complaint about Catholic persecution.[57] Charges of physical violence and more subtle forms of oppression were numerous. An article reported a dynamite explosion at the home of a Protestant missionary and the closing of a Presbyterian school.[58] When the national Catholic weekly *America* suggested that perhaps Protestants should halt some of their proselytizing activities in Columbia, *Presbyterian Life* replied that this would be a denial of true religious freedom.[59] As late as 1960, it was reported that a Roman Catholic ecclesiastical tribunal had ordered that children be taken from a Presbyterian school and confined to the care of a Catholic uncle, since their father had turned Protestant. By the concordat arrangement, the government seemed obliged to acquiesce in this "kidnap."[60] The truth or falsity of these reports is much less the concern of this study than the fact of their repeated affirmation in Protestant journals; we are concerned with the actual image of Catholicism projected on the American scene.

In a news report on changing Protestant-Catholic relations in Colombia, C. Stanley Lowell pointed to a new effort to educate Catholic priests to a friendlier relationship with other Christians. He claimed that this move began under the pressure of unfavorable publicity for Catholicism throughout the world. Lowell, moreover, stated three changes that would still have to be made. The idea of Colombia as a Roman Catholic monolith with no room for others had to be abandoned. The hierarchy would have to remove itself from politics, and the "Protestant-hating" attitude of priests would need to be abolished.[61] *Christian Century* also commented on the gradual improvement of relations in Colombia between Catholics and Protestants during the year 1958/59. But, the editorialist continued, if the Vatican were really sincere, all persecution of Protestants in Colombia would have to be halted.[62] And even though the Latin American bishops had spoken of Protestant missionaries as one of the four "deadly perils" in South America, *Christian Century* commended them for seeing the need for purification in the Catholic Church itself, rather than bloodying the opposition.[63]

Opinion among Southern Baptists reflected less optimism over the situation in Colombia. It was charged that in a period of eleven years, 112 Protestants had died for their faith in that country, 200 churches had been shut down, and 15,600 Christians had been made homeless. Although there had been slight improvement in relations by 1960, the concordat of 1953 declared that 75 per cent of Colombia was missionary territory, over which the Roman Catholic Church had absolute jurisdiction.[64] The editor of the widely read *Baptist Standard*, E. S. James, could summon up very little sympathy with Catholic lamentations about religious persecution under the new regime in Cuba. His criticisms of the State Department's white paper concerning religious persecution in Cuba were based on the fact that the U.S. government did not see fit to issue a similar paper during the height of anti-Protestant activity in Colombia.[65]

Although most of the complaints about infringements of religious liberty in Latin America centered on Colombia, other countries were also cited. Readers of the official magazine of the National Association of Evangelicals were told about a priest in Ecuador who had ordered the savage beating of a Protestant missionary.[66] In Paraguay, where there were few priests and the masses were often steeped in ignorance and superstition, Protestant missionaries were nonetheless attacked.[67]

Spain enjoyed the dubious honor of being the place of most intense anti-Protestant action.[68] A southeastern Baptist magazine described religious intolerance as rampant in Spain. Protestant churches were not allowed to look like churches, and were forbidden to publicize even the time and place of their meetings.[69] And, of course, open missionary work was not permitted. In reference to the halting of "illegal proselytizing" in Spain, *Baptist Standard*, as early as 1958, wondered how any Catholic aspirant to the presidency could resist hierarchical pressures and excommunication. If a Catholic ever became President of the United States, Baptists would have to emigrate to the moon, the editor wryly commented. But, unfortunately, he added, the Communists would probably be there sooner.[70]

Not only did the Protestant publications protest the closing of churches in Spain, but they also decried the civil disabilities imposed for religious reasons.[71] A particularly bizarre example of such penalties was the difficulty that young Spaniards had in proving that they were non-Catholics so that they could be granted permission for a civil marriage.[72] The clergy was said to have the last word in such matters. Paul Blanshard blamed such a state of affairs on the fact that an authoritarian church was in league with an authoritarian state.[73] The Spanish treatment of Protestants was a sad replica, editorialized *Baptist Program*, of Communist tactics in Hungary. In both instances, majority power blocs were persecuting minority groups, and "using the same spurious reasoning to explain away their viciousness and intolerance."[74] The usual association was then established within the American context. Readers were urged to ponder the prospects of a Roman Catholic majority in this country.

The attitude of Protestant periodicals toward the religious situation in Spain differed very little from conservative to liberal magazines. The oppressive restrictions on Spain's 30,000 Protestants were castigated: no signs on churches, no evangelical publicity, no publication of literature, no schools or youth groups, and so on. If religious liberty were ever proclaimed in Spain, some observers thought that many in the lower and middle classes would desert the Catholic Church.[75] It was also urged that Americans should not let the need for U.S. defense bases in Spain blind this nation to the flagrant suppression of religious and civil rights.[76]

Protestant pleas for justice in Spain were bolstered when 342 Basque priests protested to their bishops over violations of civil rights. The petition to the hierarchy deplored police brutality and prison terms set at the whim of the police, as well as other infringements of human rights. Dom Aurelio Escarré, Abbot of Monserrat, complained to Franco about police brutality to students in Barcelona.[77] But in general, Protestants portrayed the Spanish hierarchy as favoring a "tyrannical regime." Spain would not be drawn into the twentieth century, it was asserted, without the wider influence of the whole Catholic Church.[78] There were, however, glimmers of hope for more equitable treatment of non-Catholics. The Spanish minister of foreign affairs. Fernando María de Castiella y Maiz, who had spend seven years as a diplomat accredited to the Vatican, was working for a change in the law regarding non-Catholics. The influence of Pope John and Cardinal Bea in this affair will be discussed later. But in the eyes of many Spanish leaders, Protestantism, which they saw only through the myopic lens of an abstract Hispanic education, was synonymous with Marxism, materialism, Freemasonry, and general moral debilitation.[79] And yet, despite such a repressive atmosphere, Protestantism in Spain was reported to be growing.[80]

The condition of Protestantism in Italy was more favorable, but here, too, there were occasional complaints about the "prejudice and bigotry" of the Roman Catholic Church.[81] The Italian civil constitution provided more adequately than the Spanish for the rights of minority religious groups, but the concordat of 1929 placed the "religion of the majority of the Italian people" in a *de facto* privileged position. Moreover, the long

history of papal involvement in Italian political life was bound
to have consequences on the status of non-Catholic bodies. Thus,
the more universal orientation of the Johannine policy, in contrast to more Italianate forms of papal thought and action, will
be an important factor of the change discussed later in this study.
But in 1958 the Roman Church seemed ready to "use all means"
to frustrate the application of the Italian constitution, which
protected the rights of other religions.[82] But since the Methodist
*New Christian Advocate* was also able to comment lightly that a
bit of persecution was like a pinch of salt in spaghetti, it is hard
to conclude that the Italian milieu was as unpropitious to Protestantism as the Spanish. Yet the double standard beneath Catholic
intolerance, even in Italy, drew critical fire. When certain church
authorities condemned the building of a mosque in Rome,
*Christian Century* remarked that Roman Catholics wanted to
evangelize in Africa, but they were not willing to allow the
same privileges to Africans in Rome.[83] Such a double standard
was based on the theory that error had no rights, a position that would later receive a definitive rebuttal in *Pacem
in Terris.*

In the United States, charges that the rights of conscience
of non-Catholics were infringed arose in most acute form in the
area of birth control. The Catholic Church was accused of imposing its tenets regarding artificial birth prevention on those who
believed differently.[84] The official church, in the view of *Christian
Century*, acted as if the last few centuries had not existed. This
implied Catholic disregard for the respect for human conscience
that had been gradually developing in the West since the end of
the religious wars. It was thought that in an age of increasing
interchurch reconciliation, the Catholic tactic of forcing the
church's views on the public would impede unity and deepen
bitterness. It appeared to many that American Catholicism was
making sins—in a Catholic perspective—into crimes subject to
universal legislation.[85] For, on the latter point, there was no
public consensus supporting anti-birth-control measures. Protestants, it was admitted, had attempted a similar procedure in
the prohibition of alcoholic beverages, with national dissension

and hypocrisy as a result. The Lutherans felt that the task of the churches was to create a Christian moral climate, but not to use the machinery of government, local or national, to pursue their own specific and sectarian ends.

In the larger area of world population pressures, the Catholic Church was seen as clinging to outmoded theories, and thus contributing to the social and political problems of over-population. Protestants and others were encouraged not to allow themselves to be stopped by Roman Catholic obscurantism regarding sex from discovering more creative and humane ways of dealing with the modern demographic explosion. Artificial contraception seemed to be a far more human and Christian solution than either sterilization or abortion. These extreme methods of controlling population were resorted to more readily when birth-control information and help was not available. The Roman Catholic claim that the use of artificial contraceptives was an offense against God was answered by affirming that the real offense against God was to contribute to needless human suffering by sponsoring a primitive and rigid sexual morality.[86] In the light of the Anglican Lambeth Conference statement of 1958, which allowed for rational control of conception, Catholic idealization about "populating heaven" could only be inter-preted as "arithmetical nonsense."[87]

These theoretical considerations became acute local issues in New York and Connecticut. Official Catholicism in New York City was putting pressure on hospitals and doctors not to dispense birth-control information or services. This was inter-preted as an affront to the moral conscience of Protestants and Jews in the city.[88] In the segment of the Protestant press that was usually more outspoken in its criticism of Roman Catholicism, the New York moves against lifting birth-control bans from hospitals were characterized as a "power cult at work." The Catholic (and Democratic) majority, led by its hierarchs, was making public policy the servant of sectarian practice. This was but a sign of what would come about whenever the Roman Church gained the upper hand politically. Meanwhile, the better educated Roman Catholics seemed to use contraceptives, whereas their "near-illiterate" coreligionists, who made up the majority of Catholics, were the victims of uncontrolled sex.[89]

The Catholic Church, it was admitted, had a right and duty to influence public policy through suasive preaching and teaching. But it went beyond these legitimate Christian means and endeavored, through political connivance, to monopolize the consciences of others. Already the question was being asked as to how free a Catholic President would be from ecclesiastical direction in matters of birth-control policy.[90] The long shadow of suspicion about a Catholic in the White House was again being cast.

In Connecticut, the Catholic Church continued to support old laws against birth-control practices that now seemed out of date and harmful to the common good. In terms of the present needs of the world, *Christian Century* called the Catholic position in Connecticut inhumane, obscurantist, and immoral.[91] *Watchman-Examiner*, which mistakenly thought that the Connecticut laws had been written by the Catholic hierarchy, inveighed against Catholicism for forcing its views on others who conscientiously differed.[92] In addition to charging this violation of conscience rights, *Christian Century* challenged some of the basic assumptions that undergirded the Catholic viewpoint on birth control. How well had the Roman Church investigated the natural-law arguments themselves? How far did the ability of one church to define sexual morality extend? Was there truly a unanimity of tradition on this issue? The editorialist also predicted that Catholic intellectuals would be asking more and more questions along this line.[93]

The Roman Catholic Church at the outset of Pope John's pontificate appeared to American Protestants as an authoritarian monolith, an antidemocratic political force, and an oppressor of the rights of conscience. In addition to these criticisms, Protestant literature also concentrated on more specifically theological issues that divided Christians and caused misunderstandings.

## THEOLOGICAL ISSUES OF DIVISION AND
## MISUNDERSTANDING

Since the days of the Reformation, Protestant churches have criticized Roman Catholicism on the levels of doctrine, polity, and worship. These three aspects of theological tension were all found in American Protestant literature at the outset of Pope John's pontificate. The papacy itself, with its tenets of primacy and infallibility, continued to be a major stumbling block. The church's concept of itself as the true church was viewed as the source of Roman arrogance and intransigence, which in turn led to Rome's anti-ecumenical bias. In Protestant eyes, the Catholic laity in theory and in fact was subordinate to an all-powerful hierarchy, and the Vatican was charged with world-wide thought-control. Finally, Catholics were seen exaggerating in their worship the place of Mary to the detriment of Christ, and were accused of an externalizing and materializing sacramentality.

One of the most difficult points of doctrinal conflict, already alluded to in the section on authoritarianism, was the Catholic view of papal primacy and infallibility. Traditionally, of course, it had been a classic point of disagreement between Rome and the Reformation. But even as late as the period of this study, it had lost little of its divisive force. This can be seen from two introductory manuals on Protestant-Catholic relations, published in the late fifties and early sixties.[94] The sole headship of Jesus Christ over the church was contrasted with the supremacy of the pope. Often enough in such literature, important distinctions between the contrasting primacies were bypassed, but the general thrust of the argument was unmistakable. The sovereignty and freedom of God, together with his immediate accessibility, necessitated the rejection of the papacy, with its peculiar pretensions, as well as its mediational priesthood.[95]

On the question of the papacy, some publications were more polemical than others. A Missouri Synod magazine reprinted and stanchly approved passages from the *Smalcald Articles* and the *Formula of Concord*, which equated the pope with the antichrist.[96] The false doctrines of primacy and infallibility, the journal asserted, obscured and perverted the gospel of faith. When *Our Sunday Visitor*, a popular Catholic weekly, called the "antichrist" label a "sinister charge," the president of the Missouri Synod, John W. Behnken, upheld *Lutheran Witness*. He claimed that the papacy anathematized the very heart of the gospel: *sola fides, sola gratia, sola scriptura*, for the pope placed himself above the gospel, and enforced submission to unscriptural doctrines.[97] The foolishness of primacy and infallibility was underscored in *Watchman-Examiner*. Nor could the papal succession be proved unless the pope were willing to run the line through murderers and adulterers.[98]

As President Behnken noted, for Protestants the doctrine of primacy and infallibility subordinated the Bible to many churchly traditions or to papal fiat. In confirmation of this point, *Baptist Standard* quoted a statement of Archbishop William O. Brady of St. Paul: "The Word of God is written down in modern times in the letters of the Pope."[99] Thus Catholicism did not respect the Bible, nor did it encourage its communicants to read and study the Scriptures.[100] James Hastings Nichols summed up this charge very well:

> Once committed to the extra-Biblical tradition as actual revelation, the manifold disagreements within the tradition have pushed the Romanists inescapably to the last step, the definition that the final authority and revelation of the church is neither Biblical nor traditional but the mere say-so of the current pope-king.[101]

Thus, many Protestants found the Catholic attitude toward the pope to border on idolatry inasmuch as it raised the papacy to an office of divine institution.[102] This "divinization" of the papacy lent itself to absolutizing papal authority over all developments in the church, whether doctrinal (e.g., Mariology) or pastoral (the suppression of the priest-worker movement and the "New Theology").[103] The institution of the papacy, therefore, with its notions of primacy, but most especially of infallibility, "changes the whole substance of the gospel" for Protestants.[104]

The difficulty went much deeper than a mere failure to recognize that the pope can sin and can make mistakes in many areas—educated Protestants understood these distinctions. But it was precisely on the level of doctrinal issues that infallibility, even when the pope spoke *ex cathedra*, was firmly denied.[105] The impact of Pope John could scarcely be expected to resolve this crucial problem. But as will be seen, the Johannine papacy and Council were able to bring new insights on how the Petrine office might reflect service to the whole Christian community, rather than domination of it.[106]

Another theological obstacle to better Protestant-Catholic relations in the United States has been the exclusive Roman doctrine of being the one true church; this resulted in an ecumenical aloofness which was most gallingly evident in Rome's call to the separated churches to "return." The American Protestant attitude was succinctly characterized in 1957 by Winfred E. Garrison, a man with a long career of ecumenicity behind him, when he wrote:

> Pope Pius XI in his encylical *Mortalium Animos* voiced his opposition to "schemes for the promiscuous union into one body of all who call themselves Christians," and continued: "Federation of Christians then is inconceivable in which each member retains his own opinions and private judgments in the matter of faith . . . . Unity can arise only from one teaching authority, one law and belief and one faith of Christians." This statement is perfectly consistent with the history and principles of a church which, holding the clear-cut concept here expressed that unity requires complete uniformity, applies one or the other of the only two techniques by which that kind of unity can be attained—police methods when it can or, when that is impossible, the declaration that the church consists only of those who do conform to the requirements of its centralized authority and so by definition can never be divided.[107]

The same theme of Catholic intransigence and seeming arrogance toward other churches was echoed among Southern Baptists. Commenting on a statement of Archbishop Gerald P. O'Hara of Atlanta to the effect that Christ established *the*

church, not the churches, *Baptist Standard* saw this rigid Roman
Catholic view as the basis for Rome's resorting to force and
domination whenever possible.[108] When Catholics prayed for
unity, therefore, they asked that God might bring back, as to a
forsaken mother, all those who had unhappily departed from the
unity of the Roman Catholic Church. Catholics saw their church
as though it were standing on a pinnacle of perfection, without
need for reform and renewal. Their prayer for unity was faulty
because it did not implore God to help their own church, as well
as Protestant communions, to find a fuller scriptural basis for
oneness. For these reasons, Baptists and other Reformation
Christians could never look upon Catholicism as an authentic
Mother Church. Was this not the "mother" who tried to kill her
children at the time of the Reformation, and who now persecuted
them in Spain and Colombia?[109]

Protestants were frequently warned against entertaining
false hopes about closer union with the Catholic Church. Some
observers, like Ilion T. Jones, saw their fellow Protestants moving
naively down a one-way street to Rome, forgetting that they were
dealing with an uncompromising and unsentimental hierarchy
and papacy. Protestant kindness, self-criticism, and concessions
toward Rome were based on wishful thinking.[110] For how could
they hope for more from the pope than Martin Luther received?
This was all the more true today, asserted Professor Jones, since
the pope was a more powerful, supreme dictator than he had been
in the sixteenth century.

The perceptive editor of *Lutheran*, Elson Ruff, noted that
his church was looked upon as a possible bridge for ecumenical
rapprochement. But movement on such a bridge would have to
be in two directions; as far as Rome was concerned, all traffic had
to flow in its direction. How different was Rome's observance of
its church-unity octave from the unity prayers of the World
Council of Churches! This organization prayed for greater cooperation and understanding among Christians rather than for
a return to one particular church.[111] To the ecumenically minded
Disciples of Christ, the Catholic prayer for unity was but a sad
contradiction, for during the Chair of Unity Octave, the Catholic

Church presumed to know God's will for the churches and to prescribe the only means to unity.[112] Such presumption was itself in contradiction to the spirit of prayer, which called for humble acknowledgment of not possessing God's vision of the future of a fragmented Christianity. The correct Christian prayer for unity should ask for oneness of the church according to God's will, in his good time and by the means he chooses. In this way, one of the more distinctively American denominations, the Disciples of Christ, rejected the prevalent Roman Catholic viewpoint on Christian unity; such union would never be achieved as long as Catholicism demanded absorption of all other Christian traditions. Archbishop John C. Heenan of Liverpool represented this Catholic attitude when he insisted that the church of Rome was the one true church, and that nothing was to be gained by discussing this given belief.[113]

The movement led by Pastor Max Lachmann for reunion of German Lutherans with Roman Catholicism was criticized for conceding too much to the Vatican. "Must Protestants enter the discussion by granting in advance all that Roman Catholics need to make their claims and their empire complete, effective, and total?"[114] Such was the editorial opinion in 1959 of one of the country's leading ecumenical journals. This opposition to what seemed to be too facile concessions or easy conversion to Rome was based also on the Protestant conviction that Catholicism needed to hear the prophetic voice of Reformation spokesmen. With his own peculiar penchant for the inflammatory phrase, the distinguished church historian James Hastings Nichols affirmed this point in 1957:

> To this day the Roman Church has never been able to keep itself free from spiritual and moral rottenness except in the presence of criticism from without. Consolidated into a new sect at the Council of Trent ... Romanism has remained a caricature of the gospel in the lands of the Mediterranean and Latin America where it has been freed of criticism by Inquisition and censorship.[115]

In a more conciliatory tone, Jaroslav Pelikan underlined the importance for Catholicism to heed the voice of the Reformation. He thought that individual conversions to Rome could work a real disservice to the Roman Church, if they fixed Catholics more firmly in the conviction that their church had nothing to learn from a moribund Protestantism. Rome, insisted Pelikan, very much needed to open itself to the message of Protestantism, a message it had never really listened to.[116]

The Johannine revolution, while remaining faithful to basic Catholic tenets, will be seen to open new avenues that were still undiscovered when Pelikan and Nichols wrote these books. Under the influence of Pope John and the Secretariat for Promoting Christian Unity, the Catholic Church will elaborate a much more inclusive theology of church membership. It will pray more ecumenically, in the spirit of Abbé Paul Couturier,[117] for unity according to the manner God intends and in the time he determines. Neither of these elements can be predicted with full clarity, and they both imply an ecumenical risk, which will be new for Catholicism. Moreover, the Catholic Church will try to listen to and learn from Reformation insights. But the majority of Protestants were not aware at the outset of Pope John's pontificate that Catholicism could move in this direction.

A further dimension of the Protestant view of Roman Catholicism, evident during this time, was the subordinate and submissive state of the Catholic laity. This underdeveloped role of the laity was seen as a correlative to the authoritarian and hierarchical aspect of Catholicism. "An absolutism," remarked Nichols, "can train solid, loyal, efficient, law-abiding citizens, but it cannot train them to be *free*; it cannot produce responsible initiative in each individual layman."[118] Thus, in the Catholic Church there seemed to be little room for the growth of the responsible Christian layman who might make moral decisions for himself and take a significant role in forming church policy. The laity was described as the passive subjects of the hierarchy; they were hedged about by a clerical moral theology and a stultifying ghetto culture.[119] The clerical restraints under which the laity had to operate gave rise to a superficial, externalist morality among lay people, as opposed to a morality of personal depth. Since norms were inflexibly fixed by the hierarchy, laymen were victimized by an "authoritarian sacerdotalism and its presumptions."[120] Uniformity rather than diversity seemed to be the rule.

This stunted lay development was unfavorably contrasted to the laity's role in many Protestant churches. For them, the great apostolic commission to spread the gospel is spoken to all in the church, not just to a sacerdotal elite.[121] The Protestant minister has a special function in the church, but he is not invested with special spiritual powers; and the laity plays an even more important decision-making role. Protestants will take a new look at the possibilities for a more dynamic laity in Catholicism, however, as a result of the first session of Vatican II.

Another major blemish on the image of Roman Catholicism for Protestants was what might best be termed "thought-control." Examples were cited of the muzzling of an editor by the hierarchy in Argentina,[122] and the jailing of an editor through Vatican influence in Italy.[123] When Pope John called for certain curbs on the press to protect public morals, *Christianity Today* approved, but it went on to point out that Roman Catholic censorship also meant that much more was subject to control by hierarchical interference. This journal educed as evidence of such press control the interference of the National Catholic Welfare Conference (renamed the U.S. Catholic Conference in 1966) with copy destined for *Christianity Today.*[124] Catholicism, asserted an author in an evangelical review, was like Communism in that it suppressed freedom of thought.[125] It was also alleged that in Spanish lands the Roman Church kept the people poor and ignorant to control them better. And this thought-control was not to be blamed on the monarchy or on Spanish poverty or on any lack of intelligence, but was to be laid directly at the doorstep of the Catholic Church. Thus, Romanism opened the way to Communism in these lands.[126] Although these charges were made in an oversimplified and somewhat irresponsible way, they doubtless helped to form an image of Catholicism in many minds, especially in the South.

In the realm of books and of freedom of research, the Index of Forbidden Books and other restrictions imposed by Catholic authorities on their people were portrayed as alien to growth in

intellectual maturity and responsibility. *Christian Century*
mocked the proposed reform of the Index. For John XXIII and
the Jesuits this reform simply meant bringing condemnations up
to date, that is, adding new names to the list of proscriptions.
"Rome's determination to fetter the human mind is as active in
1959 as it was when Pius V created the Index in 1571."[127]
Catholics were said to be very eager to convert Protestants to
the Roman Church, but Catholics were not really interested in
knowing about and understanding Reformation traditions.
*Christian Century* pointed out that Catholics were not
encouraged, or even allowed, to study Protestantism.[128]

In a broader sense, it was said that Catholic thought-
control impinged upon freedom of research and expression for
Roman Catholic theologians. The Episcopal magazine *Living
Church* asserted that Rome did not trust her theologians. They
were closely regimented and seemed to carry the heavy weight
of papal utterance whenever they spoke. "Until Rome begins to
trust its own theologians and until real conversation begins
*within* the Roman Communion, it will be impossible for Rome
to talk to anybody else."[129] When the Roman Catholic Church
would be sure enough of the loyalty of its own children to have
them examine opposing views in an unbiased way, great progress
would be made on the road to eventual unity.[130] It was felt that
Pope John made important contributions to a freer spirit within
Roman Catholicism, "but it will be many years before the results
can bear fruit in a freedom of conversation across the lines of
division comparable to that which obtains among Protestants,
Anglicans, and Orthodox."[131] This was said in 1959. It could
hardly be expected then that within three years, not "many
years," freedom of expression among Catholic bishops, theologians, and students would advance significantly in Pope
John's Council.

A final blurring of the Catholic image in Protestant eyes,
as seen in the writings of the late fifties, relates to Roman
worship, and especially to devotion to Mary. The sacramental
emphasis of Catholic worship could be a valid way of approaching and experiencing the mysteries of faith, but it was also

subject to the abuses of magic. Jaroslav Pelikan felt that the
Catholic Church had not done all it could to avoid criticism
on the score of over-materializing genuine worship. In actual
practice, more stress was placed at times on sacramentals than
on the traditional sacraments of the church.[132] Criticisms of
such abuses were more severe among evangelical Christians.
It seemed that morbid curiosity about the bones of the dead
and other legendary relics not only hurt Christian worship, but
also kept nonbelievers from taking real gospel truths seriously.[133]
Religious statues were looked upon as the hardware of superstition.
They captured the imagination of the ignorant, and led
them into specious idolatry.[134] Whenever such objects were associated with events of national importance, there was usually an
outcry from evangelical quarters. This happened when a
St. Christopher medal was attached to a Vanguard missile at
Cape Canaveral. The government was thus becoming a vehicle
for Roman Catholic superstition.[135] But in a more serious context, Catholicism was urged to re-examine its sacramental
teaching, and to concentrate more fully on preaching the word.[136]
Conciliar study of Catholic liturgy would later present a more
balanced view of word and sacrament in relation to the faith
of the church and its practices.

Finally, Catholic veneration of Mary appeared to cloud
the unique mediatorship of Christ. Exaggerated and naive
piety was a special affront to Protestants, and it seemed
that, instead of correcting such abuses in devotions to Mary
and to the saints, the hierarchy even encouraged aberrations
both in Catholic literature and practice.[137] Catholic doctrines
about Mary were classed as unscriptural Mariolatry,[138] and
they spelled a new bankruptcy for the Roman Catholic Church
when they were elevated to dogmas.[139] But it is interesting to
note that although Protestants were opposed to what they
considered Marian extravagances, they were often willing to
accept a more biblical place for the Virgin Mary in their
religious outlook.[140] Some Protestants, moreover, especially
among Lutherans and Episcopalians, regretted that their
churches had reacted so adversely to Marian teachings and

practices in Catholicism. They had thus squandered a part of their own heritage.[141] But in general, Protestant scholars who were more friendly to Catholicism urged that the Roman Church re-emphasize the biblical context of Mary's place in the church, as a symbol of believing humanity.[142] Efforts along this line would also be among the fruits of the Johannine renewal.

This concludes the critical appraisal of the Catholic Church as it appeared to Protestant Americans in the early years of Pope John's pontificate. Catholicism projected an image of authoritarianism, totalitarianism, and lack of respect for rights of conscience. It also presented the theological and intellectual obstacles discussed above. Before completing this chapter on the image of Catholicism, it remains to consider some of the hopes, voiced among Protestants in the United States during the opening years of John XXIII's papacy, concerning signs of Catholic renewal that could possibly lead to closer relations with Protestantism.

## PROTESTANT HOPES FOR CATHOLIC RENEWAL

Although the main thrust of his influential book *The Riddle of Roman Catholicism* was friendly and reconciling toward Roman Catholicism, Pelikan keynoted a typical view of the Catholic Church: "In everything the church does in the modern world, this need to erect bulwarks against modernity is painfully evident."[143] And he added that "separation, alienation, ghetto" describe much of modern Catholicism. Against such a backdrop, Protestant hopes for an ecumenical *rapprochement* with Catholicism on the American scene stood out in clearer focus.

In 1958, John C. Bennett wrote on four promising factors often overlooked by Protestants.[144] First, there was more variety in Catholicism from country to country than most Protestants realized. Spanish and French Catholicism, for example, were quite distinct. In the United States, the Catholic Church, stimulated by progressive European theology, Protestant and Jewish competition, and a democratic environment, was undergoing a growth in maturity. A second factor pointed out by

Bennett pertained to the social and cultural history of American Catholics. They had had to fight for acceptance in this country. Much of the Irish Catholic aggressiveness was due to the insecurity born from struggling for recognition in a hostile land. Bennett thought that it was a significant development when the political symbol of Irish leadership changed from Boston's old-time political boss James Curley to John F. Kennedy.

Bennett found a third note of promise in the fact that Roman Catholicism in this country was divided in principle from top to bottom on the question of religious liberty, as exemplified in the very different positions represented by John A. Ryan and John Courtney Murray. Nor did such a large crack in the monolith go unnoticed by T. Otto Nall, editor of the Methodist *New Christian Advocate*. Even when the image of the Italianate papacy seemed to contradict variety in Catholicism, doctrinal changes on matters of church and state were unmistakable.[145] Finally, Dr. Bennett discussed disagreements in American Catholicism on other questions of social policy, such as attitudes toward war and toward McCarthyism.

Implicit in the above observations about developments in American Catholicism was the hope that the antidemocratic aspects long connected with the papal church would gradually be corrected. Geddes MacGregor made much of the essentially nondemocratic Roman conception of church government in contrast to a large part of the Christian world, which he saw as susceptible to a genuinely democratic church order. He accredited the centralizing and totalitarian aspects of Rome to the success of the papalist party in recent centuries. Certain aspects of MacGregor's analysis are questionable, but his view of American Catholicism is worth adverting to:

> Christians in the United States of America are in a position of unique opportunity, for if the papalist program is defeated here, it is unlikely to be triumphant elsewhere, and the Roman Church throughout the world will be obliged to re-examine her own constitution.... The outcome of such a setback to the papalist party aims would be of incalculable benefit to Christendom and mankind.... [146]

From a more balanced perspective on Catholicism, Pelikan made a similar point about Catholic possibilities in a democracy. The Roman Church, he affirmed, must learn to see the positive values of a pluralistic and democratic society. If the Roman Church definitively severed its ties with the feudal world of two swords, it would be more loyal to the deeper genius of Catholicism.[147]

After expressing Protestant fears about Catholicism in a democratic land, Robert McAfee Brown suggested that American Catholics should be more willing to air their critical differences on questions of church and state and of religious liberty.[148] And Robert D. Cross, in concluding his excellent history of liberal American Catholicism, declared that insofar as this liberal tradition, reasserted and refined, gains acceptance among American Protestants, it promises to remove old thorns from the church-state question. If Catholics could learn to approach a pluralistic and democratic culture with confidence and love, the liberal tradition in the American Catholic Church would open great possibilities for Christianity in America.[149] The full emergence of this tradition, however, was not seen as likely without a basic redirection of certain typical Catholic attitudes: "Catholics will have to ask whether a real and prolonged dialogue can take place without the ultimate risk of a possibly fundamental reorientation."[150]

One of the most promising signs for the future of American Catholicism, from a Protestant point of view, was the ability for self-criticism shown in a few, but significant, writings. John Tracy Ellis had critically analyzed the lack of intellectual achievement in American Catholicism. Walter J. Ong in his *Frontiers in American Catholicism* and especially Thomas F. O'Dea in *American Catholic Dilemma* continued this self-critical approach. O'Dea probed candidly into such faults of the American Catholic Church as formalism, authoritarianism, clericalism, moralism, and defensiveness. This ability to speak out honestly about Catholic shortcomings seemed to contradict the dominant image of a church that needed and invited no self-criticism.[151] *Commonweal* also stood out in its willingness to treat Catholic foibles freely. On its thirty-fifth anniversary, this journal of opinion was praised by the editor of *Christianity.and Crisis*, Wayne H. Cowan, for the depth and perception of its editorials. This critical review was a witness to intellectual vitality within the Catholic community.[152]

The liturgical and biblical movements in Catholicism were also influential openings toward better relations with American Protestants.[153] Proposals for a common Bible to be used by all Christians were well received; biblical scholars had been co-operating for a number of years across denominational barriers. It was, however, mainly in the more learned journals that these and other intellectual ameliorations in Protestant-Catholic relations were noted. The Lutheran theologian George A. Lindbeck discussed the evangelical possibilities of Catholic theology. He and other intellectuals were aware of new interpretations among Catholic thinkers of such doctrines as miracles, justification, and the Virgin Mary. A more historical approach to the theological enterprise in Catholicism brought a growing recognition that past thought-forms had to be understood in their own context. These same forms, furthermore, needed to be adapted, corrected, and completed according to the mentality and insights of the present. Lindbeck also noted that some Catholic thinkers viewed natural theology as following on faith: as an obedience rather than as a self-assertion. Moreover, he found a stronger tendency among Catholics to relate theology to human reality.[154]

A new trend was becoming evident in Catholic studies of the Reformation. Joseph Lortz and Louis Bouyer in Europe and Gustave Weigel in America had departed from the polemical tradition in dealing with Luther and the sixteenth century.[155] The Catholic theologian George Tavard wrote in *Christian Century*, expressing the views of such scholars as Hans Küng and Henri Bouillard on the work of Karl Barth. Tavard concluded: "... all who are concerned for Christian unity should hail the study of Barth by Roman Catholics as a token of better mutual understanding."[156]

But in terms of the total image of Catholicism as portrayed

in most Protestant publications, these intellectual hopes for greater dialogue were hardly recognized. This is especially true of the evangelical and conservative journals, which were perhaps still too locked in their own unexamined orthodoxies to take notice of Catholic intellectual developments, which probably would have been seen as a liberal dilution of fundamentals that had spread even into Catholicism.

In the area of social action there was some recognition of Catholic contributions. American Catholic bishops were praised for their stand on the race question in 1958.[157] In some places Catholics and Protestants were reported cooperating on social issues on the local level, but this was a rather rare exception.[158] News comments occasionally noted Protestant-Catholic co-operation abroad. For the first time in the history of French churches, a joint statement was issued by high ecclesiastical authorities protesting the displacement of a million Moslems during the Algerian War.[159] Communist pressures in Germany had impelled Protestants and Catholics closer together without compromising differences or dulling particularities.[160] And the sufferings of Maryknoll Bishop James E. Walsh in China under the Communists could evoke the sympathy of all who upheld the rights of conscience.[161]

Finally, in the realm of general ecumenical relations, there were, in the words of Liston Pope, whispers abroad that might someday swell into words of reconciliation.[162] *Christian Century* commented favorably on the increase of talks between Catholics and Protestants. In the ten months previous to this *Christian Century* editorial such discussions had outnumbered those held during the prior decade.[163] The Johannine influence was beginning to be felt in the United States. *Christian Century* also reprinted Robert McAfee Brown's much quoted rules for the dialogue.[164] Protestants were urged to cultivate mutual knowledge of and respect for Catholics.[165] Protestants were also encouraged to reach out to Roman Catholics, even though the latter called for a return to Mother Church. They were exhorted to give a gentle but firm testimony of one another's faults. Protestants were not to lose sight of the Protestant principle of self-criticism as applied to themselves.[166] Such self-examination would reveal that Roman Catholicism offered a creative challenge to Protestant churches to seek a wider catholicity. This self-appraisal in the light of positive elements in Catholicism would uncover for Protestants a more comprehensive world view, to replace more provincial patterns of thought. It would challenge Protestants to foster a more inclusive approach to all social classes, and could possibly spur on the urban ministry. Catholicism would also teach the lesson of a living tradition and a more vigorous sacramental worship.[167]

This degree of ecumenicity, however, represented a distinct minority of Protestant thinkers and writers when Pelikan's book was published. In this forward-looking ecumenical group were a number of American Baptists who published in their new scholarly review *Foundations*. Since much that has been quoted from Baptist journals was anything but ecumenical, it is especially noteworthy that as far back as 1958, honest self-criticism of Baptist attitudes toward Catholicism was being registered by their own scholars. William H. Hamilton wrote in 1958 that one of the most unattractive things about his denomination was a "silly anti-Catholicism on the practical level."[168] Baptists were told that they had to purchase their right to criticize Catholics at a much dearer price. This meant serious study of Catholicism past and present. Hamilton welcomed the creative leadership of the Jesuits at Woodstock College in Maryland—scholars such as Gustave Weigel and John Courtney Murray, and he maintained that Baptists could learn from them.

In a similar vein, *Foundations* stated that in the future Baptists would have to work with, not against, Roman Catholics to discover what actually does endanger religious liberty and the separation of church and state. In a remarkable article, Charles M. Fox confessed that Baptists had been too negative toward Catholicism; the time had come for a Baptist self-examination.[169] Offensive statements were to be avoided in order not to alienate liberal Catholics by intolerant treatment. Stereotypes about Catholicism had to be radically examined: the Roman Church was not a vast international machine in motion against liberty, nor was it the formidable monolith that justified Baptist fears. Fox recommended patience with Roman Catholics, since their stance was not easily amenable to new positions; and he scored what he called the besetting sin of Baptists, that of judging others. In a less detailed way, Robert T. Handy also enjoined Baptists to take up the ecumenical task, and to broaden relations with Roman Catholics. He warned that any knowledge of history would counsel against hasty optimism, but he also pointed to the change of climate that was beginning to characterize Protestant-Catholic relations.[170]

This chapter has been a general assessment of the Catholic image in the United States, especially as seen from the Protestant viewpoint. The total picture was described succinctly by Jaroslav Pelikan: "What we have now, on both sides, is a picture of the other side that is part photograph, part daguerreotype, part caricature."[171] From this study of Protestant evaluations of and attitudes toward the Roman Catholic Church, it seems necessary to conclude that at the beginning of the Johannine pontificate, Catholicism was mostly caricature and blurred photo. The negative estimates of Rome predominated, but a few perceptive analysts of Catholic life were clearly aware of creative possibilities for development. Hopeful signs were noted in Catholic approaches to social and political matters, as well as in biblical, liturgical, and other intellectual and religious pursuits.

In the next chapter the focus shifts from this general view of Catholicism in Pope John's early years to Protestant reactions to the announcement of Vatican II, and to early estimates of the personality of John himself.

# 2

# *Announcement of Vatican II and the Personality of the Pope*

The first official announcement of Pope John's intention to call an ecumenical council appeared in a curiously casual piece of understatement in the *Osservatore Romano* for January 26–27, 1959. The momentous decision was sandwiched between announcements of two more routine projects: the convocation of a Roman Synod and plans for the reform of Canon Law. For some months, the nature and purpose of the Council were unclear. At first, some thought it would be a gathering of various Christian churches to discuss ways toward church unity. Others looked upon it as a special appeal for closer relations with the Orthodox churches. The various explanations issuing from the Vatican from January to June of 1959 indicated a gradual maturation in the pope's own mind of the goals for the extraordinary event he felt inspired to convoke. By Pentecost of 1959, it became clear that Vatican II would have three general aims. First, it would be a meeting of Roman Catholic bishops to renew and update the thought and practice of their own church. Second, this renewal was intended to foster greater understanding among Christians. Third, Pope John hoped to foster a broader spirit of dialogue and cooperation with those outside the Christian orbit.

The purpose of this chapter is to examine the effect of Pope John's announced Council on a broad spectrum of American Protestant thought. Reactions will be studied under two general classifications, liberal and conservative. Such distinctions are hardly ironclad; points of view between what might be termed progressive and evangelical Protestants occasionally overlap. But the distinction is helpful and widely accepted, when it is based on differences of attitude toward theological development, ecumenicity, and the social involvement of the churches. A similar distinction between conservative and liberal will be observed in the second part of this chapter, where the personality and early actions of John XXIII will be looked at through Protestant eyes.

## LIBERAL REACTIONS TO THE ANNOUNCEMENT

It is important to understand these early reactions to the announcement of the Council in the context of Pope John's first two years, for it would be misleading to read back into this period the intense interest in the Protestant world that followed the first session of Vatican II. Although the Council had been announced in 1959, it was not really until mid-1961, with the publication of *Mater et Magistra* and the development of Cardinal Bea's Secretariat for Promoting Christian Unity, that a truly forward-looking spirit became evident in the preparations for the Council. In the first two years there were some indications that little or nothing of significance for other Christian churches would issue from Vatican II. The Roman Synod proved to be a poor adumbration for meaningful renewal in Catholicism. In addition, some of the most conservative and even reactionary curial officials were in charge of drawing up the agenda for the Council.

This helps to explain why most of the Protestant reactions to the proposed Council were either negative or very cautiously optimistic. Henry P. Van Dusen held out little hope for the efforts of John XXIII: "Pope John has shown engaging originality; it is doubtful whether he could possibly reverse, even if he wished to do so, the direction that has dominated the church's thought for most of the past century."[1] Such general attitudes among knowledgeable Protestants were rather widespread after the Council was announced. In a review of Jaroslav Pelikan's *The Riddle of Roman Catholicism*, Winthrop S. Hudson termed Pelikan's hopes for the eventual ascendency of liberal tendencies in Catholicism as "unduly sanguine."[2] In the light of the past hundred years, dominant Thomism and absolute papal authority could not be dethroned. The Roman insistence on Protestant return made any real dialogue, even in an ecumenical council, a practical impossibility. The basic difficulty in Roman Catholicism, as Hudson saw it, was an essentially utopian view of God's work through Christ in the church. In the Catholic perfectionistic view of the church, there was room only for a partial and even perverted grasp of revelation; nor was there place for a real sense of doctrinal development. Neither could Catholics understand that churchly unity was only imperfectly made manifest, and that the church stood under the constant judgment of God. In their idealistic outlook on the church, Hudson maintained, Catholics failed to see that in the church institution justice and harmony could be achieved only by various checks and balances.[3]

No pope or council could be expected to alter this. Thus, anyone who indulged his hopes for a Protestant-Catholic unity was guilty of "fantastic unreality," in the opinion of Matthew Spinka; the Roman claims were too absolute and exclusive to admit sincere openings for dialogue.[4] These negative sentiments were summed up in an editorial in *Living Church*, a journal otherwise very amenable to conversations with Roman Catholicism: "It is tragic, but true, that Rome does not yet show any signs of being ready, at the official level, to take part in the ecumenical dialogue."[5] This high-church Episcopal magazine nevertheless continued to seek dialogue with Catholicism at unofficial levels. This editorial was provoked by a news release from the National Catholic Welfare Conference that had insisted on the doctrine of the Blessed Virgin as mediatrix of all grace, and reaffirmed the strictures of *Humani Generis* regarding newer forms of theological thought.

The response of the denominational journals to the proposed Roman gathering reflected, for the most part, the cautions and

suspicions voiced in a more general way above. It was feared that
the Vatican Council would simply continue to call for a return of
submissive Protestants to Rome. This was shown in the remarks
of Edwin T. Dahlberg, president of the National Council of
Churches, who welcomed the Johannine initiative, but rejected
any "return" approach to ecumenical dialogue with Rome.[6]
Unity movements could not be accepted on conditions laid down
by one church alone. *Presbyterian Life* duly noted the Vatican
announcement, but it also cited a spokesman for the Church of
Scotland, who wanted no part of such a conference.[7] This spokesman favored ecumenism, but not on Roman Catholic terms.
*Witness*, an Episcopal review usually more critical of Rome,
called attention to an article in a Catholic paper from Scranton
that had affirmed the inability of the Catholic Church to err. In
view of this claim, the editorialist concluded, why should Protestants make such a to-do about the projected Roman Council?
Obviously, it was to be just another parochial Roman Catholic
event.[8]

In *Lutheran*, Albert P. Stauderman editorialized that the
Johannine proposal could hardly be called ecumenical. It was a
narrowly Roman assembly, subtly engineered to entice the
Orthodox back into the fold. But the latter might possibly open
Catholic eyes by declaring the friendship of Eastern churches
for Reformation communions. At any rate, continued Stauderman, it would be utterly impossible to accept Bishop Fulton
J. Sheen's assertion about the "divinity" of the Roman Church.
Before inviting others to the Council, Rome should clean its
own house in Spain and Latin America, and Christianize its laws
about mixed marriages.[9] Like the Lutheran journal, the
Methodist *New Christian Advocate* saw the Council as an appeal
for the Eastern Christians to return to Rome. "Those wise to
Roman Catholic obliquity doubt that a new breakthrough is at
hand."[10] Two years later, the same journal, though expressing
hopes for Pope John's intention to renew and purify the Roman
establishment and direct it toward unity, implied the unlikelihood
of such a result. In confirmation of this view, it quoted the conservative Jesuit theologian Charles Boyer, who had declared:

"The Catholic Church does not need any change regarding its doctrine."[11] Since Boyer taught in a pontifical university in Rome, his words seemed to echo the storied intransigence of the Vatican, and augured poorly for any parliament of churchmen held there.

The journal of the United Church of Christ remarked that mingled praise and caution greeted the pope's plan. There was praise for the forthrightness and initiative of John XXIII, whom many called the "pope of unity." But a great obstacle remained in the Roman doctrine of being the one true church. This doctrine impeded any chance for sincere dialogue, which requires a two-way conversation between equals.[12] Again, the Council seemed specially directed at the Orthodox. It was conceded, however, that despite many difficulties, any measure of success for the Vatican Council depended on the manner and spirit in which it would be conducted.

The early reactions of the influential *Christian Century* projected a dim view of Vatican II, and laid down bold conditions if Rome seriously desired the attention of Protestants. The Johannine Council would not be ecumenical in the full sense, but only a Roman Catholic meeting. Moreover, it was seen as a device to contain rather than extend the ecumenical movement. Rome hoped to broaden its own influence by staging an impressive public-relations show: "A meeting in the city of the popes, staged with imperial pageantry to show thousands of cardinals, archbishops, and bishops from all over the world worshipping, parading, and conferring in full medieval regalia—that is a public relations man's dream."[13] Readers were urged to contrast the pompous Roman affair with the approaching conference of the World Council of Churches. This would be a truly ecumenical gathering that would deal with the real social problems of humanity. *Christian Century* commented: "We need entertain no doubt as to the conclusion history will reach when it compares the two meetings."[14]

Amid these reservations about the Council, it is interesting to note that the person of Pope John was often viewed favorably. When *Christian Century* made the hard demand that the coming

Council repudiate the doctrine of papal infallibility defined by Vatican I, it nevertheless declared that John was hardly an interim pontiff; he was hoping to make history.[15] But no reunion was possible with a church which had said no to Martin Luther's attempts to bring it back to the gospel. The work of Vatican I and of Trent would have to be undone before ecumenical relations could be established between Rome and Protestantism. But history, in the estimation of Franklin H. Littell, warranted little optimism for the ecumenicity of the proposed Council.[16] Much publicity would be given to this Roman affair, but in the end it would amount to no more than a denominational synod of small importance for the rest of Christendom. If anyone needed proof of the validity of this preview of Vatican II, he had but to study the outcome of the Roman Synod launched by Pope John. *Christian Century* felt that the Synod had disturbed many Protestants and that it should alarm liberal Catholics. If this was the pope's idea of modernizing, it was certainly a backward move, a tightening of already rigid disciplines.[17] *Christian Century*, however, asserted that it was much less interested in the legalism, formalism, authoritarianism, and superstition manifested *within* the Roman Church than it was concerned with the public repercussions of the strictures of the Roman Synod, if they were applied as models for American Catholicism. What if U.S. lawmakers of the Roman persuasion were threatened by the hierarchy not to pass "laws harmful to the Church under pain of excommunication?" How could Protestants establish any meaningful dialogue with Roman Catholics if they were forbidden to read publications inspired by "Protestantism, illuminism, existentialism, atheism, and materialism?"[18] The Roman Synod seemed to confirm Protestant misgivings about the forthcoming Council.

Reinhold Niebuhr greeted the announced Council as an occasion for a wholesome conversation between churches, and he rejoiced over the humanity of the pope. But he warned that papal absolutism too easily equated an historical institution with the kingdom of God. The papacy also tended to subordinate all judgments to zeal for its own prosperity and prestige. The Roman attitude, in Niebuhr's view, could certainly be termed anti-Communist, but it was not therefore necessarily Christian.[19] This editorial, following soon on the papal announcement of the Council, reflected the rather widespread early Protestant surmise that Vatican II would be an interchurch assembly. Niebuhr also conjectured that perhaps the pope wanted to shore up Orthodoxy's resistance to Communism by reaching out to the East. Niebuhr's associate, Henry P. Van Dusen, entertained even less hope for John XXIII's Council. He reflected on the pope's interesting though problematic proposal of an ecumenical council, but he counseled that there was "no wisdom in cherishing illusions on that score."[20]

Although most of the opinions were cautious and rather negative, some optimism was voiced from more liberal elements in the Protestant press. A few months after the conciliar plans became clearer, John C. Bennett affirmed that Pope John had been a surprise to many Protestants. Overtones in Johannine statements and actions could create a better climate for Protestant-Catholic dialogue.[21] The Presiding Bishop of the American Episcopal Church, Arthur Lichtenberger, also welcomed the announcement, and hoped that it would lead to serious talks between the churches.[22] And a number of American Protestant publications quoted the remarks of the head of the World Council of Churches, W. A. Visser 't Hooft. Since his hopeful statement about the proposed Council was linked to possible developments in Catholic thought about religious liberty, it had special pertinence to the U.S. scene.[23] Visser 't Hooft acknowledged that the Roman meeting would not be a reunion council, but he thought the pope's call had spurred great interest in ecumenism among Roman Catholics, as could be seen in a marked increase of Catholic literature on the subject. In itself, this growth of interest in ecumenicity among Catholics was seen as a phenomenal event.

When it became clearer that Vatican II would be dedicated to internal renewal within Catholicism, *Living Church* was quick to sense the importance of the fact that pope and bishops would be meeting together in council. As was seen above and as will be shown below, most Protestant organs criticized the Roman Church for narrowness and exclusiveness when it became clear that the Council would be mainly a Roman Catholic affair. *Living Church*, however, found it very significant that the pope was willing to surround himself with a deliberative body of bishops. This step was looked upon as a movement toward more demo- cratic forms of church polity. Such a consultative group of bishops in the realm of government was as important as the biblical renewal that was influencing Roman Catholic theology.[24] The same journal urged Protestants to forget the misconception that the Council was nothing more than a public-relations stunt. For it was vital that Roman Catholics dialogue among them- selves, reappraise their theological positions, and reform their Canon Law; they would then be in a better position to converse with other churches. A few months later, *Living Church* repeated its interest in collegial developments within Roman Catholicism when it referred to the remarks of the then Archbishop of York, Arthur Ramsey, about the pope as *primus inter pares*. The repeti- tion of this long-held Anglican belief in the context of the coming Roman Council seemed to disturb some Protestants. Dr. Ramsey had stated that Anglicans could accept the pope as first among equals. Since the days when the church had first achieved any world-wide extension, the Archbishop said, the pope had been received as the first among his brother bishops. What Ramsey objected to was the claim that the pope is a "universal bishop" with jurisdiction in all dioceses. In light of this Roman teaching, foreseeable union seemed impossible, but Dr. Ramsey was most willing to extend his hand in friendship to Rome.[25]

Before turning to the more conservative reactions to Pope John's announcement of the Council, it seems well to reflect briefly on an inter-Protestant debate that was stimulated by the projected Vatican II. It has already been implicitly shown how the more progressive and ecumenical Protestants tried to inculcate greater openness in those of their confreres who viewed Rome with hostility. An explicit example of this can be observed in a *Christian Century* editorial which criticized a fundamentalist view of ecumenicity that had appeared in *United Evangelical*

*Action.* This journal had charged that the coming Vatican Council was part of a sinister plot for a full scale merger of the World Council of Churches and the Roman Church. *Christian Century* upbraided the evangelical journal for consistently distorting the intentions of the ecumenical movement.[26] The positive form of this exhortation within American Protestantism to greater friendliness toward the Catholic Church was exemplified by Jaroslav Pelikan. He underlined the importance for Protestantism of developing a realistic and faithful response to Roman Catholicism in light of the Council-to-be.[27]

## CONSERVATIVE REACTIONS TO THE ANNOUNCEMENT

In conservative Protestant circles, for the most part, Pope John's announcement of the Council inspired negative comments. It was seen as a ruse to entice Protestants and Orthodox to return to Rome. It also became an occasion for pointing out unacceptable Catholic doctrines and practices, and of chiding sentimental Protestant liberals who were only too willing to travel a one-way street to the Vatican. Finally, the announcement provided a chance for recalling Catholic abuses of freedom in the past and present. A few hopeful remarks were nevertheless expressed about the forthcoming Vatican gathering.

Evangelical journals of no specific denominational affiliation saw little meaning for Protestants in the papal gathering. It would simply be a great attempt "to bring the Eastern Church into submission to Rome," proclaimed the stanchly anti-Catholic editor of *Eternity*, Donald Grey Barnhouse. The Council would be an occasion at which "more great blasphemies will be promulgated as official Roman Catholic doctrine."[28] He supposed that the Vatican Council would define such teachings as Mary, mediatrix of grace and co-redemtrix,[29] and that the total result would prove even more clearly that the papacy was the Great Whore of Babylon of the Book of Revelation. But editor Barnhouse was gladdened by the invitation extended to

Rome by the World Council of Churches to come to the inter-church conference in India. When this was met with contempt in Rome, as surely it must be, it would be perfectly evident to all that "they were willing to be the lion lying down with the lamb, providing the lamb consents to be the lion's dinner."[30]

Such outspoken magazines as *Eternity* and *United Evangelical Action* also turned their fire on fellow Protestants whose liberal leanings made them "soft" on Vatican deviousness. The Council might woo Protestant "neo-pagans," who despised pure Christian teaching and hankered after church reunion at any price, but solid evangelicals knew that only a miracle could draw Rome away from its pagan practices.[31] Similar sentiments about liberal Protestants were expressed by a writer who had attended a Protestant conference to discuss relations with Roman Catholics. He accused his Reformation brethren of taking no more account of doctrine than of "annoying fleas," in their ecumenical mania to be reconciled with the Roman Church. While excoriating his coreligionists, this author revealed again the underlying fear of Rome, newly engendered by the call of a Vatican council:

> To minimize doctrine in favor of an ecumenical movement based on sentiment and good intention is to demonstrate a total refusal to face the avowed Romanist goal of state and social domination based on an inexorable pretention to be the sole guardian of all divine truth.[32]

In a calmer mood, the widely circulated *Christian Herald* echoed the evangelical reaction to the papal Council. The famous historian of Christianity Kenneth S. Latourette reviewed the history of ecumenical councils and came to the conclusion that John could hardly expect to realize his ecumenical hopes. Such a gathering might even make ecumenical relations between the churches more difficult by hardening the lines of separation. Because of the Roman Church's understanding of itself as the only true church, argued Latourette, any dealing with Protestant churches as equals was quite impossible.[33] Without such equality, ecumenism was doomed. Yet Latourette did hope for greater charity to result from the projected Council.[34] The Roman Synod cast a long shadow over the hopes that the *Christian Herald's* editor, Daniel A. Poling, might have entertained about the outcome of the Vatican Council. He quoted sections from the Roman Synod's constitution relating to the laity. They were to be excommunicated if they passed laws harmful to the church; they were forbidden to read books published by Protestants; they were not allowed to worship with "non-Catholic cults." Since the Pope had addressed this Synod, and since it was expected to be a model for other dioceses, Poling could expect little from the Vatican Council.[35]

The influential *Christianity Today* greeted the announcement of the Council with great caution and a good ideal of suspicion about its designs. What could come of such a meeting as long as it was clear that the pope's supremacy could not be questioned? He was "in possession of truth." His personal friendliness reminded *Christianity Today* of Rome's foe, the Soviet Union's Anastas Mikoyan, whose "smile seemed to promise so much, but who could concede so little because of prior commitments."[36] The editorialist concluded his somber reflections on the coming Council by quoting from Foxe's *Book of Martyrs*, wherein the saintly reformer had wished that the delegates at Trent had looked north beyond that city's lovely hills rather than down the musty Vatican corridors of heretical accretions."[37]

At other times, *Christianity Today* expressed a moderate welcome to renewal in Catholic theology concerning the Bible and the Reformation. Although any genuine unity with Rome was impossible, these developments made conversation feasible. But what could a council do to foster these beginnings? Would it not be dominated by a very conservative majority who would crush the creative minority? And would not the hierarchy simply use these new theological openings for its own narrow ecclesiastical goals?[38] Moreover, the new dialogue that seemed to be developing in the United States among Catholics and Protestants was itself cause for alarm. Such talks were off on the wrong foot, and could only lead to vapid liberalism and a kind of get-together sentimentality. *Christianity Today* opened its pages to

C. Stanley Lowell, who flayed Robert McAfee Brown for what Lowell saw as a milksop approach to Catholicism. Could Brown not see that the chasm was unbridgeable? Romanism and Protestantism were completely incompatible.[39]

*Lutheran Standard*, the organ of the American Lutheran Church, saw the pope's announcement as a call to the rest of the Christian world to "come home." It was emphasized again that this Council would not really be of ecumenical concern to Protestants, but was rather an internal Catholic venture. And even if Protestants did have a more active role in the meetings, the Roman Church was eternally fixed in its doctrines. Nothing of real significance could be altered; at most, a few trifles of Canon Law, liturgy, and discipline might be changed. Protestants were warned to beware of any ignominious capitulation.[40] A few months later, Walter G. Tillmanns, writing in the same journal, described Vatican I in a very deprecatory fashion, and doubted that any Lutheran would grace the threshold of Vatican II. John XXIII seemed to be as madonna-ridden as any of his predecessors; how could a definition of the co-redemptive role of the Virgin Mary at the next Council bring Protestants closer to Catholics?[41]

*World Call*, the Disciples' missionary journal, sounded the same note about unchangeable Rome calling for a return to the one fold. The Disciples' theory of ecumenicity meant sharing with and learning from other churches, but this was far removed from the Roman drive to absorb other communions. A limerick was cited to characterize the Catholic approach as a sort of devouring ecumenicity:

> There was a young lady from Niger
> Who smilingly rode on a tiger;
> But they came from the ride
> With the lady inside,
> And the smile on the face of the tiger.[42]

The papal announcement was heard as the roar of a famished Roman tiger.

Most Southern Baptists saw little meaning for non-Catholics

in the pope's call for a unity conference. It was simply "a plan whereby all of us can be brought into the Roman Church and become obedient to the decrees of a religio-political monarch."[43] This was another example of the early interpretation of the proposed Council as a unity conference for all Christian churches. Even though the editor of *Baptist Standard* foresaw more unscriptural decrees issuing from Vatican II, he entertained an interesting if seemingly impossible hope:

> It will be interesting to see if the Roman Church can call one ecumenical meeting and really seek the union of all believers on the basis of the Bible rather than on an insistence that all others come into that church. If they can have just one such meeting without condemning all other Christians, and without making another ridiculous decree about something that is wholly within the hands of God, then perhaps many of us will believe that it is a sincere effort and not just a new device to publicize themselves before the world as the sole representatives of God.[44]

In some northern Baptist publications, the announcement of the Council met a cold reception. If the Catholic Church was serious about healing the old rift, it would have to consider seriously such Protestant tenets as the freedom of conscience denied by authoritarianism, the priesthood of all believers rejected by hierarchical and privileged orders, and the political and religious freedom so abused by Rome.[45] But the gulf was too great between Romanism and Protestantism for these demands to be met. The pope's friendly gesture was probably an attempt to loosen the Orthodox from their attachment to the World Council of Churches.[46]

The lack of repentance in the Roman Catholic Church for its sins against others in the past was another sign that the proposed Council would not be successful. Protestants could not expect from Rome a sincere act of contrition for the Spanish Inquisition, the fires of Smithfield, and the massacre of St. Bartholomew's Day. "No conclave called by the pope would ever allow free discussion of centuries-old issues which are still alive in the world."[47] At this stage of conciliar preparations it could hardly have been suspected that Catholic repentance and a good measure of free discussion would eventually be hallmarks of Vatican II. As 1959 wore on and it became clearer that the Council would be a Roman affair, it was attacked for its lack of ecumenicity. The very summoning of the Council, maintained Daniel Eckert, showed the impossibility of its being ecumenical, because Protestants and Orthodox would not be in attendance.[48] Eckert made no mention of the Council's announced purpose, namely, the reform of the Catholic Church from within, and the possible importance of this for improved relations among the churches.

Finally, *Missions*, the missionary organ of the American Baptist Convention, echoed themes similar to those seen above. Pope John's Council announcement was just an indirect call to return to Rome. No doubt some would succumb to these blandishments, but they were "amusing" in their naïveté.[49] A few months later, in reference to Winthrop S. Hudson's *Understanding Roman Catholicism*, an editorial in *Missions* stated that the Roman Church, with or without a council, spoke for itself. Vatican I had locked it forever into a centralized, absolutist, and infallible monolith. Pius XI had clearly proclaimed in 1928, in *Mortalium Animos*, that return to Rome was the only way of reconciliation. Before him, Leo XIII, in *Sapientiae Christianae*, had demanded complete submission and obedience to the pope as to God. Catholicism was held fast in the "stranglehold of ecclesiastical authoritarianism."[50] Such interpretations of the Catholic Church made the pope's plan for an ecumenical council seem fruitless, indeed, for a large part of the American Protestant world.

## PERSON AND ACTIONS OF POPE JOHN

On coming to the papacy in 1958, John XXIII met immediate criticism, not so much for his personal actions as for the coronation ceremony, which was offensive to Protestants of nearly all backgrounds. An editorial in *Christian Century*, welcoming Pope

John to his new office, took issue with the popular press for softening the meaning of *rectorem orbis*. The editors insisted that its meaning, taken from the symbolism of the tiara, was that of ruler of the whole world, even in a temporal sense. *Christian Century* repeated what it had said in 1939 at the coronation of Pius XII:

> We salute the new pope with highest respect for his admirable qualities of mind and heart and with good wishes for a long pontificate filled with all spiritual blessings. But as to the formula of his coronation, which expressed the central idea underlying all the pomp and ceremony by which he is surrounded and which so vividly impresses the mind of the beholder, we take this opportunity of saying, in order that there may be no misunderstanding, that to us and to many millions of Protestants the world around who are joining their felicitation to ours, it is blasphemous arrogance.[51]

But a few weeks after John's elevation to the papacy, *Christian Century* felt that the new pope might present some surprises. Although he was said to be a transitional pontiff, he began to act with vigor and determination: His choice of a name and his strong pleas for world peace were cited as examples.[52] Pope John was, however, the target of some barbed polemical shafts. A new "world potentate of tremendous scope and influence" had appeared on the scene. Little was known of him except a few vague rumors of pastoral sympathy and social consciousness, noted *Watchman-Examiner*. But the editorialist saw small promise in the old man: "It is doubtful that much reform will control the new pope's policies, since only the ashes of vision remain in a man of 76 years."[53] An associate professor of church history at Southwestern Seminary welcomed the new pope with an article showing the "ridiculousness" of the unbroken line theory of papal succession. It was nothing but a myth to gloss over the immoral character of so many popes.[54] And there was no reason to praise, as some Protestants had done, the democratic trend in Catholicism that allowed the election of a farmer's son to the papacy. Such an election was no sign of real democratic process, for the people in the Catholic Church had nothing to say about the electing delegates.[55]

Criticism was not lacking even in what might be termed a more moderate press. The perceptive and open-minded Dutch theologian G. C. Berkouwer, writing in *Christianity Today*, observed that many were praising John as a modern pope, lauding his humility, realism, and humor. But Berkouwer was disappointed with the new pope's first encyclical, *Ad Petri Cathedram*, in which there was nothing new. Even though it was more friendly toward separated Christians, it simply reiterated the old "come back" theology. It gave the impression that the coming Council would attract non-Catholics back into the fold, rather than lead to serious interchurch discussions.[56]

Nor was Karl Barth encouraged by the pope's first encyclical. Amid recollections and impressions of a journey to the United States, Barth referred to Pope John's letter as "the mild yet woefully poor-in-substance first encyclical of John XXIII— which, unfortunately, may indicate that the course of the Roman Catholic Church is still not determined or even co-determined by its theological vanguard."[57] Although Pope John's intellectual dispositions were not such as to make him fearful of theological development, it should be recognized that his own theological education had in many ways been circumscribed by the narrow perspective of clerical Italy. The theological vanguard that Barth mentioned would need the stimulating and permissive environment of Vatican II before the progressives could leave the periphery of the Catholic Church and take their rightful place at the center.

But even in this first encyclical on truth, unity, and peace, Pope John was projecting his characteristic friendliness, already noted by Berkouwer. J. Robert Nelson also appreciated this quality of openness to separated brothers. Though Nelson could not accept John's invitation to return to the Roman Church, he pointed out that it was not necessary to achieve total reunion before Christians could seek together the goals of love, truth, and unity.[58]

Another disappointment for many Protestants was the suppression of the priest-worker movement in France. This bold attempt to make the church relevant again to millions of alienated workingmen had captured the imagination and admiration of many in non-Catholic circles. It was hoped that Pope John would relax the partial ban already imposed on the priest-workers under Pius XII. But these hopes were dashed when John terminated the experiment.[59] Actually, the pope's own views on the role of the priesthood, as expressed in some of his writings, reflected the spirituality of withdrawal from worldly involvements that had long dominated the church, especially in Mediterranean lands.

Pope John was criticized again for his attitude toward freedom of the press. In his attempt to curb sensationalism in journalism, he seemed to advocate extensive legal limitations on freedom of the press. He did not seem to have enough confidence in controls that the press could impose on itself. *Christian Century* had hoped that John's kindness would also reflect an understanding of democratic liberties.[60] John's openness in this respect would not be clearly manifested until the appearance of his social encyclicals, to be discussed later.

After his first year as pope, John was still seen in the antidemocratic mold that had characterized the papacy for the Protestant mind, especially since the nineteenth century. George A. Leiper, writing in *Christian Century*, commented that from John's earliest days as pope he had been praised for his *simpatia* and his "possession of a 20th century mind."[61] Thus, it was hoped that he would allow Italian politicians to make decisions free from threats of eternal damnation. But, although the pope visited the jails of Rome, he did not speak out for their reform. He had reiterated the hard line that Catholics could not vote for an official who wanted to collaborate with the Communists. Leiper concluded that no pope could ever shake off the antiprogressive and antidemocratic provisions of the *Syllabus*. For Pope John, though he might entertain some liberal ideas, was still viewed as a prisoner of a reactionary Vatican tradition and thus basically afflicted with a fear of change. The liberal thrust of Pope John's social and international outlook was not yet manifest.

In spite of such criticisms, the pope's personality was communicating itself in a remarkable way, even in the early years of his pontificate. His personal qualities were making their impact on the Protestant world long before there was really any evidence that Vatican II would succeed in being a council of reform. Prior to 1961, when John activated Cardinal Bea's Secretariat for Promoting Christian Unity and issued *Mater et Magistra*, the pontiff's actions hardly augured major church renewal. The schemata for the Council were being drawn up for the most part by curial conservatives; if Vatican II had proceeded in the curial spirit, it might have amounted to no more than a codification of the work of Pius XII and a reaffirmation of standard theology, punctuated by a few or many condemnations. And yet, before concrete papal actions changed the course of events, the spirit of the man himself was creating the climate for the changes to come.

Simplicity of mind and heart, revealed in refreshing candor and communicative warmth, were qualities of Pope John that won the esteem and affection of many Protestants. Intimations that such traits would be welcomed in the non-Catholic world were seen in the following passage from Geddes MacGregor's *The Vatican Revolution*, published in 1957:

> Little children are, indeed, as the Gospel reminds us, often wiser than their elders. They exhibit flashes of insight that astonish us. It is almost as though some supernatural agency had entered into them and spoken. But what gives little children this strange, occasional superiority in wisdom over their elders is their receptivity and freedom from prejudice. An old man may be very learned; but the cumulative prejudices of a lifetime blind him, making his learning as dust. A pope could very well have that beautiful simplicity of mind and heart that all good men love and admire in children. But if he had, its first manifestation would be an extraordinary willingness to learn from others and a striking pliability of mind.[62]

For it was precisely Pope John's openness, humility, and willingness to criticize his own traditions that helped to break down centuries-old barriers with non-Catholic Christians. An Episcopal writer saw in these papal characteristics hopes for the reunion of Catholic Christianity.[63] Although many great obstacles to such reunion would long remain, John XXIII was definitely projecting a more friendly image of the Roman Catholic Church. A year after his elevation to the papacy, *Christian Century* editorialized: "For the first time in many generations a prelate sits on the papal throne whose kindness outshines the imperial splendor of Rome."[64] Signs of a thaw in the religious cold war between Catholicism and Protestantism were in evidence. The liturgical renascence was contributing to a new understanding of the church among Catholics. The adoption of the term "separated brethren" indicated a new ecumenical attitude, and biblical studies were building a bridge between the churches. At last, there was a chance for a true dialogue in which Protestantism could teach as well as learn.[65] In a review of three books on Pope John, Wayne H. Cowan noted that "the impact of his personality on the popular mind has been greater in just one year than that of all his predecessors."[66]

Reporting from the Eucharistic Congress in Munich, Martin E. Marty noted that Pope John seemed to be cultivating the image of "pope of unity."[67] A sign of this developing image was John XXIII's much appreciated gesture of removing from Catholic prayers obnoxious references to other communities. Such terms as "nefarious sects" and "heretical wickedness" were deleted from the baptismal rite. *Living Church* rejoiced in the pope's attempt to accentuate the positive. But the editorialist also hoped that these changes in manner presaged more important changes in substance, such as the "sacrilegious" practice of rebaptizing validly baptized Christians when they entered the Roman communion.[68]

But the pope's gesture in eliminating offensive references from Catholic prayers, which was welcomed in more liberal Protestant circles, was badly received by *Baptist Standard*. Did the pope think that Baptists would join the Catholic Church just because he had removed statements that could hurt feelings? The pope and his Council had better do far more, insisted the *Baptist Standard* editor. They had better renounce the view that the Roman Church was the sole depository of God's revealed truth. If they fell short of this, they had better address their pleas for unity to "the men of Mars."[69]

The visits of non-Catholic churchmen and public officials to Pope John were also variously interpreted by the progressives and the conservatives in American Protestantism. Among many evangelicals, who tended to look askance at ecumenical efforts even within Protestant ranks, the visits to Pope John implied dangerous compromise of principle. The church dignitaries were beating a one-way path to Rome; the pope was not reciprocating with a visit to Canterbury.[70] These visits were indirectly giving credence to the Roman pretensions of being the one true church. Even if unity were possible, what would be gained by one massive church?[71] This plaint of the editorialist revealed a common fear among evangelicals of a superchurch that would dominate their freedoms and distinctive structures (and perhaps force them into social involvements not to their liking).

*Watchman-Examiner* deplored the fact that the rash of visitors to the pope failed to decry the Roman Catholic use of police power to persecute evangelicals in various countries.[72] Such abuses of religious liberty, which flowed from the doctrine of being the one true church, according to a widespread interpretation among Protestants, precluded a positive attitude among evangelicals toward the visits to Pope John. With differences between Rome and the Reformation as grave as they were, there was no room for "toe-kissing."[73]

The objections of evangelicals to the visits to John XXIII were based not only on doctrinal rejection of Roman claims, but perhaps more importantly on what were seen as implicit perils to the principle of separation of church and state. For some, the most disturbing element in ecumenical discussions was the alleged lust for temporal power among ecclesiastical bodies.[74] The meeting of John and the Archbishop of Canterbury provoked this observation.

An even sharper expression of fear for the principle of separation was voiced when President Eisenhower visited Pope John. The President should not "be received in audience" by anyone, editorialized *Baptist Standard*.[75] Even if the pope was the gentle man of admirable qualities he was made out to be, continued the editor, "he is still just a mortal man who assumes divine prerogatives."[76] Was Eisenhower visiting the head of state or the head of a church? If the former, then the issue of American cardinals voting for a foreign potentate should be raised again. If the latter, then the President should have looked into his Presbyterian creed where the pope is called "antichrist" because he impedes the course of the gospel.[77] It was fervently hoped that the President did not bend the knee to anyone, "since he represents the truest free-born of the world."[78]

Later, the visit to Pope John of Brooks Hays, a past president of the Southern Baptist Convention, caused some comment. He went, it was explained, as a private person, for the purpose of strengthening religious freedom and other freedoms around the world. *Baptist Standard* thought that he failed to accomplish this goal because he did not confront the pope with the persecutions of Protestants in Spain and elsewhere. It was of little avail to mention these infringements only to Cardinal Bea's Secretariat.[79] Only one man had all the power in the Catholic Church, the editor stated. And he somewhat naively concluded that the pope could call off violations of religious liberty by simple fiat.[80]

In the progressive segment of the Protestant press, the visits of church dignitaries to Pope John were received as an omen of better relations between the churches. When Geoffrey Francis Fisher, Archbishop of Canterbury, made his historic trip to Rome, it was acclaimed as the opening of a new era of good will and understanding between the Church of England and the Roman Church.[81] Even though the conversation between the archbishop and the pope was not about substantive matters, their meeting betokened a new spirit and held out a portent of great significance. For it was already a major accomplishment that the Roman and the Anglican Church could talk freely and openly to one another, neither seeking victory over the other, "but as fellow disciples in the service of one Lord."[82] Although the ancient barriers still stood, the ability to communicate courteously was itself a grace of God.[83] Others saw in the visit of Canterbury to Rome the likelihood that it would be easier for Roman Catholic clergymen to enter openly into discussion with Protestants in the United States. Such talks could also be more fruitfully carried on in a spirit of ecclesiastical equality and mutual respect, because of the Anglican-Roman visit and others that might follow.[84] Elson Ruff of *Lutheran* thought that a new and excellent precedent had been set by Pope John. Never before in recent centuries had such visitors been seen in the halls of the Vatican. Now that the wall of silence between Rome and the Reformation had been broken, Catholic and Protestant churches would be more free to pursue the unity that they already possessed in large measure through faith and charity.[85]

The visits to Rome of the Presiding Bishop of the American Episcopal Church, Arthur Lichtenberger, and the Moderator of the Scottish Presbyterians, Archibald Craig, further underlined the newness of this ecumenical gesture made possible by the attitude of Pope John. Bishop Lichtenberger's trip to the Vatican was explained as an effort "to reciprocate the attitude of good will and friendliness which the present pope has always shown towards those who are seeking the union of Christendom."[86] Although no doctrinal issues were at stake in the first visit of the head of a U.S. church to the pope, important implications were involved. The chief result of such a meeting was the relaxation of Catholic-Protestant tensions, and there was good hope that the Secretariat for Promoting Christian Unity might be made a permanent body, since it had been so successful under Cardinal Bea in communicating the new Roman spirit to non-Roman churches.[87]

Perhaps the most remarkable visit to Pope John was that of Moderator Archibald Craig of Scotland. It was seen as an important gesture of charity and good will from a church that had traditionally had poor relations with the Catholic Church. The editorial comment in *Christian Century* on this visit was particularly keen: "If in the face of this, Scottish Presbyterians scarcely know where to look, how utterly taken aback must many a Roman Catholic have been on observing such an attitude towards an archheretic."[88] The same journal wished that Roman Catholic hierarchs in Latin America would meditate seriously on the attitude of their leader.

During the first half of Pope John's pontificate much had

been said about inner renewal and church unity, but there was little enough assurance that these desires would be brought to fruition in the coming Council. From late 1960 on, however, with the establishment of the Secretariat for Unity and Cardinal Bea's lecture tours across Europe, the new spirit of John began to solidify. It fostered new hope among progressive Catholics for significant renewal, and it opened unsuspected vistas to Protestants for more church unity. Late in 1961, J. Robert Nelson, while passing through Rome, said that it had been his privilege to take part in some astonishingly open and candid discussions with Roman Catholics on questions of unity. He noted that it was Cardinal Bea especially who showed the most genuine concern for the unity of Christians in the truth of one gospel.[89]

Perhaps the single most significant action toward unity before the Council itself was Pope John's dispatch of five official observers to the General Assembly of the World Council of Churches in New Delhi. Roswell P. Barnes, head of the World Council of Churches in the U.S., called 1961 the year of Christian unity. One of the main reasons for this, he asserted, was the presence of these five Catholic observers at the New Delhi meeting. This action of the Roman Church "marked official recognition of regular channels and procedures for communication and consultation."[90] The change by Rome from secretiveness to openness was most welcome, as was also the choosing of delegates to New Delhi of the highest caliber and commitment to ecumenism.[91] One of these Catholic observers, Rev. John B. Sheerin, editor of *Catholic World*, was quoted in an Episcopal journal as affirming the absence of anti-Romanism at New Delhi, and as foreseeing that the statements of this conference would have influence in Rome at the Secretariat and in preparations for the Council.[92]

In this chapter, Protestant reactions to Pope John's announcement of an ecumenical council and other activities of his first years as pope have been seen, for the most part, to be negative. Even in more liberal quarters, Roman exclusivism and absolutism appeared to block aspirations for truly ecumenical relations with

other churches. The Roman Synod, the banning of the priest-
workers, and John's first encyclical were usually taken as signs
pointing against any real renewal. And yet, amid these somber
forecasts, the openness and warmth of the pope's personality
kept breaking in to keep alive Protestant hopes for a new turn
in Catholicism. Encouragement was also found in the visits of
church dignitaries to the pope, and in the Catholic participation
at New Delhi.

In the more conservative journals, neither the pope's
conciliar announcement nor his other works in the first years of
his pontificate effected any appreciable change of sentiment
toward the Roman Church. Rome was still seen as radically antidemocratic, adrift in heresies, bent on its own self-aggrandize-
ment and on the absorption of all other Christian bodies. Thus,
in these circles, the gradual gestures of friendship by other
Protestants toward the pope were viewed as compromise of
principle and as naïveté. The curtain of "Roman pretensions"
was still too thick for conservatives. Even in the person of the
pope, they could not perceive possibilities for a new look in
Catholicism.

In the next chapter, the study turns to a consideration of the
influence of John F. Kennedy on the American Protestant mind.
At first glance this subject may seem extraneous to the Johannine
revolution in Catholicism. But on closer analysis, Kennedy's
political stance, especially during the electoral campaign and
the aid-to-education controversy, was an important manifestation of new possibilities in the relationship of Catholicism
to the state and to religious liberty. Both of these elements are
key features in the renewal launched by Pope John. That the two
Johns should have come together as prominent world leaders at
the same time is truly an extraordinary convergence of history.
That both Johns were crucial in altering the American Protestant
attitude toward Roman Catholicism is the theme of subsequent
chapters.

# 3

## *John F. Kennedy and the Johannine Breakthrough*

A perennial American objection to Roman Catholicism has been its antidemocratic character. Fear of Roman authoritarianism contributed heavily to the defeat of Alfred E. Smith in the presidential campaign of 1928, and if Kennedy's success in 1960 cannot be attributed mainly to a decline of that fear (a number of other changes had taken place in American life in the intervening 32 years), a key factor in his victory was nevertheless his ability to convince many Protestants that he represented a new Catholic attitude on separation of church and state and on religious liberty.[1] These themes would also become very important features of Pope John's Council, and therefore, of his influence on U.S. Protestantism. But the 1960 electoral campaign and Kennedy's subsequent stand on federal aid to church-related schools did much to prepare Protestants in America to accept the Johannine reforms as possible and credible.

As the real possibility of a Roman Catholic candidate for President began to dawn once again on the Protestant mind, dormant suspicions and fears of Roman domination came to life. As opinion polls before and after the election showed, the Catholic issue was a primary factor in the outcome. The extensive national discussion about Kennedy's religion, launched especially in the West Virginia primary and brought to a high point in Kennedy's address to the Houston Ministerial Association, laid bare Protestant attitudes toward having a Catholic in the White House. As early as April 22, 1960, in answer to a question from Episcopal Bishop James A. Pike of California, Kennedy told the American Society of Newspaper Editors in Washington that he completely supported the Constitution, specifically its clauses on religious liberty and the separation of church and state.[2] The real battle, however, was joined in West Virginia a month later between Kennedy and the preachers. At every stop in the Appalachian country, he told the people that he would not take orders "from any pope, any cardinal, any bishop, or any priest."[3] From this West Virginia experience, Kennedy learned to meet the religious issue head on. Thus, when Norman Vincent Peale lent his prestige to a Stop-Kennedy Protestant group, it became imperative for the candidate to confront the preachers in a decisive way. Such was the setting of his famous address in Houston on September 12, 1960.

But before considering the more positive aspects of Kennedy's influence on the American Protestant mind, it would be helpful to study various reactions among Protestants to his candidacy. First, the more conservative reactions will be considered, then those from quarters generally thought of as more liberal. A similar approach will be used to analyze the federal-aid-to-schools controversy. Finally, some conclusions about Kennedy's place in the Johannine revolution will be in order.


## CONSERVATIVE RESPONSES TO JFK

Even in 1958 the prospect of a Catholic candidate was eliciting critical reactions in various journals. An editorialist in *Lutheran Witness* surmised that in 1960 the Catholic issue would come to a head; and he concluded that there was good reason for questioning such a candidate on his loyalty to the Constitution. Citing Pius IX's *Syllabus*, this author maintained that official Roman Catholic doctrine condemned the American Constitution by rejecting separation of church and state. It is interesting to note that the writer made no attempt to place the statements of

Pius IX in their own historical context, which, if it would not have destroyed their cogency, might have mitigated it. A similar defect will run through much of the polemical literature against the election of John Kennedy. A second objection to a Catholic President was the Roman Church's disregard for religious liberty in various parts of the world throughout history.[4] Thus, the two main arguments, pointing to the incompatibility of Catholicism and American democracy, were abroad in the land, and were to ring in every city and hamlet during the next two years.

The organ of the National Association of Evangelicals carried a long article that pondered the possible consequences of having a Catholic President. Such an event would mean the greatest triumph for the Roman hierarchy in 300 years. The pope's absolute sway over his subjects would be extended forcibly to the United States, imperiling religious freedom and placing the Catholic Church above the American nation. If Protestants did not firmly oppose the Catholic candidacy, the author continued, it would spell the end of church-state separation in this country within ten years after the election.[5] The following month, the same journal was back on the attack. Would a Catholic candidate approve of boycotts of public schools, as article 1374 of Canon Law demanded? Would he accept the denunciation by the American bishops in 1948 of the Supreme Court's declarations on separation of church and state? Since Catholicism was both a church and a state, how would a Catholic candidate feel about the question of sending an ambassador to the Vatican?[6] These three questions contained oversimplified assumptions that could easily have been challenged by a knowledgeable Catholic. The point in quoting them is to show how widespread these reactions were when the possibility of a Catholic candidate began to materialize.

For some years before 1960, POAU officials were echoing in many Protestant journals the same fears and reservations about a Catholic President. In 1958, *Christian Herald* published an article by C. Stanley Lowell that associated a Catholic President with school boycotts, interference in marriage and family life, strict medical codes, excommunication for those who hailed priests into civil courts, and general clerical domination of American life.[7] The national elections of 1958 presented "a fascinating and fearful demonstration" of the Roman Catholic Church's growing power in government. "Certain agencies," the journal stated, were already preparing to meet the possible challenge of a "Romanist" candidate for President. POAU was one of the most important of these agencies.[8]

Nearly two years later, when the clamor of the July nominating convention had subsided, the anti-Kennedy forces rallied for their last defense of the besieged wall of separation. From the pulpit of the largest Protestant church in the world—the First Baptist Church in Dallas, Texas—the Rev. Dr. W. A. Criswell declared: "Roman Catholicism is not only a religion, it is a political tyranny." And the preacher felt that John Kennedy would not be able to stand up to the pressures of his church should he become President.[9] Copies of the Criswell speech were eventually distributed in large quantities throughout the country.

The editorial attention of *Baptist Standard* was trained intently on the presidential campaign throughout 1960. The main theme of the *Standard*, orchestrated in many ways, was that John Kennedy was a personable and honest man as an individual, but as President he would become a "tool of the Vatican." The editor asserted that in France, de Gaulle, a fervent Roman Catholic, had given in to hierarchical pressures for aid to Roman Catholic schools. The same was destined to happen in America with a Catholic in the White House.[10] E. S. James, the *Baptist Standard* editor, believed that Kennedy was personally committed to maintaining the Constitution, although the hierarchy condemned him for it. And this same hierarchy, continued James, reserved to itself the right to control every action of its subjects. Before a Southern Baptist could even think of supporting John Kennedy, he concluded, the senator from New England would have to make a formal rejection of any allegiance to a foreign religio-political state, and he would have to pledge solemnly to defend every American citizen's freedom from domination by the Roman bishops and their clergy.[11] By April, the *Standard's* opposition to

Kennedy had become unconditional. It was "inexorably opposed to a President of the Catholic faith."[12]

Baptists were warned not to be taken in by high-sounding Catholic theories of rights of conscience. Just as Catholics taught the deceitful doctrine of mental reservation on lying, so also their statements about rights of conscience had to be carefully analyzed. Conscience was what Catholics, and especially the hierarchy, defined it to be. This meant, according to the *Standard* editor, that a Catholic President would be obliged to form his own conscience in keeping with the position of his church. Thus, the Catholic hierarchy would become the President's conscience.[13] The bishops could be expected to withold their opinions on the candidate during the electoral campaign, since premature statements from the hierarchy would only lessen his chances to win. The hierarchy was even thought to be clever enough to desist from pressuring a Catholic President, even if he were to have an eight-year term. But eventually clerical dictation would grow, and the presidency would be in the hands of the Catholic hierarchy.[14] The White House would then become the real headquarters of the National Catholic Welfare Conference. Moreover, the seeming unconcern of the Vatican was just a plot to beguile the unwary, for although Rome despised Kennedy for his liberal attitudes toward non-Catholics, the Vatican could be expected to throw all its power behind him in November.[15]

As the election neared, the *Standard* ran longer background articles to help unmask the Roman villains who were plotting to overthrow democracy. Rome had always insisted on absolute obedience, even if subjects were commanded to believe that black was white. And such obedience could be enforced by subtle coercive tactics with complete disregard for personal rights; the end of total obedience to hierarchical dictation justified any inquisitorial means. Such was the contention of Robert A. Baker, who alerted Southern Baptist readers to the perils of a Catholic President.[16] He also maintained that Leo XIII had declared the *Syllabus* of Pius IX an infallible document. Thus, a Catholic President who worked for real freedom of religious conscience, freedom of education from clerical control, and freedom from church establishment would be heretically defying his church.

A few weeks before the election, another article apprised *Standard* readers of the long history of Catholic intolerance and persecution. The author affirmed that Pius IX and Leo XIII had denounced as godless and fallacious a government of the people, by the people, and for the people. The Roman Catholic Church was officially on record as being diametrically opposed to separation of church and state, religious liberty, public schools, freedom of speech, and equality of all religious groups before the law.[17] The same writer warned Protestants not to accept at face value Catholic declarations of democratic intent. Archbishop John T. McNicholas of Cincinnati had affirmed in 1948 the basic compatibility of Catholicism and democracy. This was only a sham policy of clever expedience, for in the same year, the authoritative *Civiltà Cattolica* in Rome was restating in the boldest terms the traditional Catholic doctrine of thesis-hypothesis, which had prevailed in Catholic thought especially since the last century. According to this teaching, the ideal (thesis) was the union of church and state, and the tolerated situation (hypothesis) was the condition of a country where Catholicism was still a minority religion.

It would be a mistake to paint all Southern Baptists with the same brush. While *Baptist Standard* was reasonably representative in the Southwest, *Biblical Recorder* in the Southeast offered a more nuanced view of the Kennedy campaign. An editorial on JFK and the presidency agreed that it was unconstitutional to apply a religious test to one seeking public office. But it was not against the Constitution, the editorialist continued, to interest oneself in how a man's religious affiliation might affect the conduct of his office. The editorialist charged that in 1950 Cardinal Dennis Dougherty of Philadelphia had refused John Kennedy permission to speak at an interchurch dedication of the Chapel of the Four Chaplains.[18] The same charge was made in a question after Kennedy's important talk to the Houston Ministerial Association in September, 1960. Kennedy answered this criticism by saying that on that occasion he had been invited

to speak at an interchurch dedication ceremony not as a congressman, nor as an American, but as a spokesman of the Catholic
faith. He could not accept such a role; but as a senator or as
President he could and would attend a similar gathering.[19]

The *Recorder* also felt that it was not bigotry to be concerned
about how American funds were used in Spain, where Protestant
churches had been closed. The same concern was voiced in
Houston after Kennedy's speech. What could he do as President
to restrain persecution of Protestant missionaries in Roman
Catholic countries of South America? He answered: "I would use
my influence as President of the United States . . . to encourage
the development of freedom all over the world. . . . One of the
rights I consider to be important is the right of free religious
practice. . . ."[20] It is reported that his Texan audience broke into
applause before he could finish his whole statement.

But fears of the Catholic menace ran too deep in the
Protestant psyche, especially in the South and among evangelicals, for John Kennedy's forthright convictions to have broad and
immediate effects. Evangelical journals, for the most part, took
the line of POAU. The main thesis of these writers was that John
Kennedy as President could not be free from ecclesiastical
pressures.[21] The Roman Church would simply use him for its own
benefit. Pope John XXIII ruled by divine right, affirmed a writer
in *Eternity*, and he would use this rule over a President for the
aggrandizement of the papacy. The pope was thought to control
the political and social thought of all Catholics.[22] Many of these
writers simply ignored subtler distinctions between temporal and
spiritual authority in Catholicism. Such distinctions were either
not known, or were not thought to be honest and pertinent, or
were interpreted as masks for Catholic duplicity. At any rate,
subtleties only tend to clutter up a polemical environment.

It was customary during the election campaign for Protestant
magazines to begin a criticism of a Catholic for President by
disclaiming all charges of bigotry. Opposition to political
Romanism was not to be classified as bigotry. The charge of
"bigot" was called a Romish smear on Protestants.[23] It was of
paramount importance to warn Americans, the same editorialist

asserted, that a Roman Catholic President could turn the nation in the direction of Spain or Colombia. For the "Vatican does all it can to control the governments of nations."[24] A Catholic President would probably shackle the nation with a Roman concordat system. How could a Catholic President resist papal pressure for an entangling concordat, since it was axiomatic that every Catholic had to listen to the church or risk damnation? Did not the Roman Synod decree that excommunication would be imposed on any layman who joined a party opposed to the church?[25] Not only past history, but events contemporary to the election campaign were employed to embarrass Catholics in their protestations of freedom from clerical control of political life. The Roman Synod was one example of an easy transfer of views from one culture to another. The Puerto Rican crisis and the *Punti Fermi* issue in *Osservatore Romano*, as will be shown, also hampered the exposition of liberal Catholic views on church and state and religious liberty.

*Watchman-Examiner* and *Missions*, more representative of northern Baptists, held opinions very similar to those in Southern Baptist and in generally evangelical journals. The general contention was that a Catholic President could not be a free man. An absolute, foreign power was seeking to enhance its prestige by the Kennedy election.[26] The country would really be ruled by an infallible and totalitarian pontiff, not by an American President. Such editorial broadsides were sometimes followed by appeals to Protestants to recall their proud heritage of freedom. Their forefathers had established a land of liberty, which now protected "the enemy [that] has come in like a flood."[27] Protestants should not forget the terror of clerical domination that haunted their ancestors, who fled from tyranny to this free continent. How could they possibly countenance a Catholic President who would have to bend the knee to the pope, just as he had had to bow to Cardinal Dougherty in Philadelphia in 1950?[28]

An important book, published in 1960, was Episcopal Bishop James A. Pike's *A Roman Catholic in the White House*. This book, widely commented on in the Protestant press, received notice in *Watchman-Examiner*. Pike's main thesis was that two Roman Catholic positions existed on matters of church and state. He distinguished between the official position and the American interpretation, as expressed by John Courtney Murray. Pike considered certain issues to be more or less dead, although these same questions received much attention in the conservative Protestant press. These issues were allegiance to a foreign state, diplomatic representation to the Vatican, and federal aid to parochial schools.[29] For Pike, various informal pressures, such as moral pressures on birth-control legislation and on the President's ability to participate in interfaith activities, were more realistic difficulties. *Watchman-Examiner* ran an article that discussed Pike's analysis of Roman Catholic positions. The author reviewed the dangers of the official Catholic position, but he also maintained that if the Vatican would approve the liberal Catholic position, the "threshold of a new era" would be at hand.[30] Pike had suggested that Americans make their electoral decisions on the basis of how much they could trust the candidate to adhere to his belief in the new Catholic outlook, and on how much they could trust his church itself not to interfere in American politics.[31]

The general position of *Watchman-Examiner*, however, was that Americans could not run the risk of having a Catholic in the White House, although they rejoiced that a small group of Roman Catholics stood for a change in the official Roman position. One writer[32] quoted Leo XIII to substantiate his cautions about a Catholic President. On the question of "modern liberties," Catholics were said to be subject to the pope with an "absolute obedience." The author referred to the insistence of the Catholic weekly journal *America* on such submission during the Al Smith campaign in 1928. It is interesting at this point to note the severity and literalness with which past encyclicals were interpreted in both the Catholic and the Protestant camps. The fact that encyclicals in many respects were historically conditioned and subject to new insights and reinterpretation was not taken very seriously until fairly recently. One of the gains of Vatican II was to be a clearer grasp of such historicity and the need for reformulation of doctrine.

The main drive of *Watchman-Examiner* was strongly against the election of John Kennedy. As the campaign neared its conclusion, all the stops were pulled to block a Kennedy victory. It was reported that even such influential Catholic journals as *America* criticized John Kennedy's grasp of Catholic doctrine.[33] How could the candidate square his independence from church dictation with the teaching of John XXIII, as echoed by *Osservatore Romano*, that a Catholic could never disagree with the directives of his church? This was interpreted by the author to mean that every sector of a Catholic's life was to be governed by the commands of the hierarchy. Had not Leo XIII said that it was an error for Americans to believe that church and state could be truly separated? (The fact that Leo XIII's understanding and experience of separation of church and state were very different from those of American Catholics was not even considered by this writer.) Protestants, therefore, were entitled to their grave misgivings over the election of John Kennedy, who, according to Sterling L. Price, would have to be completely obedient to the Roman pontiff as to God himself.

Thus, *Watchman-Examiner* saw no bigotry in urging Protestants not to vote for John Kennedy. It did so because of his church and its peculiar background, and the results this might have on American democracy and freedom of religion.[34] It was necessary to look ahead, and to see what might befall this nation in the way of clerical control of thought and activity if a Catholic were to enter the White House.[35] Even John Kennedy's famous Houston speech failed to convince *Missions* that it could chance a vote for his presidency. This talk did not satisfy, because the official Vatican stand on separation of church and state was still opposed to the American view on the subject.[36]

On May 17, 1960, *Osservatore Romano* published an article under the title of *Punti Fermi* that aroused much interest in the Protestant press, and embarrassed Kennedy's efforts to project a new American Catholic attitude toward church-state relations. The Italian document, composed in the context of Communist threats to take over the Italian government, insisted on the hierarchy's rights to intervene in the political field to guide the faithful. For the more conservative wing of the Protestant press, Rome was showing its true colors. *Baptist Standard* reiterated its belief that Rome would never change until the judgment of the Lord fell on its religio-political maneuvering. This review could respect Senator Kennedy and other Catholics as persons, but in the light of such documents as *Punti Fermi*, it was violently opposed to any church "that claims the right to control the world."[37] Catholics were urged to cut themselves free from such a tyranny and from the false claims of men who arrogated to themselves the prerogatives of God. Was the Vatican over-confident about a Kennedy victory, asked the editor of the *Standard*, or was it really trying to stop Kennedy, who might actually believe what he said about separation of church and state? That an alternative other than these, and one foreign to the American political scene, might have prompted the Vatican statement hardly entered the writer's mind.

*Christianity Today* saw Rome reaffirming its political intentions in *Punti Fermi*.[38] Although Kennedy replied that he would brook no clerical dictation if elected President, the Vatican statement, if applied to the United States, would render him "a tool of the hierarchy at the peril of his soul."[39] Dale Francis, editor of the popular weekly Catholic paper *Our Sunday Visitor*, defended Kennedy, stating that there was "no likelihood that a Roman Catholic President would have to act in a manner opposed to his oath of office." But *Baptist Standard* was not at all interested in likelihoods; it wanted guarantees.[40]

In the issue of *Christian Herald* preceding the election, its well-known editor, Daniel A. Poling, reflected on the recent *Osservatore Romano* article when he stated his view on the religious issue. He asked himself whether a church that claimed to have the last word in all phases of life would not in certain circumstances pressure a Catholic President.[41] Poling not only offered *Punti Fermi* in evidence, but he also showed himself unsatisfied with John Kennedy's explanation of why he had canceled his speech at the interfaith ceremony in Philadelphia at the Chapel of the Four Chaplains.[42]

*Punti Fermi* became one of the strongest negative arguments used in the Protestant press during the final days of the Kennedy campaign. For the editor of *Eternity*, an evangelical magazine, the *Osservatore* statement was clear proof that a Roman Catholic President could not be free of clerical pressures.[43] Similarly, as the election approached, an article in *Christian Century* saw the Italian statement as an indication that Kennedy as President would have to follow Catholic policy against birth-control programs for Asian countries.[44] In *Journal of Church and State*, the *Osservatore* article was interpreted as a sign of Rome's repugnance toward more liberal American views on church and state. After reviewing past papal statements on Catholic political theory, this writer concluded that John Kennedy and his Archbishop, Richard Cardinal Cushing of Boston, were directly denying dogmatic pronouncements when they advocated separation of church and state as well as religious liberty. But this author also had the perspicacity to see these challenges issuing from the Catholic community of America as harbingers of serious Roman Catholic rethinking on the subject of religious liberty and church-state relationships.[45]

Another embarrassing instance of clerical intervention in political affairs occurred in Puerto Rico in the final stages of the U.S. electoral campaign. The Catholic bishops of the island formed a party to oppose the re-election of Governor Luis Muñoz Marín, because of his stands on birth control, religion in the schools, and common-law marriage. Kennedy had been forthright in his condemnation of these episcopal maneuvers, but what was one man, asked *Biblical Recorder*, against the power of the Vatican and its infallible head?[46] It was not enough for 165 prominent Catholic laymen to support Kennedy's position, when official Rome continued to be silent about these ecclesiastical machinations. At home and abroad, the Puerto Rican debacle opened the eyes of many to both the doctrine and the practices of Rome.[47]

The Puerto Rican action was held up as an example of what the American bishops would do, if they were ever driven to the wall. The United States was well advised to watch "what a desperate section of the Roman Catholic Church will undertake when existing political parties thwart its will."[48] The only reason that there was no Catholic political party in the United States rested on the conviction of the hierarchy that it could control the existing political parties without calling them "Catholic."[49] The clear implication of these editorials was that a vote for John Kennedy was a vote for the Catholic bishops, who in turn would tell Americans how to vote.

Kennedy confronted the religious issue even more directly after a group of prominent Protestant clergymen met in Washington on Septemper 7, 1960, to form the National Conference of Citizens for Religious Freedom. Also known as the "Peale Group," these ministers made it clear that, despite Kennedy's claims to the contrary, his religion would make him unacceptable for the presidency. Kennedy was to give his famous answer to this charge in Houston, Texas, the heartland of those who opposed him on religious grounds. The Houston speech reiterated in a specially dramatic way what he had said in West Virginia and elsewhere. The substance of his talk can be summarized by quoting his own words:

> I believe in an America where the separation of church and state is absolute—where no Catholic prelate would tell the President (should he be a Catholic) how to act, and no Protestant minister would tell his parishioners for whom to vote—where no church or church school is granted any public funds or political preference ... an America that is officially neither Catholic, Protestant nor Jewish—where no public official either requests or accepts instructions on public policy from ... any ... ecclesiastical source ... where there is no Catholic vote, no bloc voting of any kind ... and where religious liberty is so indivisible that an act against one church is treated as an act against all.[50]

During the question period that followed, he was asked if he would urge Cardinal Cushing to forward his (Kennedy's) endorsement of separation of church and state to the Vatican. He answered that just as he would accept no clerical dictation in his office as President, so also he would not presume to tell the pope what to do. In brief, he maintained that should an irreconcilable conflict arise between his conscience and his responsibility as President, he would resign that office.[51]

Kennedy's stand in Houston was one of the crucial phases of his successful campaign. It was difficult to estimate how many believed his claim or thought that he could carry it out if elected. But it was generally conceded that he had won wide applause and sympathy through the Houston address, which was replayed on TV across the nation for the rest of the campaign.[52] It was impossible to measure what effect this film had on the millions who saw it. But it helped to divide the citizens legitimately concerned about Kennedy's views from those who opposed him on more emotional grounds.[53] It is also interesting to note that Theodore C. Sorensen, special counsel to President Kennedy, read the Houston speech over the telephone to John Courtney Murray before it was delivered. The Kennedy team wanted to avoid loose wording that might cause a furor in the Catholic press.[54] Since Father Murray was destined to be one of the principal architects of a key Johannine document on religious liberty, it seems legitimate to acknowledge John Kennedy's contribution to rendering the new Catholic stand credible to American Protestants. Through Kennedy's campaign and presidency, millions became aware of possibilities in Catholicism for new views on church-state and on religious liberty.

But these new openings in Catholic thought penetrated the Protestant consciousness but slowly. The immediate reactions to the Kennedy election were quite somber in the segment of the Protestant press under consideration. For *Christianity Today*, the JFK victory meant that the American dream had become hazier because of the Roman Catholic power displayed in Catholic bloc voting.[55] After reviewing some of the reasons for the Kennedy triumph, *Watchman-Examiner* could only ask itself dismally: What happened? It was not at all clear on that day what the future had in store for this democracy.[56] Although protesting loyalty to the new President, some Southern Baptists were especially apprehensive about the "frightening development" of Roman Catholicism in the United States. Now that one out of five Americans was a Catholic, there was real danger that this nation would be led in the direction of Colombia and Spain. Protestant evangelicals were called upon to resist the "bold, aggressive, astute" plan of the Catholic Church, which had maneuvered a man into the powerful office of President.[57] It seemed probable that the hierarchy would not interfere with the presidency for at least four years, but as time went on, no such assurances could be assumed.[58] For some Lutherans, who were traditionally more conscious of creeds, the great danger of the Kennedy election was not that a Catholic American had entered the White House. Rather, the grave peril for the nation consisted in "its [Catholicism's] false doctrine, which destroys the souls of men."[59] Lutherans were now specially called upon to meet the challenge of Rome with conviction and stronger faith.

## LIBERAL RESPONSES TO JFK

In this section, the word "liberal" is used in a general sense to characterize those Protestant voices which cautioned about the possible dangers in a Roman Catholic being President, but also manifested a distinct openness to the creative aspects of having a Catholic in the White House. Thus, the liberal opinions extended from cautious and critical to open and receptive. Certain journals, as will be seen, revealed both ends of the "liberal" continuum. At times, the only difference to be noted between the "liberal" and "conservative" reactions to Kennedy and his Catholicism was not so much the substance of negative views, but rather their tone and context. In one case, the opposition appears more reasoned in argumentation and even able to be convinced otherwise; in the other case, the rejection of Kennedy and his religion reveals a greater emotional dimension of fear and stridency.

A Disciples of Christ journal, *Christian*, concluded that it could not support a Roman Catholic for President in 1960. Although the journal could recognize certain mitigations of traditional Catholic stands in the political realm, it found the Roman Church still antidemocratic in its orientation. The pope had too much to say about social and political issues, and his voice carried too much weight with Catholics. Especially in the area of federal aid to parochial education, a real danger existed with the election of a Catholic President.[60] The Disciples' mission magazine also acknowledged with favor Kennedy's opposition to a Vatican ambassador and to public funds for parochial schools. But the editors felt that real doubt existed whether the candidate held the historic view of American democracy or whether he would allow himself to be influenced by hierarchical pressures.[61]

Kennedy himself seemed to hold liberal views, noted an Episcopal editor, but he thought it was especially unfortunate that the only Roman Catholics with whom Protestants could cooperate were those not loyal to official Vatican views.[62] Even those observers who sympathized with John Kennedy as a loyal American saw behind him the shadow of the papal curia, which had not changed much since the days of Pius IX. It was, therefore, not possible to vote for this candidate.[63] The Houston speech was praiseworthy, but Kennedy was urged to go further and proclaim that all were free to worship and profess their faith, and were not merely tolerated. He was asked to tell the Roman Church not to force on others its opinions concerning birth control and medical ethics.[64] Although Kennedy had indirectly acceded to these requests in his Houston talk, he was exhorted to confront concretely his church's official positions. Kennedy would probably have replied to this, as he did in Houston, that he did not think it proper to tell his church what it should hold.

But the problem of tight control of private opinion in Catholicism continued to make Protestants hesitant about voting for a Catholic President. The Roman Church claimed to teach authoritatively only in matters of faith and morality. But what important human question was not also a moral issue?[65] Moreover, in *Punti Fermi*, the Vatican had affirmed the right of the hierarchy to direct and form the views of the laity. This

Roman statement would surely make many Protestants hesitant about voting for a Catholic President, who, even as a layman, would be subject to Vatican dictation.[66] Although this allegation was not fully warranted in terms of American and European experiences of church and state, the *Punti Fermi* document nevertheless acted as a strong catalyst when it was dropped into the caldron of an American presidential campaign already stirred by religious friction. For the *Osservatore* article seemed to support a widespread Protestant view that a Roman Catholic's primary loyalty was not to God, but to the hierarchy. The private conscience of a Catholic was thought to take second place to ecclesiastical loyalties.[67] Thus, despite the attractive qualities of John Kennedy, the voice of POAU sounded very convincing when it spoke, in quite liberal journals, about the perilous ambiguities of the Catholic stand on church-state.[68] Almost apologetically, Methodists urged their fellows not to support a candidate whose church showed such a great rift between official and unofficial positions on separation and liberty.[69]

The influential *Christian Century* followed the campaign very closely, and frequently repeated that it was not a matter of bigotry to question seriously the possible influence of Catholicism on an American President. This review decried the intolerance toward John Kennedy shown by certain fundamentalist writers.[70] It denounced "political anti-Catholicism," and it defended the Roman Church against the bogus Knights of Columbus oath, a purely fictitious piece of polemics that had also been used against Al Smith in 1928.[71] Nevertheless, the editors of *Christian Century*, while guarding against a bigoted and unthinking stand, were not generally in favor of a Kennedy victory.

The evidence seemed to weigh too heavily against the candidate's religious background. In that office which symbolized much of what America was and should be, a Catholic could not be trusted. As far back as the spring of 1959, *Christian Century* was questioning the religion of a candidate whose hierarchy showed so little respect for American pluralism and separation of church and state. Furthermore, the freedom of all the churches seemed in danger because of Rome's doctrine of being the one true church.[72] This review maintained a consistent policy as the election neared. Without bigotry, it could look on Catholicism's tenets as a departure from the tradition of the United States. The candidate's relation to such a church demanded examination.[73]

In addition to the *Osservatore* article, *Punti Fermi*, two other examples of clerical dictation assumed considerable importance in *Christian Century*'s evaluation of John Kennedy. These have been referred to above: the interfaith dedication ceremony at Philadelphia and the action of the Catholic bishops in Puerto Rico. These examples of hierarchical interference were made the most of in an article by Harold A. Bosley published in *Christian Century* just two weeks before the election. Bosley admitted that Kennedy and other American Catholics like him had attained a deep respect for church-state separation and religious liberty. But he did not feel that the official Roman Church had developed sufficient maturity to understand and accept openly the deepest meanings of freedom in a democracy. Bosley seemed to express the views of the editors of *Christian Century* when he stated that he could not vote for a Catholic candidate for President until the Vatican officially admitted the doctrine of religious liberty.[74]

Moving left in the liberal spectrum of Protestant opinion about the election of a Roman Catholic as President, we find a sizable minority of open and even favorable attitudes. Just one week before the West Virginia primary, Dean Francis B. Sayre, Jr., of the Washington, D.C., Episcopal Cathedral and thirteen other nationally known Protestant leaders issued an open letter to their fellow pastors. In an attempt to stem the more prejudiced reactions to the Kennedy nomination, these ministers said: "We are convinced that each of the candidates has presented himself before the American people with honesty and independence, and we would think it unjust to discount any one of them because of his chosen faith."[75] Among the most active groups that worked for fair play and rational discussion in the campaign were the National Fair Campaign Practices Committee and the National

Conference of Christians and Jews. Though neither of these organizations could be called Protestant in the strict sense, their highest leadership and many of their members were Protestants.[76]

An important segment of the Protestant press expressed very balanced, and at times friendly, views about a Roman Catholic in the White House. The perceptive editor of *Lutheran*, Elson Ruff, did not think that clerical pressures on a Catholic President would be excessive. Ruff stressed the pragmatic aspects of Roman Catholic relationships to political persons and regimes, underlining the adaptability of Catholicism over a long period of history. Although Roman Catholic political theory, Ruff asserted, was badly in need of updating, this church had been hurt too many times in the past to insert itself quickly and unthinkingly into politics.[77] If the Roman Church were to put great pressures on Kennedy as President, and if he were to yield, Catholicism would suffer a terrible setback in the United States.[78]

Ruff was more worried about the bitter divisions that were being caused among religious groups during the loud campaign than by the perils of hierarchical domination over Kennedy. This rupture of charity among the churches could cloud agreement on more important things, such as the basic belief in one faith, one Lord, one baptism—here again the Lutheran concern about doctrinal matters was evident.[79] Another Lutheran writer repeated Ruff's approach to the Catholic issue in an interesting review of Bishop Pike's book *A Roman Catholic in the White House*. Albert R. Ahlstrom criticized Pike for keeping the question on the level of ideology, although he praised him for his presentation of the two main Catholic views on church-state and religious liberty. Ahlstrom thought that Pike should have paid more attention to the American way of trial and error, which had made itself felt on the Catholic Church in this country. Catholics in America were more affected by their firsthand experience of separation of church and state than by theories about it.[80]

Both *Presbyterian Life* (representing northern Presbyterians) and *Presbyterian Outlook* (southern Presbyterians) rejected any bigoted anti-Catholicism.[81] Catholics were not to be seen as constituting an undifferentiated monolith in their political views. Kennedy and many other American Catholics had repudiated traditional church-state theories, and had embraced the progressive opinions of American Catholic theologians. These Catholics needed encouragement rather than negative criticism, which would only deepen their minority complex. Thus, Senator Kennedy's Catholicism was not to be considered a barrier to his election, although Protestants had both a right and a duty to look searchingly into traditional Catholic positions. But since Kennedy had repudiated such aspects of the older tenets as the view of a privileged relation of the church to the state, limits on freedom of speech and worship, and public support for parochial schools, he was to be judged on his own merits.[82]

It was also asserted that in other nations, such as France and Germany, Catholics held the highest posts without detriment to the rights of other religious groups. The perspective of American Protestants would be distorted by a narrow-minded anti-Catholicism that lost sight of creative dialogue between Protestants and Catholics both in Europe and America. Although the traditional concept of church-state relations was firmly entrenched at the center of the Roman Church, it was hoped that Pope John might be able to modify it, if and when his Council took place.[83]

Although the Methodist *New Christian Advocate* ran its share of POAU articles before the 1960 election, its editor, T. Otto Nall, showed himself broad-minded on the issue of a Catholic President. In 1959, he prepared a list of questions that Methodist bishops might be advised to ask the candidates. The most important questions, he felt, were these: Would a Catholic President consider all religions equal before the law, and would he be opposed to the establishment of any one church as the official, or state, church? But Nall also proposed that Protestants examine their own consciences with such queries as these: Do Protestants underestimate the complexity of Catholicism and identify it with the Spanish type? Do Protestants identify

Protestantism with Americanism, and are they sitting too lightly to the dangers of secularism?[84] Nall thought Protestants should not deny the growing recognition of democratic values in the Catholic Church. Further, Nall affirmed that Protestant Americans had at times been as badly confused as Catholics on questions of church-state. The wall of separation had been wrongly interpreted to mean the absence of any cooperation between church and state.[85] He reminded Protestants that American Catholics, bishops included, held liberal church-state opinions in the very face of Rome. Although Protestants usually thought these liberal Catholics to be few, it seemed to Nall that they were many. Catholics showed considerable independence of Rome, and the supposed changelessness and "infallibility" of the Catholic Church were more elastic than American Protestants allowed themselves to believe.[86]

Among Episcopalians, opinions were generally open to a Catholic entering the White House. They were, of course, clearly aware of Roman traditions on church-state, but Kennedy's statement on the question seemed "so definite, detailed and precise that it is difficult to doubt his sincerity and his ability to be guided and controlled only by the Constitution of the U.S."[87] *Living Church* stated that it would support a qualified Roman Catholic for President. This review maintained that it was as strongly against Spanish clericalism as against secular dictatorships. But France and Germany had experienced no suppression of democratic rights under Catholic leaders; this fact was more indicative of what Kennedy would do in the White House than were citations from the canons of St. Gregory or from nineteenth-century popes.[88] *Living Church* disagreed with POAU charges that Rome was to be feared as a political force. History revealed that the Catholic Church did not crush national interests, and as a religion it had nurtured its share of great Christians.[89] Moreover, readers were reminded that important liberal views on church-state carried much weight among American Catholics.[90]

A strongly worded article in *United Church Herald* called any Protestant refusal to consider the Roman Catholic candidate on his merits both undemocratic and un-Christian. Even though there were grounds for questioning official Roman pronouncements, a Catholic President would not mean Vatican control of the White House.[91] Similarly forceful views about the positive aspects of a Catholic President were echoed by John C. Bennett. He admitted the Protestant fear that the Catholic Church would use the high office for its own aggrandizement. But in view of the more open Catholic theory on religious liberty and church-state relations, Bennett felt that a Catholic President could deal very effectively with these questions. After pointing out that a Catholic President might adopt various methods of approaching the birth-control question, Bennett asserted that a Catholic might also reflect the well-developed Catholic moral teaching on social justice, the just war, and communal concerns, as opposed to more individualistic views.[92]

In an answer to questions posed by the editors of *New Republic* early in the campaign year, John C. Bennett made a significant distinction among three Roman Catholic views on religious liberty. One was the traditionally dominant curtailment of religious liberty; the second consisted of the pragmatic approach of American bishops, who, for the most part, did not explicitly renounce the traditional position, but stressed the values of the American way of separation; the third view was that of those Catholics who were radically rethinking the traditional Catholic position.[93]

Such an ability to distinguish carefully the positive and negative aspects of Roman Catholic public policy made Bennett a particularly acute observer and interpreter of Catholicism in America. In the same article, he predicted that Catholics could be expected to work for severe divorce laws, but not to impose their views of birth control on others. He thought that Catholics would continue to seek public funds for parochial education; as will be seen in the next section, *Christianity and Crisis*, under Bennett's leadership, supported certain auxiliary benefits for Catholic schools while opposing direct federal aid. He foresaw no clear Roman Catholic international policy that would adversely affect the United States. On the contrary, Bennett claimed that Protestants had an exaggerated fear of the role of the pope in American affairs. Such people failed to recognize the variety in Roman Catholic views and in actions from country to country. For all these reasons, *Christianity and Crisis*, while warning against the dangers of bloc voting, urged Protestants not to vote against a Catholic simply because of his religion.[94]

Bennett was not unmindful of past and present Roman Catholic policies that caused grave concern and even fear among Protestants. Catholics had themselves to blame for cultivating a monolith image, for the absence of public debate among their church leaders, and for failing to repudiate the more rigid aspects of church policy. But Bennett was among those Protestants who criticized Norman Vincent Peale and others for focusing only on the negative aspects of Catholicism. These Protestants seemed to want to place the Catholic Church, during the Kennedy presidential campaign especially, in the worst possible light. Such critics stressed the authoritarian and totalitarian episodes of Catholic history, refusing to grasp the civic freedom of the Catholic layman and the inner dynamic of change within Catholic teaching and practice.

Bennett underscored an interesting correlation between religious opposition to the Catholic candidate and the somewhat more latent opposition based on attitudes toward social questions. Many of the most violent attacks on Kennedy came from those who would not have voted for any liberal Democrat, regardless of his religion. These critics often came from parts of the country that were the most backward on the issues of civil rights and social justice.[95]

Shortly after Kennedy's election, Bennett asserted that if he proved to be a good President, this would have a "most salutary effect on interfaith relations in our country."[96] He saw the Catholic vote less as a religious bloc vote than as a minority vote of those who wanted to remove the stigma of not being able to attain the presidency. For Catholics, said Bennett, the election victory was a sign of their full acceptance into the mainstream of American life. The fuller consequences of Kennedy's victory and the relationship of his presidency to the Johannine renewal in Catholicism will be discussed in the fourth and final section of this chapter. But before considering the Kennedy break-through in American Protestant thinking about the Catholic Church, it is important to study what might well be termed the second great religious issue of his presidency: the question of federal aid to parochial education.

## THE CONTROVERSY OVER AID TO CHURCH-RELATED SCHOOLS

Just before the inauguration, a Kennedy task force completed a plan for extensive federal aid to public schools, but with no provisions for private or parochial schools. Almost immediately after the Kennedy proposal was made known, Cardinal Francis J. Spellman of New York attacked the plan. In denying aid to Catholic students, he said, the new program "blatantly dis-criminated" against them.[97] Thus, President Kennedy's first year in office was to be the testing ground for important aspects of the religious issue that had seen so much a part of the electoral campaign. Would he succumb to hierarchical pressures? Would he maintain the traditional church-state separation in the area of education? Much of Kennedy's influence on Protestant attitudes toward Catholicism hinged on his answers to these questions.

Catholic devotion to parochial schools in the United States had been in part the defensive reaction of an alien, immigrant population to the Protestant ethos of the public school. It had also been a religious response to the growing challenge of secularism in the public schools. Although Protestants were not oblivious to the latter danger, they were generally committed to the public school system for its intellectual, moral, and democratic values. A common criticism of the parochial school in America centered on its alleged divisiveness of national unity and purpose. Moreover, American Protestants have been almost unanimously opposed to any direct aid to parochial schools, seeing such aid as a violation of church-state separation and as the beginning of ecclesiastical establishment and preferment.[98]

The conservative wing of the Protestant press reacted strongly against renewed Catholic attempts to "make the public treasury the target of its inordinate demands."[99] The National Catholic Welfare Conference was seen as spearheading the Catholic lobby in Washington to openly defy the principle of separation of church and state. Only an aroused citizenry could resist this "mounting Romanist determination."[100] Despite its arguments that double taxation in education is discriminatory and constitutes an indirect denial of parental rights, and that Catholic education is a public service, the Roman Church was characterized as a privilege-seeking minority. It would settle for some gains in school financing, always looking forward to the day when it could achieve majority status and then persecute other religious groups. Thus, *Christianity Today* saw once again the fulfillment of the dictum: Rome never changes. The new politico-educational maneuvers of the hierarchy were judged to be part of Rome's determination to make secular governments its own agents for ecclesiastical gain.[101]

But in the midst of these sharp criticisms of the Catholic Church, and especially of the American hierarchy, the first Catholic President was consistently praised, even in the most conservative segments of the Protestant press, for his interpretation of church-state separation. Kennedy was gradually diminishing the perennial Protestant fear that a Catholic President would necessarily be subservient to the bishops. It was to Kennedy's credit, editorialized *Christianity Today*, that he resolutely refused to be pressured by his church into altering his deepest constitutional convictions.[102] *Christian Herald* applauded the President's stand on the educational controversy. Kennedy was proving to all Americans, thought Dr. Poling, that a Catholic President could withstand pressures from the Roman hierarchy.[103] Also noteworthy in the Protestant view of American Catholics was the effect produced by Catholic laymen who were critical of the hierarchy's approach to the debate on aid to parochial schools. *Christian Herald* quoted the editors of *Commonweal*, who believed that "violent pronouncements" on the school-aid question by bishops had intensified religious antagonisms. It seemed clear that a powerful and perhaps growing tendency was developing among Catholic laymen to speak out in honest dissent. This was a healthy sign.[104]

The Catholic attempt to secure federal funds for their schools caused the Protestants to rally around President Kennedy and to encourage him to hold firm in his resolve.[105] Cardinal Spellman was generally cast in the role of the villain. He was described  as leading a massive attack on the tenet of church-state separation, driving a divisive wedge between Catholics and Protestants, and presumptuously demanding that non-Catholics pay for Catholic schools.[106] It appeared to some that the Cardinal, in the name of the hierarchy, was already trying to exploit the victory of a Catholic, and use him for the aggrandizement of the Roman Church.[107] Cardinal Spellman was accused of wanting to introduce into the United States the "dismal pattern" of European sectarian school systems.[108] This would lead only to interchurch strife, the destruction of the public school's unifying power, and the recrudescence of the deepseated fear of Roman Catholic political maneuvering in the nation.[109]

Some writers rose in defense of the public school system, which was seen as neither godless nor academically inferior. It was also more of a deterrent to Communism, they claimed, than the Catholic school, since the latter was under such totalitarian control.[110] The Catholic Church was dedicated to a policy of political subterfuge through which it would gradually exploit the public schools. The machinations were subtle, proceeding from bus transportation to hot lunches to school texts, and on to complete control.[111] If Catholic parents complained about double taxation, they had only themselves to blame. Private education was their choice; it was not imposed on them. Could they not emulate the Lutherans and Baptists, who did not ask a penny from the government?[112]

When it became clear that the Kennedy education bill was doomed, the Roman Catholic Church was charged with sacrificing the national welfare in education because Catholic demands were not met. *Eternity* stated that the bishops knew what they wanted. When they could not get it through their Washington lobby and Congressman John McCormack, they saw to it that everyone else would be equally deprived.[113] The Roman Church was prepared to flout the commonweal if it did not get its "pound of flesh." It would never be satisfied until it had imposed Roman Canon Law concerning Christian education upon American civil laws.[114] But *Watchman-Examiner* stood firmly behind President Kennedy, who had demonstrated that a Catholic President could protect the deepest convictions of those outside his church.[115]

In the South, the same alarm was sounded over hierarchical manipulations of the educational dollar. It was illegal, maintained the Texas *Baptist Standard*, for the federal government to give financial aid to sectarian religious education. Furthermore, it violated the profound convictions of American Protestants, who did not want to support Catholic schools with their tax money, especially since this would constitute taxation without representation. For the citizenry would have no control over the teaching or administration of the Catholic schools for which they were being asked to pay taxes. The *Standard* also feared that government funds for church activities would mean government dictation to the churches. This would destroy church-state separation and cut the roots of religious liberty.[116]

Baptists were urged to resist the relentless pressure of the Catholic hierarchy for government aid to their schools.[117] For the struggle was much more than a passing conflict between Catholics and Protestants; it represented a life-and-death war between those who were intent on turning the public schools into a clerically-dominated European system and those who cherished the essential values of the American public school.[118] For the Southern Baptists, this great battle had only been stalemated when Cardinal Spellman and his fellow hierarchs succeeded in killing the education measure in 1961.[119] The next session of Congress was to experience another round in the school-aid controversy. But even in May, 1961, the entire Southern Baptist Convention, meeting in St. Louis, passed a resolution praising the new President for his stand in support of religious liberty and separation. Wicklein quoted one of the delegates, who said: "Jack Kennedy is making a pretty good Baptist President." [120] Of course, it must be admitted that Kennedy's stand on the education issue was the politically wise thing to do. If he had given in to Catholic pressures, he would certainly have alienated most of the Southern Baptist voters in 1964, as well as many more moderate Protestants. But however mixed his motives, Kennedy's views on the relationship of church and state were consistent. On this point, a close friend and adviser said:

> The death of his aid to education bill, however, was accompanied by one of the most far-reaching changes in American politics effected during the Kennedy years. To a much greater extent than had been true the previous November, the ban on Catholics in the White House was dead also. John Kennedy had demonstrated that a Catholic could withstand the full pressures of the hierarchy on a bill of real significance to both sides, and he was toasted from Protestant pulpits throughout the land. One of his most violent opponents in the campaign a few months earlier, for example, Dr. W. A. Criswell of Dallas, called upon his flock "to stand behind President Kennedy and the Constitution." Even the POAU reported that it was "extremely pleased with President Kennedy" whose "strong stand ... will reassure and inspire all who believe in the separation of church and state...." [121]

Sections of the Protestant press, which on other issues frequently took a more liberal position, were almost unanimously opposed to Catholic endeavors to obtain government funds for their schools. Elson Ruff, editor of *Lutheran*, commented that the education controversy was another example of the Roman Catholic Church's long history of demands for special favors from governments. If the federal authorities agreed to subsidize Catholic schools, Ruff affirmed, the church situation in the United States would be drastically changed. But he believed that President Kennedy would be intensely loyal to the basic principles of the Republic,[122] even in face of another assault on American principles by Cardinal Spellman.[123] Lutherans were exhorted to write to their congressmen protesting the Catholic move, which was seen as impairing the freedom and independence of church schools. For government funds meant government control of policy in the schools. After the education bill failed in Congress, the hierarchy's pressure tactics were likened to those of the Puerto Rican bishops during the campaign.[124]

In official statements, groups of important church leaders opposed federal aid to parochial schools. Such declarations were made by the Methodist bishops and by the General Council of the United Presbyterian Church (U.S.A.).[125] The voice of POAU resounded widely in the Protestant press against the Catholic bishops as an "overt political force on the American scene."[126] These were the words of C. Stanley Lowell, whose pen was ever active during the school-aid debates and before.[127] An interestingly liberal note in *Christian Advocate* was sounded in an article criticizing the methods of POAU at a time when the magazine was reflecting POAU conclusions on the education issue.[128] But the Methodist Bishop of Washington, D.C., John Wesley Lord, attacked the Catholic endeavors as bolstering through government funds a system of education that did not contribute to democratic living.[129]

*United Church Herald* found it ironical that a Roman Catholic President was locked in combat with his own bishops over the education bill. The bishops' efforts were interpreted as showing great disrespect for the principle of separation of church and state. Had not the bishops in 1948 called the separation principle a "shibboleth of doctrinaire secularism"? The editorialist, Andrew Vance McCracken, admitted that a risk of secularism, which most Protestants deplored, existed in public education; but that risk had to be taken to preserve a free society. He concluded: "One might wish that the monolithic Catholic community of today were more sensitive than seemingly it is to the essential values of our free democracy and free institutions."[130]

*Christian Century* maintained a constant barrage of criticism along the lines already seen in other reviews. The usual points were repeated: the Catholic Church was an aggressive hierarchy flexing its muscles, a religio-political institution seeking control of the American government, and a totalitarian mentality with small regard for democratic principles and institutions.[131]

Cardinal Spellman's request for help in nonreligious facilities was judged a ruse. What control would local authorities have over these facilities? Could non-Catholic teachers and students find a place in such state-aided Catholic schools? It was clear to *Christian Century* that Cardinal Spellman was just using the non-religious facilities argument as a dodge to get federal support for the Roman Catholic Church.[132]

But during this intense conflict of opinions, the President's image was gradually improving in Protestant eyes. In one of those paradoxes of history, the American Catholic Church was winning while it was losing. The loss was one of esteem among those Protestants who viewed the Catholic efforts to secure government funds as a recrudescence of callous, undemocratic power plays. But Kennedy's firmness of purpose and independence of judgment was gaining a long-range advantage for American Catholics. For it was dawning on Protestants that a Catholic could actually be a free President of the United States. Thus, *Christian Century* found itself in the strange position of defending a Catholic President from criticisms advanced in a review edited by Jesuits, *America*. After Kennedy's first year in office, *America* had discussed the President and the Catholic Church, implying duplicity in the President's conduct. It was not a question of the Catholic Church and the President, countered *Christian Century*, but rather of the President and the nation. Kennedy had to be faithful to the Constitution, as interpreted by the Supreme Court, and faithful to his own conscience.[133] When the federal-aid-to-education bill was being resuscitated in 1962, *Christian Advocate* reopened its critical commentary on organized Catholic efforts to obtain government subsidies. But at the same time, it praised Kennedy for standing firm. Through the din of the educational battle, a new image of the American Catholic statesman was emerging.[134]

Perhaps the most creative approach to the Catholic requests in the education controversy was to be found in the pages of *Christianity and Crisis*. Its editorial opinion, advanced by John C. Bennett, was also stanchly opposed to direct government aid to parochial schools, and it seemed to him that the tactics of the Catholic hierarchy were raising old fears among many Protestants. But Bennett, unlike many of his confreres in Reformation churches, was truly sensitive to justice for the children in parochial schools. Although direct aid was unacceptable, Protestants had a responsibility to explore ways of helping parochial schools through such auxiliary benefits as bus transportation, free lunches, class texts, and medical services. Various "shared-time" programs were also encouraged.[135] This indirect aid was based on the premise that the principle of separation did not mean that Catholic children in parochial schools were to be separated from the nation's concern. Bennett criticized fellow Protestants for being too negative in their attitudes to the Catholic quest. They were content to reiterate the principle of separation without searching out new ways to meet in justice some of the needs of children in parochial schools. The end result of such negativism would be the repeated defeat of an education bill that was important for all the nation's schools.[136]

As the thinking of *Christianity and Crisis* developed on the question of educational aid, the whole staff of the review declared by 1963 that the issue for parochial schools had entered a new phase. It was no longer to be judged on the basis of ideology, but rather on the practical merits of the requests without admitting such direct aid as would infringe upon the traditional separation principle.[137] That the whole question should have shifted, in the minds of the editors of *Christianity and Crisis* at least, was a significant event. Without intending to narrow this development to a unique cause, it seems reasonable to assert that the decline of ideology was in part due to a new-found trust in a Catholic President. Ideologies often rest on absolutist and static premises. Such ideology can be a defense mechanism, hardly ever subjected to serious scrutiny, but convenient as a weapon to wield against an enemy that conjures up old hates and fears. For American Protestants, these evil premonitions connected with Catholic power were most intense in the vision of a Roman Catholic President as the subservient tool of clerical designs. For a number of Protestants, this bad dream began to fade when John Kennedy said no to the bishops of his own church.

## THE KENNEDY INFLUENCE

The point of studying the impact of President Kennedy on the American Protestant mind has been to show how the Kennedy breakthrough related to the Johannine revolution. It is important to stress, however, that the influence of President Kennedy on American Protestantism was not directly and causally related to Pope John. As has been indicated, a liberal school of American Catholic thinking on church-state issues had long been growing through the American experiences of Catholicism. Kennedy would probably have had the same effect on Protestant thinking even without a John XXIII in the papacy. But what is truly remarkable is the convergence of a John Kennedy and a John XXIII in the same moment of history. Kennedy's position on church-state and religious liberty would eventually be in line with the progressive thinking on these subjects which Pope John would make possible through his Council. This historical convergence helped to foster a new image of the Catholic Church in Protestant eyes. In this sense, John Kennedy as President had an important relationship to the total impact of the Johannine changes.

To draw this correlation more tightly together, the concluding section of this chapter will first summarize the positive effects of Kennedy's presidency on American Protestants, a topic already touched on in the course of the chapter. The summary will, however, introduce new references. Second, a closer association of Kennedy and John XXIII in the Protestant mind will be examined. And finally, some later evaluations of Kennedy will underline the importance of his role in the wider Johannine influence of altering the Catholic image in the eyes of American Protestants.

A year before the presidential campaign of 1960, when the dangers to religion and democracy envisioned in the election of a Catholic President were being reviewed, glimmers of hope for positive contributions from a Catholic candidate were noted. It would be heartening, editorialized *Christianity Today*, if Kennedy could initiate a movement in his church to repudiate those things that make his fellow American Catholics objects of suspicion in public affairs.[138] In what was both a conjecture and a desire, *Churchman* stated that John Kennedy as President might have a greater influence on Roman church-state views than Rome would have on him.[139] If he used his presidential power responsibly, not favoring Catholics, it would perhaps be the last time in American history that a President's religion would stir up so much comment.[140] As the passions of the campaign died down, Elson Ruff reflected, the Roman Catholics could seize the opportunity to show how serious they were about religious freedom under all circumstances. And Protestants could observe what really happened when a Roman Catholic became President.[141]

Even in conservative circles, rays of hope shone for a better day in Catholic-Protestant relations in America through the Kennedy victory. The fact that a Catholic could be elected was interpreted as a triumph for the spirit of religious liberty in the land. And it represented a new era for American Catholicism, since Kennedy was expected to foster liberal Catholic views, which, it was hoped, would be promoted by Pope John's Council.[142] The Kennedy administration could set new milestones in the story of church and state in America, and bring about a "modification of Catholic doctrine and practice relevant to freedom of religion."[143]

The Kennedy impact on American Protestants in his stand on aid to education has already been adequately reviewed. Suffice it here to cite briefly a few comments expressed in *Baptist Standard*. While Nelson Rockefeller, who was from a long line of Baptists, gained Roman Catholic support for his candidacy in New York by holding out aid-to-student grants for private schools, John Kennedy was standing fast on his promise not to succumb to hierarchical pressures. "That is the picture," commented E. S. James, "and many of us won't forget it."[144] The *Standard* felt that no President since Lincoln had been so tested as Kennedy was in his first weeks in office, when he was pressured by the hierarchy on the education bill. Although such an estimate smacks of hyperbole, it does bring out Kennedy's influence in Southern Baptist areas. On various occasions Southern Baptists wired the President, commending his courage and statesmanship.[145] In spite of the political aspects of these Baptist gestures, the message was registering that a Catholic President could uphold separation and religious liberty as forcefully as a Protestant.

The southern quarterly *Journal of Church and State* made some acute reflections on the Kennedy phenomenon. The principle of separation of church and state was so well established in American tradition that no Roman Catholic President would be able to uproot it. Like other religious groups that had immigrated to this country from Europe, Roman Catholics had been conditioned by the American ethos of practicality and secularity. Old European dogmas about union of church and state would be ineffectual to alter this American conditioning of Catholicism.[146] In another article, W. Stanley Rycroft reviewed the unfortunate effects of clericalism in the Catholic Church's involvement in political and social history. But the same author believed that President Kennedy would

> ... in God's providence, dramatize to this nation and to the world the fundamental importance of the separation of church and state, that a spiritual church, whether it be Roman Catholic or Protestant, or any other, is the only kind of church which can guarantee freedom from the baneful influence of clericalism, a blessing which any church should learn to cherish.[147]

President Kennedy and Pope John XXIII were at times directly linked in the influence they exerted on the American mind. Claud D. Nelson affirmed this relationship when he wrote in 1961 that Catholics were experiencing a new sense of emancipation in two respects. John Kennedy was breaking the barrier that had kept Catholics out of the White House and thus out of full acceptance in American life. And John XXIII, by calling a council and by projecting a fresh image of the papacy through his own personality, made Catholics feel freer to converse and criticize. The fact that they felt more free, concluded Nelson, meant that they were more free.[148] Such a change in Catholicism could not but have an effect on the Protestant outlook toward the Roman Church. This indirect influence of Pope John and President Kennedy was evidenced again in 1962 when President Kennedy received the Brotherhood Award of the National Conference of Christians and Jews.[149] Both pope and President were champions of a brotherhood wider and deeper than that which more narrow and provincial Catholics had previously projected.

Recent biographers of President Kennedy do not fail to relate Pope John and President Kennedy in their influence on the non-Catholic evaluation of the Catholic Church. The noted historian and presidential aide during the Kennedy administration, Arthur M. Schlesinger, Jr., remarks that Kennedy "felt an immense sense of fellowship with Pope John XXIII, but this was based more on the Pope's practical character and policies than on theological considerations."[150] Both men made their marks in the practical order: one as a political, the other as a pastoral practitioner. But Schlesinger's next comment could have applied to Pope John as well as to President Kennedy: "Still, his basic attitude was wholly compatible with the sophisticated theology of Jesuits like Father John Courtney Murray, whom he greatly admired."[151]

Something of the close relationship between the two Johns can be seen in the reflections of an English political commentator two years after their deaths. Henry Fairlie wrote:

> The identification—"He was as much our President as theirs"—was astonishingly strong. I found my mind returning to the almost similar identification when Pope John XXIII had died a few months before. "He was as much our Pope as theirs," people of all religions had felt able—almost bound—to say. Neither of them had held office for long, yet both had become universal symbols. . . . The world gazed on them and felt hope.[152]

But the impact of both pope and President on the American mind is perhaps best described by the close confidant of President Kennedy, Theodore C. Sorensen:

> Partly as a result of John Kennedy's example—and the example of another John whose brief tenure as Pope overlapped Kennedy's

brief tenure as President, but who by tragic chance died before
they could meet—the Catholic Church in this country became less
subject to recriminations from without and more subject to
reform from within.[153]

Tributes to Kennedy from conservative Protestant quarters
after his assassination are worth noting, for these testimonials
are of more moment than the encomiums to personal virtues
which might be expected after such a tragic event. On the day of
the assassination, E. S. James wrote:

> President Kennedy was not a Baptist, but it is safe to say that
> Southern Baptists have had no better friend in the White House.
> He defended the principle of religious liberty for which many
> Baptist forefathers gave their lives. The editor of this magazine
> probably knew him about as well as any gospel minister in America
> knew him. We gave it as our opinion last February that he was a
> man of courage, integrity, and faith in God; and we shall ever
> remember him as such.[154]

E. S. James's meeting with President Kennedy the previous
February had been an extraordinary example of the President's
influence on a leading Southern Baptist who had been among the
stanchest foes of a Catholic in the White House. James had
complimented the President on his adherence to church-state
separation and on his unbiased appointments, and later
described the man he had formerly thought would be a tool of
the Vatican:

> ... our President is a man of faith who is characterized by great
> intelligence, much ability, strong convictions, and profound
> courage.... This editor was remarkably impressed with his
> apparent sincerity, his gracious and understanding spirit, and his
> eagerness to be President of all the American people.[155]

A former president of the Southern Baptist Convention,
Brooks Hays, also revealed his deep respect for John Kennedy's
important contribution to religious understanding in America.
Shortly after the President's death, Hays commended him as a
sincere and practicing Christian who wanted to be President of

all the people, regardless of their religious ties. He also affirmed that the President had defended church-state separation and religious freedom as well as any of his predecessors. Shortly before the President's assassination, Hays had received from him a thank-you note for the gift of *The Baptist Way of Life*. In inscribing the book, Hays had referred to President Kennedy as "belonging to the soul of the Church—Baptist, that is—for his devotion to freedom and to the biblical idea of universal love linked him to us as well as to his Catholic people."[156]

*Christianity Today* affirmed that "Kennedy had kept his promise to the nation and had held the line on the church-state issue."[157] And in a later review of his administration, *Journal of Church and State* stated that with "unusual intelligence and integrity" he had left a notable legacy to church-state relations in the United States. In 1960, many Protestants believed that the election of a Catholic President would mean the end of a free church in a free state, but Kennedy had disproved this assumption. Moreover, the real legacy was not just his election, but his utterances and positions as President, especially in the aid-to-education controversy.[158]

In concluding this chapter, it would be well to cite briefly the estimates of Kennedy's influence on the American religious milieu as seen by his principal biographers. Commenting mainly on the presidential election, Theodore H. White wrote:

> In the long sight of history, John F. Kennedy cast his appeal, *above all*, to the overwhelmingly Protestant majority of the American people, and ran uphill to convince them that whatever differing pasts and heritages they brought to 1960, they shared a common future and common conviction for the years ahead.[159]

These common convictions pertained in large measure to a salutary separation of religion from national government. On this count, as Sorensen points out, Kennedy was true to his word. There was no religious favoritism in his selection of appointees, no fear of ecclesiastical pressures, no divided loyalty of any kind, and no ambassador to the Vatican. He vetoed a bill on censoring obscene literature, not because he favored such literature, but because the bill labored under grave constitutional defects. He showed no hesitancy in attending a Protestant service in his capacity as President, as when he went to Congressman Sam Rayburn's funeral in Texas or when he attended a prayer breakfast with evangelist Billy Graham. He even met privately with Paul Blanshard in the White House to discuss church-state matters. When he visited Pope Paul, he shook hands, but did not kneel or kiss the pontiff's ring. And, finally, remarks Sorensen, the only mass held in the White House during his administration was celebrated on November 23, 1963.[160]

Arthur M. Schlesinger, Jr., remarks that the President showed little knowledge of or interest in Catholic dogmatic traditions. Nor did he consciously try to apply the papal social encyclicals to the American scene. But he had a great respect for the kind of religion that could transcend the barriers of parochialism and narrow individualism, a religion that "can challenge the purpose and performance of the nation-state" and contribute something meaningful to the universal needs of society. On this broad vision, Schlesinger comments:

> This was not in the mid-fifties the typical attitude of American Catholics; but if Kennedy was not a typical American Catholic, his example helped create the progressive and questing American Catholicism of the sixties. Above all, he showed that there need be no conflict between Catholicism and modernity, no bar to full Catholic participation in American society.[161]

This breadth of vision and concern for the spirit and needs of modernity is a further link between Pope John and President Kennedy. It was part of Kennedy's appeal to Protestants and others in America and abroad. It was also, as the next chapter will show, part of Pope John's impact in his monumental social encyclicals, *Mater et Magistra* and *Pacem in Terris*.

# 4

## *Two Social Encyclicals: Johannine Universalism*

Chapter 2 dealt with some of the earlier phases of Pope John's efforts toward Christian unity: the announcement of the Ecumenical Council, the visits of non-Catholic churchmen to Rome, the establishment of the Secretariat for Unity under Cardinal Bea, and the sending of official observers to the meeting of the World Council of Churches in New Delhi. These developments represent a second circle of Pope John's interests, in addition to the first circle of intrachurch renewal. A third circle, that of justice, peace, and unity for the whole of mankind, seemed to take on a greater urgency as John's pontificate progressed. The Berlin crisis, the revolutionary births of new African nations, and later the Cuban blockade were major examples of the constant threats to the brotherhood of mankind. In the context of these events, Pope John's social encyclicals, *Mater et Magistra* and *Pacem in Terris*, reflected his deep concern for the issues of world justice and order. The reaction of American Protestants to these documents will be studied in this chapter. It affords still another indication of the American Protestant response to Pope John.

*Mater et Magistra*, issued on May 15, 1961, was in many ways a continuation of the social teachings of *Rerum Novarum* (Leo XIII, 1891) and of *Quadragesimo Anno* (Pius XI, 1931),[1] but Pope John's encyclical also reflected and stimulated important developments and innovations in papal social teaching. Conscious of the new developments in technology and in urban and rural life, as well as in international responsibilities, Pope John went well beyond his predecessors in appreciating and accepting contemporary "socialization." Not to be confused with socialism, "socialization" meant for Pope John the growing interdependence of men which had given rise to various patterns of group life and activity and, at times, to social institutions established on a juridical basis. Socialization affected both private and public spheres of life. It was both the cause and the effect of growing state intervention.

Pope John accentuated the positive values to be derived for personal and societal development in the more interdependent life of modern nations and organizations. Neither Leo XIII nor Pius XI would have been prepared to accept welfare-state tendencies as readily as Pope John was, although he also pointed out the dangers in these trends to the integral development of the human person. The protection and growth of the person was a basic Johannine emphasis, seen in his endorsement not only of natural law, but especially of natural, inalienable human rights. Underlying these rights was his paramount concern for human freedom. Thus, man was not to be considered simply as the object of the blind forces of socialization, but rather as a being capable to a large extent of freely shaping the patterns of evolving socialization, through individual and group efforts.

*Mater et Magistra* continued to uphold the rights of private property, a constant theme in papal social encyclicals. The right to own and use property expresses the dignity of man, who controls inanimate creation, and helps to preserve his economic and political freedom. But Pope John went beyond these arguments for private property to stress the importance of both the social dimensions of property rights and the primary value of human labor. For property is external to the person, but human work is both external and internal to man, as his personal manifestation in the natural world. From this more personalist standpoint, John advocated man's rights to just remuneration for his labor and also to some participation in the process of decision-making.

Some observers wondered why the pope did not explicitly denounce Communism in the encyclical. This would have been contrary to his spirit of open dialogue with all men, and it would also have contradicted the important distinction, to be made more clearly in *Pacem in Terris*, between an unchanging ideology and changing historical movements and persons. His answer to Communism was a positive one: to show that the church was deeply concerned with the freedom, dignity, and development of the human person, not merely in some supernatural sphere, but in his this-worldly existence. Other new aspects of the pope's concern were his extended treatment of agriculture, a socially and economically depressed vocation in many parts of the world, and his views on the new and the old, the rich and the poor nations. This Johannine thrust was oriented to abolishing an exaggerated dualism between religion and the world, and to securing just conditions for the development of free persons.

For the most part, Protestant reactions to this encyclical were meager, when compared with the later response to *Pacem in Terris*. Of course, the second encyclical spoke to the world after the first session of Vatican II, which had aroused a new ecumenical awareness toward Catholicism among non-Catholics. Moreover, *Mater et Magistra* was not of a nature to arouse either great antagonism or enthusiastic approval, for many of its goals had also been sponsored in documents of the World Council and the National Council of Churches. More than ordinary intellectual background and perspicacity were needed for a full perception of the creative advances of the encyclical. In addition, the encyclical appeared when national attention was largely focused elsewhere: on the struggle for civil rights, the aid-to-education controversy, the Eichmann trial, and preparations for the New Delhi conference of the World Council of Churches.

By far the greatest portion of Protestant reaction consisted of either straight news coverage of the letter's issuance, or of general statements about its importance and meaning. E. S.

James admitted in *Baptist Standard* that the encyclical had some good things to say, but he characterized the letter as "an instrument of religion," not a charter for international relations[2]—a reference to a South American statesman who had quoted from *Mater et Magistra* before the United Nations. James found such conduct offensive to many non-Catholics; the suspicion that Rome was using the encyclical for political gain was strong. Although *Christianity Today* spoke of *Mater et Magistra* as one of the great social documents of our time, it also warned its readers to beware of Rome's political intentions. It would be to the advantage of the Vatican to have the rich nations of the world help the poorer ones, especially in Latin America where the Roman Church was both entrenched and imperiled. Why, wondered the editorialist, were so many Catholic nations poor and illiterate?[3]

The general comments, however, were generally favorable. In a year-end review of significant happenings in Roman Catholicism, Ralph L. Keiper, writing on "Roman Catholicism" in *Eternity*, felt that *Mater et Magistra* would "become an outstanding social document of our era."[4] The well-known Methodist preacher Dr. Ralph Sockman saw the document as a comprehensive and generally correct appraisal of the world's ills, and Dr. Lawrence L. Durgin, a New York Congregational minister, was quoted as saying that the encyclical "challenged our imagination and our responsibility."[5] Kyle Haselden, then managing editor of *Christian Century*, compared the pope's letter to the New Delhi "Message of the World Council of Churches." He thought that such a comparison would be embarrassing for the WCC from the viewpoint of both style and content.[6]

A few publications went beyond surface comments to probe the content and significance of *Mater et Magistra*. Reinhold Niebuhr called it a "formidable document . . . a welcome extension of this (the Catholic social) doctrine to the new era of a technical civilization."[7] Niebuhr reflected on the amazement in some Protestant quarters that such a "reactionary" church could advocate such advanced policies as the welfare state, social insurance, and aid to underdeveloped countries. Niebuhr judged that this amazement stemmed from ignorance of the Roman Catholic grasp of the social substance of human existence. In Niebuhr's view, the Catholic Church in traditionally Catholic territories had skipped the whole period of classical *laissez-faire* economy, and to some extent had also avoided the national parochialism of Hobbes and Luther. Thus, Catholicism had been able to preserve many of the organic and social elements of the medieval synthesis, and to bypass the extreme individualism of both the Protestant and the modern-secular ethos.[8]

Although these broad Niebuhrian generalizations would seem to call for numerous qualifications, they tie in well with the observations of Professor Paul Ramsey of Princeton University. Ramsey commended the pope for making the universal common good, an obviously social point of view, the controlling idea of his encyclical. Pope John's doctrine of private property, according to Ramsey, was a clear manifestation of the social dimensions of the new papal teaching.[9] In the Johannine outlook, individual private property had become a derived right, for it had become much clearer than in the days of Leo XIII that in theory and practice the use of property was inevitably social or common. The challenge was to bring about an equitable private and personal participation in that common use.[10] Pope John had given the primacy not to principles of innate natural right of ownership, but to principles concerning the universal common good. In past Catholic social teaching, the need for public ownership and use of certain kinds of property had not been denied, but it had been much more circumscribed with cautions than in Pope John's attitude toward socialization.

Henry B. Clark, writing on "Can Property Be Private?" in *Christianity and Crisis*, reflected on Ramsey's views of private property as treated in the encyclical. Clark thought that, despite Ramsey's claims to the contrary, the pope's basic views on property rights negated the liberal advances of the encyclical. Clark understood papal thought on private property to uphold absolute private rights, in keeping with a long Catholic social tradition, as opposed to the social responsibility of those rights.[11] At best, Clark affirmed, Roman Catholic social thought was ambiguous on whether ownership and use of private property were determined mainly by the common good or by individual private rights. He felt that *Mater et Magistra* suffered from the same ambiguity, for it seemed to make family welfare the principle criterion for property rights. This, thought Clark, was a far too "notoriously parochial unit of loyalty." But a closer reading of the encyclical seems to indicate that Ramsey was closer to the truth than Clark in interpreting the Johannine attitude toward private property and its social dimensions.

Ramsey rightly saw that the pope's attitude toward property in *Mater et Magistra* stemmed more from a proper understanding of the principle of subsidiarity than from absolutist views about individual property rights. Subsidiarity meant the preservation of personal initiative, in both individuals and subordinate groups, to provide freely for the common good. Persons operating through their legitimate groupings in society were not to be ultimately determined by individual property rights, although these were to be respected according to law. In the Johannine perspective, there appeared to be a move away from a more external, static, and reified view of property rights to a more personal, communal, and dynamic conception. Therefore, Ramsey asserted, Pope John could welcome degrees of socialization that would not have been accepted by Leo XIII, as being opposed to strict individual rights of property and individual independence.

Thus, there was an important shift of viewpoint in John XXIII from the individual and social character of work (the thing produced or private property) to the individual and social dimensions of the person's labor and his human initiative. Ramsey saw that for John the this-worldly aspects of human labor, as a manifestation and development of the person, were of paramount importance. In this light, one could reflect on whether Reinhold Niebuhr's criticism, in the context of the encyclical, of the exaggerated dualism between natural and supernatural in Roman spirituality was truly valid.[12]

Although the question of private property caused some disagreement among Protestant commentators on the encyclical,

Pope John's attitude toward agriculture and the underdeveloped nations met with strong approval. It seems fitting in retrospect that a son of peasants from Sotto il Monte should have been the first pope to concentrate his concern in such a specific way on the depressed condition of many agricultural communities in the world. The encyclical considers agricultural issues related to taxation, credit banks, social insurance, price protection, and the promotion of ancillary industries.[13] Ramsey and Pelikan both noted the importance of this Johannine concern,[14] and A. Dudley Ward underlined the close similarity between the encyclical's treatment of rural issues and that of the General Board of the National Council of Churches.[15] Methodist Bishop Marshall Reed agreed with the pope that inadequate machinery and selfish attitudes were responsible for a good portion of the world's hunger. He felt that "the pope's encyclical is right in harmony with the idea of stewardship."[16]

Reinhold Niebuhr rejected the view of the professional anti-Catholics that the Roman Church was a pernicious monster in modern society. He saw it rather as an impressive survival from medievalism, a survival that had managed to apply its ancient wisdom to the comfort of a harrowed generation in a nuclear and technical age.[17] At the same time, Niebuhr claimed that Rome dealt better with perennial problems; it was embarrassed by new historical developments, such as the current issues of war and population control. On the question of birth control, this renowned scholar echoed the views of many Protestants that Catholicism was frozen in an outdated morality that betrayed the Roman Church's inability to extricate itself from a feudal order and mentality.[18] In *Christian Century* Niebuhr thus described Pope John's attitude toward birth control in *Mater et Magistra:*

> All this oblique appreciation of Catholic social theory vanishes and becomes unambiguous criticism when the new encyclical betrays the Achilles' heel of human frailty and displays dated rather than eternal wisdom.[19]

*Christian Century* left no doubt about its views on the encyclical's birth-control policy. The editors called it "an archaic, demonstrably ineffective and harmful remedy to the ordeals and the perils which an accelerated population inflicts on the human race."[20] Pope John did not overlook the rising birth rate in some countries and the lowered infant-mortality rate resulting from advances in modern science, nor did he ignore the imbalance between growing populations and the inadequacy of agriculture and other forms of production to provide for more people. But, while urging the development of scientific means of production, the pontiff held the line on the traditional Catholic doctrine on limitation of births, although he did reinforce the need for responsible parenthood. The pope's stand drew a regretful comment from Dr. Truman B. Douglass, executive vice-president of the Board of Home Missions of the Congregational Christian Churches: "It is regrettable that Pope John should so courageously have demanded all-out aid for underdeveloped nations, then denied them succor for one of their most acute problems—population control."[21]

The Protestant view on birth control was stated in brief by the General Board of the National Council of Churches in a booklet, "Responsible Parenthood." It held that most Protestant churches agreed that contraception and periodic continence were both morally acceptable when the motives were right. Professor Ramsey further maintained that Protestants stressed the Genesis doctrine that in marriage two shall become one flesh, which "states the unitive purpose of marriage and places sexuality in the context of personal covenant for the attainment of its final, primary, and highest end."[22] Catholicism, on the other hand, seemed to stress, as did the pope in *Mater et Magistra*, the biblical commands "Increase and multiply" and "Fill the earth and subdue it." But a more radical reason for the Catholic immobility on this issue, Ramsey indicated, was a rigid natural-law perspective that locked the Catholic mind into a biological determinism. Although Niebuhr appreciated certain aspects of Catholic natural-law thinking, he, too, criticized its rigidity and metaphysical determinism in reference to birth control.[23]

Another widespread Protestant criticism of *Mater et Magistra* was based on what might be called its authoritarian tone. Ramsey felt saddened that the liberal thought and wise action of the encyclical needed to be directed by "an intrinsically deplorable obeisance to ecclesiastical positivism. . . . "[24] For Niebuhr, Roman doctrine, even when fundamentally sound, was always presented with a note of pretension. He thought that this was inevitable when a human and historical institution claimed eternal, transhistorical, and divine validity.[25] Thus, Niebuhr asserted, one could not expect even from Pope John an admission of indebtedness to modern learning for advances in Roman Catholic teachings. These doctrines were always presented as known from time immemorial in the Catholic heritage.

The Protestant reaction to Catholic authoritarian ways, discussed in the first chapter, was revealed again in criticisms of what seemed to be a dictatorial spirit in the encyclical. *Dialog* welcomed the pope's ideas, but bridled at this "presumption" of being teacher of all.[26] *Lutheran Standard*, too, was bothered by the seeming assertion that the pope must have the last word in social and theological matters.[27] *Living Church*, which was customarily open and favorable to Roman Catholic thought, also decried a certain overly authoritarian tone in Pope John's letter. The editors described it as the voice of a maternal church dictating to an obedient and paternalistic state. This did not commend itself to men brought up in an atmosphere of freedom.[28] Another closely related observation of *Living Church* was that the Catholic Church in this document as in others seemed to lack a sense of the intractability of sin. The encyclical seemed to imply that all would be well if only right belief and reason prevailed. This strain of utopianism in Catholic writings seemed to deny that the Catholic Church also stood under the constant judgment of God.

In general, the Protestant press defended *Mater et Magistra* from attacks of ultra-conservatives.[29] A cryptic remark by Truman B. Douglass summed up the attitude of many Protestants towards right-wing criticisms of *Mater et Magistra:*

> It is interesting to speculate how the encyclical would have been received by members of the House Committee on Un-American Activities and the John Birch Society if it had been issued by the

churches [Protestant]. Fortunately, His Holiness is not likely to be accused of being a fellow traveler.[30]

John C. Bennett hoped that the influence of *Mater et Magistra* would help change the American mind about the "utterly self-defeating character of the intransigent forms of conservative anti-Communism."[31] And Ramsey, in a similar vein, ventured to hope that the encyclical would be the occasion for a repression of "do-it-yourself McCarthyism" on local, state, and national councils of churches. Perhaps the universalist outlook of Pope John might even devolve on Protestants and others to help them fashion the nation's policy in the light of the universal common good and solidarity of all men.[32]

Two months before his death, Pope John issued his second social encyclical, *Pacem in Terris*, one of the most remarkable documents in modern papal history. It was widely acclaimed and commented upon by scholars and statesmen in the religious and secular realms. For the first time, a papal letter was addressed not only to Catholics, but to "all men of good will." The pope's language was less involved and ecclesiastical than was normal in encyclicals;[33] in clear and sincere words, John sought to realize his growing desire to speak to all men, especially those in the "third circle," that is, outside the Christian community. In some respects *Pacem in Terris* repeats *Mater et Magistra*, but the second encyclical was a natural complement to the first. *Mater et Magistra* had dealt largely with social and economic questions; *Pacem in Terris* spoke to more political and international issues.

*Pacem in Terris* fired the imagination and awakened the dormant hopes of the vast majority of "men of good will."[34] Pope John did not stress the abstract idea of natural law so much as the natural rights of persons to develop in real freedom. He left no doubt about his preference for democratic participation in civic and social life. He strongly affirmed an inviolable liberty of conscience in religious matters, and advocated the fullest possible education for all men. In a ringing plea for peace, he urged an end to the arms race, and the building of the United Nations into an effective instrument of world peace. He unequivocally supported the efforts of international organizations to succor less privileged peoples, and he risked a daring new opening for dialogue with Marxists and other unbelievers. This latter aspect of Pope John's universalism was not well received by some of his more timorous fellow Catholics. Protestant reactions to the encyclical can be divided into those of general recognition and acclaim, and those of critical analysis.

For the most part, *Pacem in Terris* was favorably received in the Protestant press. *World Call* noted that the "encyclical has received more comment in church magazines than any message from any individual in recent years."[35] The readers of *World Call* were invited to give the pope's letter their special attention, and not to let old prejudices about Catholicism deafen them to this progressive message. After listing examples of the wide coverage given to the letter, *Witness* also urged its readers to become acquainted with the pope's thought. This review mentioned the various social and political problems treated in *Pacem in Terris*, and praised Pope John's leadership.[36] *Churchman, United Church Herald*, and *Christian Century* were also among those journals that encouraged their readers to study the papal message. The very fact that so many Protestant editors recommended study of the encyclical was itself a significant change of attitude toward documents of the Roman Church.

This new openness to Catholic statements would seem, at least partially, to have flowered in the climate of dialogue created by the first session of Vatican II, as will be seen in the next chapter. But it was also the result of the intrinsic merits of the encyclical, and it reflected the open personality of Pope John himself. *Churchman* was impressed that the Vatican statement radiated so much universal good will, and that it avoided a certain self-centered propaganda for the Roman Catholic Church. For these reasons, the editors of *Churchman* found *Pacem in Terris* unique among papal letters.[37] *United Church Herald* was moved not only by the perceptive blending of Christian ethics and practical suggestions for peace, but also by the friendly and conciliatory tone of the "ecumenical pope." The editors felt that it was one of the most important documents of our time.[38]

*Christian Century* noted that the 25,000 words of the encyclical, appearing in Holy Week of 1963, "breathe compassion, faith and hope."[39] Howard Schomer, writing in *Christian Century*, remarked that the document showed John to be more than an ecumenical peacemaker of notable humility and sincerity: he was also a bold, creative political thinker. After commenting favorably on such topics of *Pacem in Terris* as the solidarity of races and nations, the reduction of nuclear dangers, and the establishment of an effective world political authority, Schomer concluded: "Pope John XXIII has given unprecedented Christian leadership on the all-dominating question which the living generation must now answer: Will we carry history towards increasing peace and justice, or will we end history in the most absurd of all wars?"[40]

But even *Pacem in Terris* did not escape criticism in a few very conservative journals for being a clever papal plot to enhance Roman authority. The Vatican's appeal to groups outside its own sphere suggested that the common goal of world peace was being used to extend the influence and authority of the Roman Church.[41] Furthermore, the same editors felt that the pope, like the rest of today's religious prophets, had forsaken the role of leading men to peace with God to follow the illusory dream of peace on earth. It is interesting to note the strong dichotomy in this type of evangelical thinking between individual salvation and churchly involvement in human social structures. The more apocalyptic *Moody Monthly* emphasized the appearance of the antichrist in the pope's vision of a centralized world authority. And his conciliatory gestures toward the Communist world were interpreted as a foreshadowing of the apostate church of the end-time, which would lead men astray. Because of his concern over merely temporal matters, Pope John was termed a humanistic religious leader, one who had compromised Christianity by worldliness.[42] But such criticisms of *Pacem in Terris* were in no way characteristic of the main current of American Protestant thought.

Among the more perceptive analysts of the encyclical, the pope's stress on natural rights was seen as a significant development. Reinhold Niebuhr saw the main significance of *Pacem in*

*Terris* to be Pope John's incorporation of the modern democratic natural-rights theory into the traditional natural-law theory. Niebuhr described the latter as a system logically deduced from a static and a historical concept of human *nature*. In contrast, the natural-rights theory, based on Stoic eqalitarianism and Lockean democracy, stressed in a more intuitive way the rights of individual *persons*. Neither theory was originally historical, but the rising classes in modern democracies availed themselves of the natural-rights theory. In this outlook, the rights of individuals were emphasized more than the duties, but Pope John managed to weave rights and duties together in a responsible relationship of mutuality.[43] In the responsible context of God-given rights implying duties, John could advocate the modern view of rights arising from the dignity of the person: such rights as those of conscience, of emigration, and of a just wage, and the rights of women, minorities, and poor nations.

The stress on human rights was widely noted in the Protestant press. Herman F. Reissig, an official of the United Church of Christ, pointed out the similarity of Pope John's views on human rights with those expressed in the United Nations's declaration on human rights. This writer underlined the pope's up-to-date thought, since these were the rights of modern democratic societies. Reissig also commented on Pope John's special commitment to democratic forms of government, which at the same time did not canonize any particular regime. This was typical of the balance and sagacity of the encyclical.[44] Moreover, as Robert McAfee Brown remarked, this new appreciation in a papal document of the natural rights of democracies was a manifestation of creative growth in understanding the implications of natural law. For in addition to repeating the usual natural-law norm of the common good, Pope John made much of the criterion of "the dignity of the human person."[45] This represented in papal teaching a shift in emphasis from the traditional natural-law accent on "nature" to a deeper appreciation of "person" as a fundamental ethical criterion. Paul Tillich did not overlook this aspect of *Pacem in Terris* in his general assessment of the encyclical:

My first reaction to the encyclical is the general one that its appearance is an important event in the history of religious and political thought and may have practical consequences for man's historical existence. Most valuable seems to me the way in which is emphasized throughout the document the ultimate principle of justice, *the acknowledgement of the dignity of every man as a person*, from which follow his rights and obligations in the manifold encounters of man with man. (Italics added.)[46]

A number of Protestant thinkers criticized *Pacem in Terris* for what they saw as a certain utopianism. Reinhold Niebuhr thus assessed the encyclical: "The difficulty with this impressive document is that the church ... speaks as if it were a simple matter to construct and reconstruct communities, not by organic processes of history but by an application of 'the sense of justice and mutual love.'"[47] Niebuhr saw this optimistic view of world order as more Pelagian than Augustinian; the encyclical seemed not to take seriously enough the sinfulness of human self-interests. Reason constituted only one motive of men's actions; national interest, mutual suspicion, hostility, and fear were equally significant springs of action that must not be overlooked because they were unpleasant.[48] In the same vein, *Christianity Today*, although it referred to *Pacem in Terris* as "masterful and historic," pointed out that the Roman Catholic natural-law view inclined toward an exaggerated optimism about man, without giving due consideration to the pervasiveness of evil.[49]

This reaction to the encyclical manifested a good example of the classic Protestant sense of human selfishness and depravity, in both individual and group contexts. The *peccator* of the traditional Reformation maxim, *simul justus et peccator*, tempered the following response of Paul Tillich to Pope John's invitation to all men of good will:

And one should not appeal to "all men of good will" as the encyclical does. One should appeal to all men knowing that in the best there is an element of bad and that in the worst there is an element of good will. ... This view of the ambiguity of man's moral nature ... should distinguish genuine hope from utopian expectations.[50]

Paul Ramsey expressed the same criticism. He thought that *Pacem in Terris* paid slight heed to the moral ambiguity in the human situation; the natural-law perspective, for which Ramsey's writings have shown much respect, tended to attribute too much to "the perfect order of the universe."[51] Besides the traits of moral evil in man, Niebuhr affirmed that human differences of culture and aspiration would make one question the harmony derivable from Pope John's "community of mankind."[52]

Thus, for these observers, though the encyclical stressed many important positive elements, it did not come to grips sufficiently with the moral ambiguities of power in political affairs. Ramsey thought that this failure in the pope's letter made it sound a trifle too much like a document of the turn-of-the-century liberal Protestant tradition. The papal treatment of disarmament was disappointing in that it jumped rapidly to the desirability of disarmament, but was less clear in helping to discover the criteria to be employed by the various nations during the long interval in which they seek to order their relations with one another.[53] There was no quarrel with the desirability of universal disarmament, especially of nuclear weapons, but the pope did not take seriously enough the need for "immediate security" that confronted both sides in the nuclear dilemma.[54] To these Protestant thinkers, schooled in the realism of neo-liberal Protestantism, Pope John's letter on peace was overly idealistic in its treatment of disarmament and in its hopes for what the United Nations could really accomplish. Brown warned against the "premature disillusionment that such idealism might engender,"[55] but Niebuhr underscored the role of this idealism as a general motivation for human conduct rather than as a specific guide.[56]

Pope John's defense of the right of religious liberty for all men was very well received among Protestants. His statements were seen as the clearest affirmation in any papal document of a person's right to believe and profess, privately and publicly, according to an upright conscience; and "upright" meant an honest, not necessarily a correct, conscience. The pope distinguished clearly between error and the person who errs. Such a one was to be treated in keeping with his dignity as a human person, and thus allowed to worship God according to the dictates of his conscience. Ramsey saw the pope's stand on religious liberty as a great gain for Protestants.[57] Niebuhr voiced a common Protestant hope that the pope's declaration on religious liberty would leaven Latin Catholicity in general and Spanish Catholicism in particular.[58] The suppression of religious liberty, as seen in the first chapter, was a constant Protestant complaint against the Catholic Church. Pope John's championing of the rights of conscience was therefore viewed as an impressive step toward greater church unity.[59]

Going beyond ecclesiastical affairs, Robert McAfee Brown applied the pope's declaration on freedom of conscience to international relations:

> That these distinctions are of utmost importance in the relation between ecclesiastical bodies is beyond dispute. And it is here being emphasized that they likewise set forth the fundamental basis on which relationships between men and nations, in other than the ecclesiastical sphere, must also be ordered.[60]

But a new difficulty, not adequately handled by the encyclical, was raised when one nation in its internal affairs engaged in actions that seemed to threaten the good of all. According to *Pacem in Terris*, citizens had a right to resist coercion and tyrannical abuse of their rights. "But how," asked Brown, "and in what ways, is the defense of this principle to be extended beyond the internal life of a state and made a responsibility incumbent upon the community of states?"[61] And what measures would the United Nations, for example, be justified in taking against South Africa's racial policy, or even against that of certain U.S. states? Such questions were not much illumined by the encyclical.

Despite these shortcomings, an influential segment of the Protestant community in the United States lauded the pope's important distinction between ideology and historical movements. John C. Bennett, a long-time critic of militant, crusading anti-Communism and an advocate of the need to recognize that there are different kinds of Marxism, praised Pope John's distinction. Ideologies as such remained constant, but historical movements in society were subject to profound changes, since historical conditions were constantly evolving. Here was the principle for Pope John's controversial "opening to the left," stated now in a solemn papal pronouncement. Bennett thought that this statement might prove momentous in the light of the Catholic Church's past tendency to deal with Communism almost exclusively on the level of ideology. "*Pacem in Terris* may be the most powerful healing word that has come from any source during the Cold War."[62] Bennett also believed that a better chance existed for ecumenical discussions on Cold-War issues between Roman Catholicism and the non-Roman churches now that Pope John had moderated the militant anti-Communism of the past.

Other Protestant commentators saw in the pope's new attitude toward Communism a positive and effective way of resisting its appeal. By avoiding denunciatory statements about Communism, the pope was content to focus on the principles for building sound societies of justice, charity, and freedom. Such nations would be able to combat the perils of the Marxist system, while developing their own sound social and political structures. This was a way to refute Communism without self-righteousness, and all Americans were exhorted to take this approach.[63] The same point was made in *Lutheran Standard* by a writer who claimed that the pope had thrown a psychological bomb into Catholic circles by his attempt at a rapprochement with the Communists.[64]

Indeed, many Catholics of more conservative stamp were troubled by the pope's willingness to talk to Communists and by liberal interpretations of his statements in *Pacem in Terris*. *Churchman* quoted Paul H. Hallett, a conservative columnist for the Catholic *Denver Register*, who maintained that Pope John did not endorse the UN, nor did he urge coexistence with Communists.[65] Most American Catholics had been trained in an uncompromising opposition to Communism since the days of Pius XI. Disturbed by John's fresh approach to the issue, they termed the pope a good and visionary man, but unrealistic. But Pope John was in a true sense more realistic than the "prophets of doom." Instead of hurling the old anathemas in the same old way, he was sensitively aware that historical contingencies effect important changes in human groups, however unchanging their ideology may be. In the context of the encyclical, the pope was not seeking to compromise with, much less to deny, the evils of Communist theory and practice. Rather, as a realist, he knew that some middle way had to be found between surrender to the Communists and nuclear annihilation. He was attempting to fashion a more creative and positive Christian response to Communism.

As has been said, *Pacem in Terris* did not escape serious Protestant criticism. In addition to the demurrers already mentioned, Paul Tillich felt that the encyclical did not take sufficient cognizance of non-Western traditions, in which the principle of the personal dignity of man was not ultimate. Tillich proposed no ready answers for the Western Christian, who was more and more frequently confronting the East. But he believed that "only a prolonged mutual interpenetration, in which the West must take as well as give, can change the situation."[66] Another source of disappointment for some analysts was that neither *Pacem in Terris* nor *Mater et Magistra* gave extended treatment to the problem of racial justice. The broad principles dealing with minorities were certainly applicable to the question of race, but the lack of a more explicit study of the racial dilemma was regretted.[67]

What is particularly important to understand about these Protestant criticisms of Pope John's letters is that for the most part the whole tone and intent of the criticism had shifted. The negative observations by some American Protestant commentators were not the polemical barbs of old. They were, on the contrary, constructive criticisms that could just as well have been made of Protestant social and political statements. Thus, much of the analysis of these encyclicals had moved from the polemical to the ecumenical. Here again was evidence of the Johannine breakthrough. His universalism, as revealed in his two social encyclicals, was shattering the Catholic monolith image in Protestant eyes. Although his encyclical *Mater et Magistra*, issued in 1961, had afforded the same opportunity.

> ... Pope John's latest letter has caused men of good will who think of the Roman Catholic Church as an ossified monolith capable only of the most parochial, self-centered ideas to revise their views completely.[68]

In this quotation, the charge of Catholic exclusivism and self-centeredness was confronted in the Protestant mind with what the chapter title calls "Johannine universalism."[69] Other modern popes had also addressed themselves to the more general problems of humanity. But Pope John was able to communicate his concern for the larger problems of mankind in a more convincing way than his predecessors had been. An indefinable quality of credibility adhered to John's concern for the whole world. He did not seem to be directly concerned about getting the world "back into" the visible confines of the Roman Church. He went out into the world to aid it in whatever way it needed to be helped. Perhaps what rendered his actions more credible to the non-Catholic mind was that he was willing to take the risks involved in the new Catholic outreach. Endorsing a concrete world organization like the UN implied a willingness to work within the structures of an imperfect institution in which many philosophies of life clashed with the Catholic outlook. His "opening to the left" risked an important shift in church-state relations in Italy, but this was of lesser interest to him than peace between the two opposing world blocs. One felt that he was as concerned about the welfare of Soviet Premier Nikita Khrushchev as he was about the well-being of the College of Cardinals. His ability to distinguish in concrete gestures between false philosophies and their human adherents, subject to the changes of history and personal contacts, permitted Pope John to communicate a new kind of Catholic universalism. This was, indeed, a modern revolution in the Catholic attitude toward the world. This broader ecumenism, mirrored especially in John XXIII's two social encyclicals, had a considerable influence on the American Protestant attitude toward the Roman Catholic Church.

*Pacem in Terris* was Pope John's last legacy to mankind. It appeared in the spring of 1963, two months before the pope's death and five months after the conclusion of the first session of Vatican II. The encyclical on peace was a continuation of the Johannine spirit that had, to the astonishment of many inside and outside the Catholic Church, come to pervade the first session of the Ecumenical Council. The impact of those late months of 1962 in Rome constituted a great turning point in the American Protestant view of the Roman Catholic Church. The next chapter concentrates on the first session of Vatican II, which became in Christian history a watershed dividing the post-Reformation polemic from the contemporary dialogue between Catholicism and Protestantism.

# 5

## *Vatican II, Session One:*
## *A Turning Point*

As the first session of the Second Vatican Ecumenical Council neared, the volume and intensity of the preparations indicated that an important event in Roman Catholic history was in the offing. The preparatory commissions had compiled fifteen tomes of suggestions for renewal from all parts of the Catholic world. Position papers for conciliar discussion were nearing completion, and Pope John used many of his speaking occasions to focus attention on the coming Council. But even as 1962 wore on, there was no real assurance that Vatican II would do much more than codify and ratify traditional Catholic positions and modern papal statements. Perhaps there would also be some condemnations of ideologies and movements. The fact was that nearly all the preparatory commissions were headed by curial conservatives, and their preparatory drafts were often heavy with scholastic abstractions and juridical formulations.

Cardinal Bea's Secretariat drew up a progressive schema on ecumenism that contrasted rather sharply with the other preliminary documents. And while the conservatives slowed the reforming initiatives coming into Rome, Cardinal Bea crisscrossed the continent, stirring interest in renewal and giving hope to the progressives. Bea's talks were moderate, guarding against compromise of doctrine and radical reform, but they also reflected the Johannine openness to separated Christians and to the world. Bea made much of the incorporation of all Christians into Christ through baptism, and of the consequences for unity that followed from this theological belief. In the days just before the opening of the Council, many Protestant leaders had made cordial and religiously rewarding visits to the Secretariat for Promoting Christian Unity in Rome. Other Catholic thinkers, through books and lectures, were also stirring latent desires for renewal within the Catholic community. Hans Küng and Yves Congar played a significant role in this awakening.

As Vatican II entered its final months of preparation, what were the attitudes of American Protestants toward it?[1] This is the first of two main questions to which this chapter addresses itself. The second question pertains to Protestant reactions during and soon after the first session. In both sections, it will be necessary to study more closely the various responses along the conservative-liberal continuum among American Protestants.

## CONSERVATIVE VIEWS PRIOR TO THE COUNCIL

In more conservative Protestant quarters, the approach of Vatican II did not greatly alter the negative views that had greeted the announcement of the Council, as seen in Chapter 2. The Council continued to be interpreted as a Roman plan to direct all non-Catholic traffic to the Vatican. There was no hope for better Protestant-Catholic relations as long as the papacy persisted in being the antithesis to the gospel. Furthermore, the classical theological objections to Roman Catholicism had lost none of their force in these conservative Protestant circles. But at the same time, a little more ecumenical openness was detectable among conservatives than had been evident when Pope John announced his intention to convene the Council.

A few months before the Council began, E. S. James viewed dimly his fellow Protestants who sought an audience with the pope. It was a sorry sight for him to see Protestants responding so eagerly to the pope's invitation to "return." How could they return to where they had never been? James predicted that it was not likely that many Baptists would attend the Roman gathering. They had little affinity for church councils, especially when they were denied a voice in them.[2] Pope John's Council, remarked the editors of *Missions*, was just another call to return, to be lured into the Roman fold so that it might be aided in its struggle against Communism.[3] And why should Protestants bother with a council in which all would be decided beforehand by the Roman authorities? Ecumenism was what they determined it to be—return; nothing would change because of the Council.[4]

*Watchman-Examiner* repeated a similar theme just before the start of the Council. Again it was claimed that Protestant observers would have no part in the formulation of conciliar policy. How could there be any serious exchange of views with those who spoke with divine authority and infallibility?[5] When the Baptist World Alliance, meeting in Oslo, Norway, declined the Vatican invitation to send official observers to the Council, *Watchman-Examiner* reflected approvingly:

> To sit, therefore, as a tolerated guest, cultivated with ecclesiastical blandishments, impressed by exclusive power and its age-long panoplies; voiceless, and as ignorant children coming to school to learn, is to feed the solemnity of an alien creed.[6]

Besides, commented the same editors, Baptists spurned organizational ecumenism and held for spiritual unity among Christians.

Implicit in this anti-organizational ecumenism was the fear of a superchurch. *United Evangelical Action* expressed the uneasiness of the National Association of Evangelicals toward the Vatican Council in a cartoon which showed Martin Luther firmly proclaiming: "Here I stand," while a group of ministers were portrayed rushing toward Rome, saying: "Here we go."[7] *Christianity Today* said that they were playing into the hands of the Romanists, who saw this Protestant movement to the Council as a great homecoming.[8] In the same review, the day after the Council began, a major article maintained: "Rome will never take a single step of real consequence towards unity."[9] Although Rome demanded the return of "Protestant prodigals," the sad truth, according to the writer, was that Rome, by departing from the Bible, had itself become the prodigal—for biblical faith, it had substituted power and infallibility.

The enthusiasm about the new ecumenical trends in the Catholic Church evident in some Protestant groups, such as the World Council of Churches, was classified as dangerous naiveté. Contemporary Protestantism was said to be suffering from "ecclesiastical elephantiasis" in its rush toward organizational ecumenism.[10] This naive ecumenism was maintained even in the face of Vatican proclamations against undermining Roman teaching about the one true church. Another writer in *Christianity Today*, J. D. Douglas, recommended that travelers on the Rome Express should read Edmond Paris' *The Vatican Against Europe*, which underlined the relationship between the Axis powers and the Roman Church. Protestants were encouraged to calculate the price of easy ecumenicity with Rome. Douglas cited, in support of his cautions, a statement by J. W. Draper, a professor at New York University during the late nineteenth century: ". . . the claims of the Roman Catholic Church imply a rebellion against modern civilization and an intention to destroy it. . . . To be able to submit themselves to these claims, men need the souls of slaves!"[11] It was wishful thinking to suppose that such Vatican policy had changed just because a friendly priest had invited a minister to tea.

A flurry of articles in *Christianity Today* in the weeks preceding the Council seemed dedicated to protecting Protestants from the ecumenical clutches of Rome. It was even argued that Tridentine Catholicism was closer to evangelical Protestantism than the latter was to liberal Protestantism. For between Catholics and evangelicals there was some agreement about the early councils and the fathers,[12] but the reason that liberal Protestants were seeking reunion with Rome, in the eyes of C. Gregg Singer, lay in the fact that both modern Catholics and progressive Protestants were basically Pelagians and humanists. Both had thrown off the classic Christian faith.[13] Thus, there was no reason for sentimentality among Protestants toward the latest Roman gestures, simply because Hans Küng had written a book.[14]

Not only was Catholic ecumenism a snare, but the Vatican Council offered little hope for many conservative Protestants, because the pope represented a denial of the gospel of Christ. Although this criticism was hard to apply to Pope John, it was, nevertheless, applicable to the papacy itself, according to certain Protestant thinkers. While the first session of the Council was in progress, *Eternity* ran an article against the exaltation of a mere man as the vicar of Christ. Such idolatry was a negation of the gospel, and entailed the elevation of the mediational Catholic priesthood to a powerful but un-Christian place in the church.[15] In another conservative journal, the good dispositions of Pope John as an individual were recognized, but the glorification of the papacy was attacked as diminishing the role of Christ. The Roman Council represented only a change in practice and tactics, not any sincere alteration of principle. Thus, no real reconciliation with genuine Protestantism was possible unless Rome were willing to return to the gospel.[16] Although many Protestants, the author maintained, had forsaken the true principles of the Reformation, evangelicals were urged to remain loyal to them.

In the early days of the Council, *Christianity Today* published a few severely anti-Catholic articles. Perhaps the most biting of these was a piece by J. D. Douglas, who described the papacy as a reactionary and domineering force in history. It could never be expected to change in its role of opposing the Enlightenment and demanding the submission of the intellect. Douglas cited Gladstone to the effect that papal Catholicism was hostile to intellectual liberty and incompatible with modern civilization.[17] Papal claims were based on a tendentious apologetic; they were maintained by arid legalism and commercialized rites; they demanded blind loyalty to Rome, not to God. A short time later, Addison H. Leitch tried to shake Protestants back into a sense of reality. Had they forgotten that not long ago their fathers believed Rome and its pope to be the "Whore of Babylon" and the antichrist?[18] Vatican II aroused in this author only cynicism and sadness. He admonished his fellow Protestants not to raise their hopes about the Council, but rather to look to Spain and Colombia where they would see the true colors of the papal monster.

Some opposition to the papacy was less violent, but equally clear. The good qualities of Pope John as a man seemed almost to obscure the classic understanding of the papacy, and therefore to ccnstitute an even more insidious pitfall for unwary Protestants. They could only deny the evil claims of the papacy by which the pope became Peter and called for total obedience.[19] Earlier in the year, the same writer had set as a condition for better Protestant-Catholic relations the rejection by Rome of the pope's primacy and infallibility.[20] If the Roman Catholic Church made itself truly apostolic by such a rejection, then real conversations might begin. In the same vein, E. S. James editorialized on the Vatican Council. He was willing to pray that some good would come of it, but Rome had to change radically before Baptists could take it seriously. If Rome were willing to return to the Bible as the unique churchly authority and renounce its human dogmas, Baptists would go anywhere to meet Catholics. No "barrage of propaganda from the imperial city" could change these conditions.[21]

It is interesting to note here the radical character of the demands made on the Vatican Council by the more conservative spokesmen in American Protestantism. This contrasts sharply with the willingness of more liberal or progressive Protestant thinkers to rejoice over partial gains in conciliar theology and practice. Without going too far afield in speculating on the reasons for this clear difference, perhaps two tentative causes may be suggested. First, a lack of real contact with Catholics as persons, as well as with newer developments in Catholic theology, might account partially for the fixity of the conservative demands. Conservatives, who usually did not have close contacts with the church they were criticizing, were constrained to resort to classic patterns of polemical criticism. A second reason may have stemmed from a defensive attitude on the part of the rigidly orthodox. Feeling their own orthodoxies under attack from modern thought, both religious and secular, conservatives frequently could not risk moving even slightly from their fixed positions. Therefore, they felt compelled to demand that Catholics reject long-held doctrines and embrace the tenets of evangelical conservatism. Whatever may be the correct explanation for the radical demands by conservatives, this inflexibility was evident not only in their attitudes towards the papacy before the Council, but also in other theological issues.

When Cardinal Bea and theologian Hans Küng spoke of reformulating Catholic doctrines, whose understanding was historically conditioned and only partially adequate, Philip E. Hughes, writing in *Christianity Today*, found such moves inadequate.[22] He felt it necessary to correct radical deformations of doctrine. He noted, however, that certain reforms in Catholic worship, although not dealing with basic doctrines, could be helpful to interchurch relations. But, Hughes continued, Protestant churches had long since reformed their own liturgies; one may note here another trait of conservatives—that of seeming to be beyond the need for reform in their own traditions.

Closely related to the demand for radical changes in Catholic doctrines was a conservative tendency to oversimplify Catholic positions, and thereby to reject them absolutely. An example of this was to be found in an already mentioned article by C. Gregg Singer, in which he refused to see that any meaningful unity could issue from possible conciliar changes, because Catholics subordinated the Bible to the church, taught no assurance of salvation, made sacraments necessary for salvation, and denied the finished work of Jesus Christ by establishing a sacerdotal clergy.[23] The distinctions and nuances necessary to grasp these Catholic doctrines, as they are understood by reputable theologians, were ignored. In a similar way, James G. Manz devoted two columns a month for six months before the Council to a systematic and radical rejection of Catholic teachings.[24] In his oversimplified views, the mass was not a gift of God for Catholics, but an act of man; veneration of Mary meant a belittling of Jesus; and prayers directed to saints implied an unscriptural glorification of the righteousness of works.

Thus, as the Council opened, the general trend among conservative reviews was to reject the false doctrines of the Catholic
Church, while admitting that an atmosphere of friendship was
of some value. *Lutheran Standard* reminded its readers that they
should not cease to point out the wrong teachings of Catholicism,
such as those concerning Mary and the papacy. But Lutherans
were encouraged to pray for the Vatican Council in their
churches, even though the Milwaukee Convention of the
American Lutheran Church had turned down a resolution asking
prayers for the Council.[25] *Watchman-Examiner* also welcomed
the new human fraternity with Catholics, but insisted that the
truth needed to be stanchly defended. Evangelical Christians
could not be expected to return to a state church, to man-made
hierarchies, and to the practices, pretensions, inventions, and
false doctrines of the Roman Church.[26] At the same time, POAU
kept up its drumfire against the more practical, political aspects
of Catholic teachings. C. Stanley Lowell bore down incessantly
on Catholic canons regarding marriage, schools, and birth
control. At the start of the Council, Lowell warned Protestants
against sentimental dialogue, maintaining that "bibulous
ecumenism needs correction."[27]

This section on conservative reactions just before the
Council would be inadequate without mention of a growing
openness toward some developments in the Catholic Church.
The Johannine ferment in Catholicism, both in its personal and
doctrinal dimensions, was not lost on the American Protestant
evangelical. Even in conservative quarters, an important change
had taken place since Pope John's announcement of an
ecumenical council three years before. After stating the usual
cautions about Protestantism slipping from its Reformation
heritage into a kind of sentimental ecumenism, James W. L. Hills
welcomed recent friendly Roman Catholic gestures. As an
example, he cited Pope John's call for unity, truth, and love.
Evangelicals were to love Catholics and to realize that everything about the Roman faith was not false.[28] Two articles in
*Lutheran Standard* just previous to the Council were open and
friendly to the new Catholic venture.[29] In the same issue,

C. Umhau Wolf praised John XXIII's significant appeal to "separated communities" of Christians in his address convoking the Council, *Questa Festiva.*[30] Wolf also noted the increase of books on Protestant-Catholic relations, and he urged even more study in this area.

Another facet of conservative openness to the impending Council was an appreciation of various aspects of Catholic renewal which the Roman gathering might effect. *Lutheran Witness* cited the hopes of Roman Catholics themselves for a greater decentralization of authority, a clarification of the doctrine of infallibility, and a continuance of the new approach toward "separated brethren."[31] The Dutch theologian G. C. Berkouwer, writing in *Christianity Today*, called on Protestants to show keener interest in the possible future shape of the Roman Catholic Church. He asserted that the "New Theology," partially curbed by *Humani Generis* in 1950, was far from dead. He pointed to the move away from scholasticism toward a new biblical emphasis in Catholic theology, and to the new ecumenical openness that was replacing the earlier exclusivism.[32] In *Baptist Standard*, E. S. James commented favorably about the conciliar hopes expressed by the Catholic editor Philip Scharper. Scharper had advocated putting an end to the Constantinian legacy of church-state imbroglios, stressing inner commitment rather than outward conformity, abandoning the costumes, customs, and privileges of a Byzantine era, and reaffirming biblical authority. James saw this as the finest statement to come from a Roman Catholic editor "since the day the Roman Catholic Church departed from New Testament teaching on so many vital matters."[33]

A final feature of the growing openness toward Roman developments among American Protestants of more conservative bent revealed itself in a new willingness to allow the Roman venture to engender self-criticism in Protestant ranks. Protestants from Free-Church traditions were encouraged to take a new look at recent ecumenical developments, and to reassess their own place in these movements.[34] As the Council opened, Herman Sasse predicted in an article in *Christianity Today* that Pope John and his Council would make all Christians think again about dogmas. The discussions in Rome about scripture and tradition, the nature of the church, and the place of Mary would be occasions for all the churches to listen more intently to their Lord.[35] In the same issue, the editors offered a sincere prayer for the Vatican Council, and confessed their own sins against unity. Their prayer was for eventual unity in faith, liturgy, and witness.[36]

Thus, as the Council fathers gathered in Rome, their task was still viewed in a negatively critical way among most conservative-evangelical Protestants. But even in these circles, an important advance could be noted in interest about and openness toward the Roman enterprise. The sheer volume of commentary in conservative journals about the Catholic Church increased enormously. But of greater moment, the Johannine impact was being felt even among those who had grown up with a vision of Rome as the "Whore of Babylon."

## LIBERAL VIEWS PRIOR TO THE COUNCIL

It may be well, for the sake of clarity, to repeat briefly how the word "liberal" is being used in this context. It refers to journals or individual authors who generally held a less polemical stance toward the Catholic Church, although they could be seriously critical of it. For the most part, they were more open to theological development in the light of modern secular learning, and thus less tied to rigid orthodoxies. They were also more involved in ecumenical endeavors among Protestants, and concerned themselves more fully with the moral dimensions of social and institutional reform. Again, all these indicators must be placed in a continuum of various attitudes; no single journal or author can be too narrowly pigeonholed.

The questions posed in this section are similar to those put to the more conservative wing of American Protestants in the first part of the chapter. First, what was their general attitude toward the imminent Roman Council? Does this attitude indicate a development in interest, knowledge, and expectancy regarding the Catholic Church? It is important here to contrast the muted hopes for Catholic renewal seen in the comments of a few liberal Protestants quoted at the end of Chapter 1, and their firmer hopes for better Catholic-Protestant relations with the announcement of Vatican II. After discussing general developments and movements in Catholicism as seen through Protestant eyes in the summer and fall of 1962, specific doctrinal issues will be treated. Here the question will be: What theological and moral problems did Protestants consider vital for conciliar debate?

It was clear by 1962 that the Ecumenical Council would not be directly concerned with interchurch union, but rather with Catholic renewal from within. How far this critical self-examination would proceed was indeed hard for both Protestants and Catholics to determine. But the editors of *Christian* wished Vatican II well, and hoped that its efforts would bring an end to bitter Catholic-Protestant antagonisms. They prayed that Christ might make the church one, even though chances for reunion seemed remote.[37] Despite the fact that the Vatican radio had denied that the slightest concessions could be made by the Council and affirmed that hardly an iota of truth could be found in other traditions,[38] Vatican II was seen as opening the Catholic Church to new contacts with Protestant churches.[39]

Kenneth Scott Latourette thought that the impending Council might stiffen the barriers between Christians by emphasizing certain Catholic doctrines, but he also believed that the bishops might stress a deeper Christian spirituality that Protestants could share.[40] The editors of *Dialog* expected no dramatic proclamations from the Council, but they hoped for new directions. The very summoning of Vatican II was a great surprise after Vatican I, whose declaration of papal infallibility appeared to have made future councils useless. Moreover, Hans Küng's *The Council, Reform and Reunion* had introduced Protestants to a too-little-known evangelical wing of Roman Catholicism.[41] Because of these developments, Protestants were urged to rid themselves of misconceptions about Catholicism.[42] There were enough serious obstacles dividing Catholics and Protestants without making relations more strained by irrational prejudices. Even though the Roman concept of "return" bothered many Protestants, it should not be allowed to blind them to the positive expectations from the Council, for God worked his will despite human obstacles. Thus, the Methodist editors of *Christian Advocate* exhorted their readers to adopt a prayerful and receptive attitude toward Vatican II.[43]

It was widely felt that Pope John's Council could either chart new paths or end in a dismal acceptance of the status quo. *Aggiornamento* had by this time become a stock word even in the Protestant vocabulary, but expectations needed to be tempered lest disillusionment set in.[44] Protestants had no right, said Roger L. Shinn of Union Theological Seminary in New York, to expect the Council to ratify the Protestant Reformation. Rather, they ought to hope that Vatican II would be genuinely, but generously, Catholic. If the Council managed to speak with an awareness of the temper and the needs of the times, Protestants would listen to it with great sensitivity.[45] For the ecumenical contacts between Protestants and Catholics in the United States since the beginning of Pope John's pontificate had prepared the ground for such sensitivity across denominational lines.[46] Bible study, ecumenical services, and conversations between Catholics and Protestants were part of this new climate of dialogue.

Invitations to non-Catholic observers to attend the Council were seen as a refreshing concern for the whole of Christendom.[47] In contrast to some of the more conservative Protestant commentators, who looked on the observers as naive status-seekers, the editors of *United Church Herald* judged that the presence of observers betokened a major step forward in the ecumenical movement.[48] Only a few years earlier, such a move by Rome would have been inconceivable. *Christian Century* was well aware of the importance of this new gesture. This journal criticized certain Orthodox churches and the Baptist World Alliance for isolating themselves from the Vatican Council for what were judged to be obscure reasons.[49]

The welcome accorded to Protestant observers at the Council, as well as other ecumenical advances, were attributed mainly to the influence of Pope John and Cardinal Bea, who, during 1962, had become familiar figures in the Protestant press, as even a casual checking of indices reveals. The establishment of Bea's Secretariat for Promoting Christian Unity was termed the most notable implementation of John's often expressed desire for Christian oneness.[50] Without this agency, the famous visits of non-Catholic church dignitaries would have been impossible, and the new phase of Catholic cooperation with the World Council of Churches could never have been achieved. One of the many Protestant visitors to Cardinal Bea's Secretariat was Dr. Harold E. Fey, then editor of *Christian Century*. After his interview with the Cardinal, Fey pointed out the importance of the Roman unity venture: "One has only to talk with younger priests and church officials to discern that already the concern of Pope John and Cardinal Bea for all baptized Christians has started renewal within the church."[51] The whole of Fey's favorably oriented interview with Bea is a striking instance of a profound change of view in a well-known Protestant writer who had frequently criticized the Roman Church.

Also evident in Protestant views just before the Council opened was a growing awareness of the impact of Pope John as a personality and a leader. *Episcopalian* spoke of his warmth, spontaneity, and outgoing qualities.[52] He was described as the most ecumenically minded and conciliatory of twentieth-century pontiffs.[53] Professor Ralph D. Hyslop of Union Theological Seminary in New York was criticized in Protestant circles for his extraordinary praise of Pope John. Hyslop stated that if it were true that Christ had chosen to keep his church free from fundamental error through papal authority, "the embodiment of the doctrine in a person is at this moment in history most persuasive in the person of John XXIII."[54]

Furthermore, the attractiveness of John's personality was complemented in Protestant eyes by his ecumenical actions. Shinn called them "Pope John's spacious purposes."[55] John had introduced a new tone into the ecumenical dialogue even if he had not modified Roman claims or demands in regard to unity.[56]

Before the conciliar discussions about ecumenism, most observers, Catholic as well as Protestant, had not realized that changes more profound than merely ones of tone and manner were afoot in Catholic theology. Pope John, as *Witness* clearly foresaw, wanted to advance by small practical steps to prepare the way for larger strides.

In one of the first books by a Protestant author to analyze the approaching Council, the Anglican Canon Bernard Pawley rejoiced not only that it was to take place, but also that "the present pope who has given such a new spirit to the possibility of union" would preside.[57] And Claud D. Nelson, an American Protestant ecumenist of note, reminded Protestants that any event vitally affecting the life of a church as large as the Roman Catholic would have important meaning for other churches. Nelson stressed the central role of Pope John in the coming Council, for "by creating a climate favorable to the participation of Catholics in dialogue—attentive listening and honest speaking—across confessional lines, the announcement of the Council has already substantially contributed, at least temporarily, to the cause of Christian unity."[58] Thus, in liberal Protestant circles, the Second Vatican Council gave high promise of becoming a crucial turning point in Protestant attitudes and actions toward the Roman Catholic Church.

Among the specific issues that Protestants hoped the Council would deal with, papal primacy and infallibility were high on most lists. Some observers of the Council from afar, like the well-intentioned editors of *Churchman*, thought that the Roman Catholic Church should simply deny papal infallibility, and thus remove barriers to unity.[59] Others did not resort to such explicit advice, but restricted themselves to asking the Council Fathers not to widen the split in Christendom, already so riven by such doctrines as that of papal infallibility.[60] Still others, like Walter Leibrecht, writing in the ecumenically open Lutheran periodical *Dialog*, were even prepared to accept some form of papal primacy, but infallibility provided too great an obstacle; it was seen as absolutizing church pronouncements in a way that excluded necessary historical correctives to human statements.

Infallibility also appeared to eliminate the need for Christian repentance on the part of the whole church, and seemed to remove the church as an institution from being under the constant judgment of Christ.[61]

Certain perceptive Protestant thinkers, however, could see in the events scheduled for the fall of 1962 a beginning of important implications for the doctrine of the papacy. The very calling of the Council was in itself an argument against extreme interpretations of teachings on infallibility. Not only did this convocation imply the need for consulting the whole church through the bishops, but it also indicated that updating of the Roman Church meant renouncement of human claims to perfection.[62] This observation of Claud D. Nelson was also made in a slightly different context by Robert McAfee Brown, who hoped for a clarification at Vatican II of the meaning of infallibility. After Vatican I's strong insistence on papal infallibility and after Pius XII's definition of the dogma of the Assumption, there seemed to be no need for a future council, for everything could be handled by papal fiat. But despite this, the very summoning of this ecumenical council was fraught with implications contrary to any concept of one-man rule.[63] If this was only an implicit ecumenical advance, it certainly was not to be overlooked in Protestant calculations for the coming Council.

A few Protestants delved into deeper theological territory where the key could be found for a renewed understanding of papacy and infallibility in Catholicism. Brown was aware that a new appreciation of infallibility lay in the direction of putting the doctrine into the context of God's promises to the whole church. Speaking through the whole believing community, God would keep the church from error in those matters essential for salvation. Thus, infallibility was to be understood primarily in the setting of the whole church, and only secondarily in terms of the Petrine Office, which endeavored to reflect correctly the belief of the community.[64] But a rethinking of dogma on many levels required the breaking of a static pattern of theological thought that had pervaded most Catholic schools in modern times.

Protestants of the caliber of Professor George A. Lindbeck
were able to perceive the currents in Catholic thought that were
opening up new dicussions of dogmatic bases. He pointed to
such developments as Hans Küng's work on Karl Barth's views
on justification, John Courtney Murray's rethinking of Pius IX's
position on church-state relations, and the new scriptural
exegesis that distinguished between history and symbolic interpretation. Lindbeck realized that Catholic as well as Protestant
theologians were studying revelation in its meaning as event,
prior to propositional elaborations. The historical events of
revelation could never be adequately understood by logical
deductions, but depended on progressive insight in a community
of faith, witness, and study. Thus, the whole concept of infallibility implied at best a partial grasp of the mysteries of faith
revealed in historical events. Lindbeck insisted that the new
Catholic theologians were loyal to their tradition, and he maintained that they constituted the greatest opening in Catholic
thought since the Council of Trent. Because of this, he was able
to say as early as 1961: "Reactionary voices seem unlikely to
dominate the coming Council. It will tacitly approve the return
to sources and the greater openness to the modern world."[65]

Lindbeck and others were able to see through the supposed
dogmatic intransigence of Rome, because they understood the
meaning of "development of doctrine" as it moved to the forefront of Catholic consciousness. This theory of development had
been brilliantly articulated in the nineteenth century by John
Henry Newman.[66] But after the scare of Modernism, developmental thinking in the Catholic Church was pushed into the
background, and for a considerable time it was tinged with an
unorthodox hue. In the days prior to the opening of the Council,
however, not only progressive Catholic thinkers in academic
circles were teaching the incompleteness of doctrinal formulations, but as high a church official as Cardinal Bea was proclaiming the same views in public. Lindbeck named this trend the
"evangelical revival" in Catholicism, as opposed to the static
tendencies that had created the image of monolithic Roman teaching. Such supposed theological unity in the Catholic Church

was misleading, as the Council itself would manifest.[67] The Anglican Bernard Pawley hoped that the Council would admit inadequacies in the formulation of doctrine, and be willing to discuss doctrinal questions with non-Romans.[68] His hopes were partially met in Pope John's opening address to the first session of the Council. John clearly distinguished between the substance of revelatory beliefs and their doctrinal formulations.

An important corollary to rethinking the place of the papacy in the Catholic Church were the movements toward decentralization of authority and the definition of episcopal collegiality. These themes were widely discussed in the Protestant press as desiderata for a Roman renewal that would lead to better relations with Reformation churches.[69] Elaboration of the true place of bishops in the church in their collegial function would contribute to a new understanding of the relationship between the bishops and the pope.[70] It would become clearer that the bishop was not simply a representative of the pope in a given locale, but rather one whose consecration made him a representative of Christ to his people. The Catholic Church would have to ask itself again about the relation between the pastoral responsibilities of both pope and bishops for the whole church as well as for a particular diocese.[71] The centralization of authority in the Vatican, especially since the last century, had helped to foster the Catholic monolith image in the eyes of many Protestants. Thus, more autonomy for bishops and national or regional episcopal bodies would be welcomed by Protestants as leading to greater initiative and freedom in Catholicism.

Closely related to Protestant hopes for decentralization and collegiality was a desire for a renewed understanding of the role of the laity in the Catholic Church. As was seen in the first chapter, a constant Protestant complaint about the Roman Church was its clericalism, and the correspondingly minor place accorded to the layman in ecclesiastical decision-making, worship, and witness. Clergy-laity relations, according to Robert McAfee Brown, constituted an ultimate division between Protestants and Catholics.[72] The growing role of the laity in the Catholic Church was seen as a kind of ecumenism-at-home that would have far-reaching effects on relations with other churches, for it would mitigate the notion of "hierarchical totalitarianism" that engendered mistrust among non-Roman Christians. Such were the views of the editors of *Living Church* a few months before the start of Vatican II.[73] They quoted Cardinal Koenig of Austria, who emphasized the layman's task not only in the liturgy, but also in his witness in the temporal order. The Cardinal had also discussed the laity's part in choosing bishops and pastors. These were, indeed, novel accents from Roman authorities, and they raised hopes in the Protestant mind for an authority structure in the Catholic Church that would give increasing prominence to significant dialogue between clergy and laity.

Beneath this theological rethinking remained the core problem concerning the nature of the church. Protestants were asking whether the Roman understanding of the church would move in the direction of greater inclusion of Christians through baptism and faith, or whether exclusivist views would prevail. Here was a basic issue for the future of ecumenism. For the ecumenical thaw would soon freeze again if the Council were to identify the Mystical Body of Christ with professed membership in the Roman Catholic Church. What would the Council say about Protestant membership in the church, and about the value of Protestant worship, ministry, and witness? Although Lutherans, as Kristen E. Skydsgaard affirmed, would have to say no to certain Roman claims, they could gladly answer yes on many issues precisely because they and Catholics were all members of one People of God.[74] And yet, it was not clear to Protestants whether the Roman Church would advance beyond the church-membership position in Pius XII's encyclical *Mystici Corporis* of 1943 and the official Roman responses during the Feeney controversy of 1949.[75] In the latter perspective, Protestants could be saved through their implicit desire for salvation, in the manner of the heathen, but they could not be said to belong to the one true church.[76] The editors of *Dialog* also doubted that the Catholic Church would recognize the ecclesiastical status of the non-Roman churches, since the Holy Office kept insisting that reunion meant return.[77]

In spite of these doubts about the coming Council's attitude toward other Christian communities, many Protestants were encouraged to hope for significant changes in the Catholic understanding of the church. Perhaps Rome was ready to terminate its isolationist view of who belonged to the Mystical Body.[78] Although official statements from Vatican congregations still echoed the "return" thesis, a whole new climate of openness was developing toward the explicit recognition that all Christians through faith and baptism belonged to the church.[79] Even the use of "return" (*reditus* or *reunio*) in papal statements was not intended simply to mean a return to the Catholic Church as it was now, but as it might some day be when renewed by God's action.[80] This was a particularly perceptive evaluation of Catholic ecumenism before the Council.

Similar hopes for a broader understanding of membership in the church were voiced by other Protestants. Harold E. Fey, after his above-mentioned interview with Cardinal Bea, stressed the importance of baptism, which incorporated men into the church.[81] Thus, among some Protestants there were sound expectations that the Council could, through a wider vision of membership in the church, come to appreciate more adequately the Christian character of Protestant bodies as churches. By respecting Protestant faith and baptism, the Council could acknowledge the means of grace in Protestant worship, ministry, and witness.[82] "We belittle the Roman renewal," warned Lindbeck, "... at the peril of scoffing at the work of the Holy Spirit."[83] Elson Ruff also underlined the significance of the new Roman use of the term "separated brethren." This was more than euphemistic phrase, Ruff felt; it connoted a deeper grasp among leading Catholics of the nature of the church. The pope seemed convinced "that some genuine Christian faith and life survive among the separated brethren."[84]

In an important article, Paul Tillich explained the priestly-prophetic polarity in the nature of the church, a needed tension that lent new significance for Protestantism to the approaching Council. In stressing the priestly element of the church, Catholicism ran the constant risk of suppressing prophetic criticism of its structure and doctrine. It tended to absolutize the human and historical, making them speak with what Tillich felt was an unwarranted divine authority. Although Protestants were cautioned against these dangers in Catholicism, Tillich maintained that the Catholic Church had permanent significance for Protestants. For Protestantism needed the Catholic sacramental orientation to keep the prophetic element from straying into cultural activism and moral utopianism. For sacramentalism implied an appreciation of the church which preceded individuals and was the basis of their experiences as well as a corrective for them. Second, Protestantism could profit from the notion of authority in Catholicism. Tillich did not mean the legal authority of Canon Law nor hierarchical authority as practiced in the Catholic Church, but rather the sacramental aspects of authority. As a sign of God's presence in the church, authority could help people to listen more readily to the prophetic word. Third, while avoiding any magical aberrations, Protestants could gain from the Catholic sense of the symbolic. The mystical presence of the divine in symbol would protect Protestantism from the pitfalls of intellectualism and moralism. Finally, Catholic approaches to philosophy might contribute clarity and a stronger correlation between faith and reason. "In the final analysis," asserted Tillich, "the prophetic type of Christianity cannot live without the priestly type, nor the eschatological without the sacramental."[85] Coming on the threshold of Vatican II, this article emphasized the deeper longings of perceptive Protestants for a successful Catholic rethinking of the nature of the church.

Perhaps the most widespread Protestant hope for Vatican II was for a clear statement at the highest level of Catholic respect for religious liberty.[86] As the first and third chapters of this study have made clear, suspicion of Catholic theories on toleration of other religious groups has been a major obstacle to better relations between Catholics and Protestants. American Protestants harbored strong misgivings about the official Roman attitude toward religious liberty.[87] Claud Nelson did not see in 1961 how any profound changes could take place on the question of religious liberty and the rights of conscience,[88] but he did see grounds for hope that the Council would reflect progressive viewpoints in contrast to those that emanated from the Curia or from the Roman Synod. As the Council opened, Lindbeck looked for an improvement in the Catholic interpretation of religious liberty, but he cautioned against hoping for the impossible.[89] He was vividly aware, however, of how great a contribution toward unity would result if the Council rejected the use of political power for ecclesiastical purposes.[90] Stephen Neill hoped that the Council would speak out unequivocally for religious liberty, and thus improve relations between the churches in missionary lands;[91] and Canon Pawley stated that one of the things that most distorted the Roman Catholic image in the eyes of other Christians was its attitude on freedom of conscience. To many, the Roman Church appeared inimical to the natural liberties of man in the political, intellectual, and religious realms.[92]

Another subject that Protestants wanted to see raised in the Ecumenical Council was the place of Marian veneration in Catholic worship. Mariology and its cult were a sore point for Protestants, as has been previously noted, and the issue came to the surface again in Protestant reflections on the coming Council.[93] Those who were aware of biblical and liturgical developments in the Catholic Church during the twentieth century thought that these trends could, under conciliar influence, act as curbs to exaggerated Marian cults.[94]

Two other aspects of Catholic renewal, though mentioned less frequently than other topics, entered into Protestant aspirations for the impending Council: mixed marriages and social reform. The Catholic canons regarding mixed marriages gave grave offense to a sense of justice and charity among many Protestants.[95] The Catholic laws were seen as an infringement of the liberty of conscience of the non-Catholic partner, and as a form of clerical dominance of family life. George Lindbeck, one of the most knowledgeable commentators on Roman Catholicism, saw little hope for a change in Catholic canons concerning mixed marriages, although he believed that such a change would contribute much toward Christian unity.[96] However insoluble certain theological problems might appear, Catholic-Protestant cooperation in social, political, and economic reform was viewed as a promising area of the Council's deliberations.[97] *Mater et Magistra* offered a rich field for collaboration among the churches.[98] It was hoped that the Council would declare itself in precise statements concerning the morality of race problems and of war, subjects that had received disappointing treatment in the otherwise admirable *Mater et Magistra*.[99]

By the fall of 1962, therefore, a great deal of interest in Pope John and his Council had been generated among American Protestants. Catholicism had never been subject to such intense scrutiny in the Protestant press in America, except perhaps in a more polemical way during the presidential campaigns of 1928 and 1960. In the more conservative segments of American Protestantism, the promise of Pope John's Council was largely hidden by a deep-rooted suspicion of one-way Catholic ecumenism, of a gospel-denying papacy, and of classical theological barriers erected in the sixteenth century and carefully guarded into the twentieth. Yet even among the conservatives, new rays of hope for the Council, not noticeable in 1959 and 1960, were beginning to break through. A turning point was reached when the thought began to dawn that the Roman Church was not as impervious to the action of the Holy Spirit as had once been believed.

In more liberal circles, expectations for significant renewal in Catholicism, though guarded, tended generally to be optimistic. Interest in Pope John and his Council certainly ran high; all the principal journals carried extensive coverage of the preparations for and prospects of Vatican II. Pope John and Cardinal Bea became symbols of the great ecumenical importance of the coming Council. New openings were seen as real possibilities in such thorny areas as papal infallibility and primacy, episcopal authority and lay intitiative, religious liberty, and the veneration of Mary. Other questions pertaining to doctrine, worship, and witness in Catholicism received an attention alive to new promise. The serious preparations for the Second Vatican Council were even challenging Protestant churches not to rest satisfied with their own status quo.[100] The Reformation itself could become an obstacle to the constant reformation needed for an ever vital Christianity, if the new thaw in Protestant-Catholic relations were allowed to pass without concern and commitment.[101]

When Pope John entered St. Peter's on October 11, 1962, to deliver his opening address to the assembled bishops of the Catholic world, the turning point to which he was to allude in his talk was beginning to be reached. Against the "prophets of doom," some of whom were close to him in Vatican circles, John XXIII proclaimed a new optimism. The Council was to be optimistic about reforming the Catholic Church from within, about reaching out in a new ecumenical spirit to separated Christians, and about a wider concern for peace and justice among all men. Providence, Pope John said, was leading human society to a turning point:

> It seems to us necessary to express our complete disagreement with these prophets of doom, who give news only of catastrophes, as though the world were nearing its end.
>
> In the present state of affairs, *now that human society seems to have reached a turning-point*, it is better to recognize the mysterious designs of divine Providence which, passing through the different ages of man, and his works, generally against all expectation, achieve their purposes and guide all events wisely for the good of the Church—even those events which seem to conflict with her purposes. (Italics added.)[102]

Under the Johannine influence a new turning point was also being reached in Protestant-Catholic relations in America. The first session of Vatican II, both in its preparations and in its realization, was to become the pivot for a new phase of Christian ecumenism. But to perceive this change more fully, it is necessary to study Protestant reactions to the first session of the Council.[103]

## CONSERVATIVE REACTIONS TO THE
## FIRST SESSION

It would have been naive and unrealistic to expect only favorable views on the Council from American Protestants, especially from those of more conservative-evangelical tendencies. What is surprising and significant is the fact that negative criticism of the first session was generally so moderate in tone. Moreover, the negative comments were outnumbered by positive evaluations, even among conservative sectors of Protestant opinion. Unfavorable analyses clustered around two topics: the lack of radical doctrinal change in the Council, and the ecumenical pitfalls into which so many unwary Protestants were in danger of stumbling.

Anthony F. Vasquez, writing in *Watchman-Examiner*, admitted that Pope John radiated a warm, affable, and dedicated personality, but he also asserted that the Council failed to touch on such important issues as infallibility, Marian devotions, and indulgences. If these things had been once and for all defined, what chances existed for real Christian unity?[104] Immediately after the first session, the editors of *Watchman-Examiner* termed it a "piece of ecclesiasticism" that had successfully captured the front pages. It had done nothing to re-examine the fundamental issues of Rome's political ambitions, its Mariolatry, its privileged priesthood, and its exclusive right to interpret the Bible.[105] Thus, the reforms under way in Rome were seen as merely ecclesiastical or disciplinary, but not as penetrating to the deeper doctrinal issues. When the millions of words were distilled, noted the assistant editor of *United Evangelical Action*, the question would still be: Does Christendom have an infallible pope or an infallible book?[106] *Baptist Standard* published similar reflections on the debates on scripture and tradition at the first session. There was little hope that the Catholic Church would ever say that the Bible was more important than papal encyclicals.[107] This was, to be sure, an oversimplified view of Catholic teaching concerning scripture and tradition, even for the most nonprogressive circles. Such rigid and inadequate views of Catholic doctrine made it doubly hard for these commentators to perceive the subtle but momentous developments that were actually taking place in the Council's understanding of Catholic theology. A classic example of this inability to break through stereotypes in grasping Catholic movements was a comment in *Christian*, a journal otherwise fairly well disposed toward the Catholic Church. Its editors maintained that the most significant happening during the first session of the Council was the insertion of St. Joseph's name into the canon of the mass.[108]

The dangers of organizational ecumenism were of great moment in the conservative-evangelical outlook, and these fears were only increased in the minds of some observers of Vatican II by what appeared to be the Roman hoodwinking of their fellow Protestants. These eager ecumenists traipsing to Rome were being taken in by the blandishments of clever bishops. On returning to their own countries, these Protestants would then be less opposed to the spread of Roman Catholicism.[109] It was to be hoped that the Protestant observers would come to see that the Roman Church was still a closed corporation whose "social and political objectives are as completely hidden as ever."[110] The "return" theme was as prevalent in Rome as ever, noted J. D. Douglas in an early report on the Council. Protestant potentates, he asserted, were naively streaming to the papal quarters, hat in hand, because they had been called "separated brethren." The term suggested to Douglas some sort of leprous body.[111]

Shortly after the first session, an evangelical missionary commented critically on the new Protestant friendship toward Rome:

> The wishful thinking of some naive Protestants notwithstanding, the Second Vatican Council is not likely to produce results that will make a Protestant-Catholic union an early possibility. Some Protestants seem to drool at the prospect of becoming one with Rome again, but having been a missionary in Latin America; I can assure you there is no enthusiasm for this south of the border.[112]

Reflecting on the fact that some Baptists like Stanley I. Stuber and J. H. Jackson had decided to attend the Council, E. S. James, the editor of *Baptist Standard*, mused: "We cannot understand why some Protestants were so excited over an invitation to observe a meeting of this kind."[113] For he saw the primary purpose of the Council as the reunion of the "separated brothers," despite a few conciliar attempts to talk about liturgy and revelation. Cardinal Bea called the presence of observers at the Council "a miracle," but James called it a mirage. "If there were a single sign of a move by Rome towards a better understanding of Protestantism during the first session of the Council, it has not been made known." James felt no compulsion to allow himself to be "dined and entwined" by the astute bishops.[114]

But these criticisms were overshadowed by more favorable comments on the Council. It was indeed unexpected to read in conservative Protestant circles that Vatican II would be the most important religious news story not only of the year, but perhaps of the twentieth century. The same editors reported that even Paul Blanshard had spoken in Rome about a "hopeful era of understanding" opening between Catholics and others.[115] Protestants had found a new flexibility and charity in the Roman Church that they did not anticipate.[116] And this new charity could not be reduced to an opportunistic blandishment; rather Rome was at last evincing a sincere openness towards non-Roman churches.[117] Most commentators noted that although serious doctrinal differences between Catholics and Protestants remained unresolved, the remarkably more friendly atmosphere created by the Council would permit separated Christians to work together in a more meaningful way.[118]

For the editors of *Lutheran Witness* nothing contributed quite so much to this new climate as the Catholic admission of guilt and unworthiness, and a sincere spirit of repentance.[119] G. C. Berkouwer was also much impressed by the Catholic recognition of the church as a congregation of sinners. These views, which had become prominent in the theology of such European writers as Küng, Rahner, and Urs von Balthasar, had now entered into the spirit of the Council.[120] Protestants could readily embrace this new approach of the Catholic Church, which implied not only knowing the beliefs of others but also knowing what others *think* the beliefs of one's own group to be. It meant, too, that Protestants should endeavour to speak of their religion in understandable language, and that they should avoid everything offensive and merely polemical, while fostering constructive criticism.[121]

The Roman liturgical renewal indicated a deepening appreciation among Catholics of sincere and meaningful worship.[122] The liturgical movement was militating against Roman pomp, and it was undergirding more spiritual attitudes toward grace and the sacraments.[123] Protestants also rejoiced that the Council was searching the scriptures in an attempt to deepen its understanding of the meaning and transmission of revelation. This renewed inquiry into the Bible, noted a Lutheran writer, should spur Protestants on in their efforts to witness to the "pure gospel."[124] The fact that liberal voices in the Council were invoking modern, scientific ways of interpreting the scriptures challenged evangelicals to ask themselves to what extent they could employ the concepts of form criticism and salvation history.[125] Commenting on the debate at the first session over the one- or two-source theories of revelation, G. C. Berkouwer pointed out that the tension in Catholicism between the teaching authority of the church and modern biblical exegesis remained. But he also affirmed: "When men begin to read scripture in new ways, it is not possible to predict the outcome."[126]

Pope John and his Council marked another advance in the eyes of conservative Protestants: a greater respect for religious liberty in certain Catholic lands. The mission-minded evangelicals were especially sensitive to infringements of their right to profess their beliefs publicly. In analyzing what the Council meant for Protestants, Stanley I. Stuber predicted an increased Catholic dedication to the principles of religious liberty.[127] *Christian Advocate*, a journal not usually listed as conservative, but, like most Protestant reviews, very much concerned about religious liberty, recorded the conciliar progress on this subject. Its editors noted that Cardinal Bea, on behalf of the pope, had urged the Spanish bishops to manifest a more ecumenical spirit toward other Christian communities.[128] *Christian Century*,

reporting that the Spanish minister of foreign affairs, Fernando
María de Castiella y Maiz, was taking his plea for religious toleration to Pope John for approval, expressed appreciation that the
Vatican did not seem to agree with traditional Spanish views on
religious liberty.[129] As has been seen above, Clyde W. Taylor was
a more typical voice of evangelical-conservative Protestantism.
Although he took a very dim view of ecumenical efforts among
many Protestant churches and the Roman Church, he was
astonished by a new spirit of religious freedom developing in
Spain:

> However, this Council has created one amazing by-product. The
> ecumenical winds have blown some unbelievable freedoms to
> Spain. All but three or four of the long-closed Protestant churches
> are now open. Evangelical marriages are being allowed....
> Evangelicals have now been promised liberty to have their own
> publishing houses and schools. There is no doubt that the chang-
> ing climate in Spain is a reflection of the Vatican Council on the
> Spanish hierarchy.[130]

In the light of previous opinions voiced by Taylor, this is a truly
arresting admission.

But beyond the developments of the Council, the single
most impressive phenomenon in the new Catholicism was, for
the evangelical mind, the person of John XXIII. His personality seemed to penetrate the still formidable barriers between
Catholics and evangelicals. For them, the "surprising Council"
owed its success to John XXIII.[131] J. D. Douglas, who was
severely critical of the ecumenical overtures surrounding Vatican
II, noted that instead of being an interim pope, John XXIII had
established a "remarkable climate of good will, which would
have been incredible a decade ago." Douglas felt that John's
"attitude of charity" was very different from that of past
popes.[132] The first inkling that *Watchman-Examiner* might be
mellowing a bit toward Rome and the Council was a recognition
by its editors that a start was being made to rectify the religious
ills and misunderstandings of 400 years. "There is no doubt
that Pope John opened the way to such a possibility...."[133]
Like John F. Kennedy, but for different reasons, Pope John was

able to elicit the admiration of Southern Baptists. Glenn Hinson, writing in *Baptist Program*, the publication of the Executive Committee of the Southern Baptist Convention, affirmed that the key act of John XXIII was the convening of the Ecumenical Council. Pope John's acts "are creating a new image of the church as reflected in the supreme pontiff. The new image is one of fraternity and brotherly love. There has been no similar image since 1870."[134] Although this writer found many reasons to be apprehensive about the Catholic Church, the Johannine orientation was seen as the direction for better Protestant-Catholic relations.

## LIBERAL REACTIONS TO THE FIRST SESSION

If the first session of Vatican II heralded a momentous turning point in the attitudes of conservative Prostestants toward the Roman Church, the change was even more clearly marked among liberal American Protestants. One of the keynotes of this change sounded at both ends of the Protestant spectrum, was the transformation of the age-old Catholic monolith image in Protestant eyes. After the early sessions of the Johannine Council, the editors of *Lutheran Witness* wrote that as the Council Fathers worked to modernize their church, Protestants would be compelled to update long-cherished opinions and fixed ideas about the Roman monolith. The dictum "Rome never changes" was becoming unreal in light of the serious renewal underway in Rome.[135] A new openness, flexibility, and charity were beginning to change the image of a tyrannical and unbending Rome.[136] Journals like *Christianity and Crisis*, which generally took a more ecumenical stance toward the Roman Church, had on previous occasions challenged the Protestant stereotype of a Catholicism frozen against change. The first session added cogency to the challenge, and brought this periodical to a clearer awareness of the diversity within the Catholic Church. For the growing evidence that the progressive wing of Catholicism was not a weak minority, as some had feared, the editors of *Christianity and Crisis* said: "We can but give thanks."[137]

An important element in the monolith image of Catholicism, as discussed in the first chapter, was thought-control. Catholics were charged with lock-step thinking, formed and directed by the absolutely unified voice of the hierarchy. When the first session of the Council revealed that serious differences of opinion could be publicly aired not only by lay Catholics but by bishops, a long-held Protestant stereotype began to fade. The Baptist commentator Stanley I. Stuber stressed the fact that Vatican II was not a rubber-stamp council; freedom of speech and action were clear traits of the Roman gathering.[138] This freedom of discussion, said the editors of *Presbyterian Outlook*, was destroying the monolith image of Catholicism. The Council was writing a new and vital chapter in ecumenicity which would be important to the whole Christian church.[139]

Protestant reactions of appreciation for free debate in the Council were widespread. That Catholic bishops should be seen disagreeing with one another was viewed as a healthy corrective to the timorous regimentation usually associated with the Roman Church.[140] William J. Wolf, writing in *Episcopalian*, spoke of the "sheer marvel" of free deliberation at Vatican II,[141] and Jesse M. Bader, general secretary of the World Convention of the Churches of Christ (Disciples), found himself most impressed at Vatican II by respect for the gospel and by freedom of discussion.[142] During the first session, an official observer, Douglas Horton, underlined the Council's democratic procedures, although he wondered whether the prepared schemata would tend to close the minds of the Fathers.[143] As the first session progressed, he was to see the conservative draft on divine revelation strongly attacked by progressive bishops and withdrawn for radical revision.

Thus, the open discussion at Vatican II not only weakened the stereotype of Catholic thought-control but also helped to counter the accusation of antidemocratic practices (see Chapters 1 and 3) so often hurled at the Catholic Church. This newly fostered democratic orientation among Catholics impressed the editors of *Christian Century* during the Catholic University of America controversy a few months after the close of the first session of Vatican II. When four well-known Catholic thinkers were banned from speaking at the university because of their progressive views, a tempest of reaction swirled through the pages of the Catholic press. *Christian Century* found it encouraging that Catholics were more willing to talk publicly about their divergent views.[144]

The two main topics of debate during the first session, liturgy and divine revelation, also drew favorable comments from liberal Protestant quarters. Lindbeck saw many vistas of understanding opened up by the new insights into Catholic worship. He praised the trend toward communal worship as a corrective to individualistic tendencies in Catholic spirituality, and he noted the importance of emphasizing the presence of Christ in the scriptures and in the community as well as in the Eucharist. The symbolic meaning of Catholic rites was receiving a whole new development, and intelligibility and participation were accordingly becoming more essential, as contrasted with more externalist ways of conceiving the sacraments. Adaptation of worship to various cultures and decentralization within the liturgy were also seen as significant advances with ecumenical overtones. For these changes in liturgy were indirectly diminishing Roman conformism, and were also giving the laity a more meaningful role in church life. Although Lindbeck felt that the new conciliar document on worship did not stress sufficiently God's constant judgment on the church, he held that the new Catholic directions in worship presaged other developments toward better Protestant-Catholic understanding.[145]

Protestants responded favorably in two ways to the Council's approach to the questions of the liturgy and of revelation. First, the content of the conciliar documents themselves won praise, as seen in Lindbeck's comments above. Even the schema on revelation received commendation, if rather obliquely. The preliminary draft, with its scholastic distinctions between scripture and tradition, was defeated, thus giving hope for a new document that would stress the unicity of revelation in

Christ, as transmitted through the channels of scripture and apostolic tradition. In addition, the withdrawal of the conservative document gave rise to hope for progress in related areas: biblical research according to scientific methods, and more sophisticated views of inerrancy and inspiration. Second, Protestants found the victory of the liberals at the Council in matters both of liturgy and revelation to be a stunning surprise.[146] The renewed interest in biblical interpretation and in the meaning of worship was described by the well-known Presbyterian educator and ecumenist John A. Mackay as a resurgence of evangelicalism in the Roman Church.[147] Protestant elder statesmen like Mackay had never expected to see such stirrings in the Catholic Church they had known for so long.

Pope John had contributed very meaningfully to a new image of the Catholic Church among Protestants when he invited official observers to Vatican II. To grasp the impact of this gesture on Protestant thinkers, it is helpful to listen to the reactions of James Hastings Nichols, some of whose severe, and at times even bitter, criticisms of Catholicism were recorded earlier in these pages. Nichols termed it a "brilliant decision" of Pope John to invite Protestant and Orthodox observers to the Council, and to give them a place of honor. This observer commented on the great courtesy shown the non-Catholics, and he asserted that the observers exerted a marked influence on the bishops.[148] The hospitality of Cardinal Bea's Secretariat toward the observers was widely recognized and appreciated.[149]

The Harvard professor George H. Williams, one of the official observers, portrayed the high moment and the source of this new Roman hospitality when he described the visit of the observers to Pope John's residence. When the pope pulled up an ordinary chair and sat on a level with the observers, Williams thought: "Pope John is not setting himself up as someone over us. He is with us."[150] Both Nichols and the Swiss biblical scholar, Oscar Cullmann, reiterated Cardinal Bea's phrase that the presence of non-Catholic observers constituted "a true miracle." Moreover, both of these observers remarked that the Protestant and Orthodox guests also became full participants in the informal discussions and commission deliberations. The observers' views were taken seriously, and played an important part in the final form of various documents.[151]

Pope John's Council was characterized by Protestants in such terms as "new era," "new climate," and an irreversible "step forward" in ecumenical relations. The doctrine-conscious *Lutheran* was explicit about the deep differences that still existed, but its editor, Elson Ruff, maintained that "never since 1521 has there been a friendlier spirit between Protestants and Roman Catholics than now."[152] In a series of articles in *United Church Herald*, Douglas Horton expressed his optimistic hopes for a permanent change of direction and of climate in Protestant-Catholic relations.[153] The editors of *World Call* saw the Council as one of the most important religious events of our time. It was a kind of fellowship not seen in many generations, which had brought deeper understanding and keener appreciation among both Catholics and Protestants. If it were to achieve no more than this, it would still have been a highly significant event.[154]

Harold E. Fey of *Christian Century* viewed the Council as a moderate "turning point" in Protestant-Catholic relations.[155] He was happily surprised to find that the progressives constituted a majority at the Council, for he had previously believed that the conservatives would be in the ascendancy. By the end of the first session, the editors of *Christian Century* were referring to it as the year's most outstanding event, and as a tremendous extension of the ecumenical movement.[156] The Council seemed to portray a Vatican without walls showing a new openness to the outside world, Christian and non-Christian. After only the first session, it was clear to these editors that a real renewal had already taken place in Roman Catholicism.

The Methodist editors of *Christian Advocate* depicted the Vatican Council as the beginning of a new era in the search for unity among Christians,[157] and Methodist Bishop Fred Pierce Corson hailed the Council as a milestone in the ecumenical movement: "We shall be separated after the Council, but our hope is that we shall not live side by side as entire strangers."[158] The Presbyterian James H. Nichols also spoke of the Council as having brought about a "new situation." It is particularly noteworthy to cite the views of this observer, whose books had shown him such a firm opponent of Roman Catholicism:

> Nevertheless, we now have a new situation. The transformation in the relations of Roman Catholics to other Christians which has been effected by the Vatican Council is astounding, in Cardinal Bea's phrase, "a true miracle." Who would have believed it possible five years ago, or three?[159]

Among Episcopalians, the meaning of the Council for the work of ecumenism was grasped at an early date. Preaching in San Francisco's Grace Cathedral, Lord Fisher of Lambeth, the former Archbishop of Canterbury, noted that a quiet reconciliation between Rome and other Christian churches was progressing. He himself had responded in a spirit of friendship to Pope John's invitation to visit the Vatican. Lord Fisher said of the spontaneous outpouring of good will and the establishment of Rome's Secretariat for Promoting Christian Unity: "It cannot now be undone."[160] Shortly after the Council began, the editors of *Living Church* wrote about a new "Roman Spring." No great doctrinal changes were expected, but they foresaw an increased openness to the Holy Spirit, a readiness to communicate with other Christians, and a deeper charity and humility of expression.[161] Looking back at the first session at which he had been an official observer, the biblical scholar Frederick C. Grant noted that despite the small visible results of the 1962 session, it had represented a forward step that could never be retraced. Protestant-Catholic relations, according to Grant, would never be the same again.[162] A few months later, the same observer declared that a new age of ecumenical relationships could be brought within range of possible achievement as a result of the Vatican Council.[163]

The new direction of Roman Catholicism in Pope John's Council and its effect on the Protestant mind were neatly summarized after the first session by the pseudonymous author Presbyter Anglicanus:

The whole world has received with enthusiasm and thanks-
giving the intelligence that the Roman Catholic Church has
begun to become other than they thought it was; that it is in fact
pulsating with new life and vitality, and struggling, in many
places, to free itself from shackles which the centuries have imposed on it; that the forces which made for renewal are very
much stronger than they were believed to be.

Here again the facts can be made to prevail over speculation.
The Roman Catholic Church is officially, at its highest levels,
behaving differently from the manner in which it was seen to
behave only a few years ago. What was a rigidly authoritarian
automaton, passively under the control of the papacy and its
departments, has suddenly become a dynamic force in the hands
of a worldwide episcopate, reaching out to listen to the needs of
its sheep, seeking for a way in which to bring the laity into
partnership with the hierarchy.

The whole of Christendom has been glad to observe a desire
for real ecumenical encounter showing itself in the debates. Perhaps most of all, it has rejoiced in the new possibility of real,
friendly relationships with Roman Catholic neighbors which can
now be free from embarrassment and from the danger of
compromise.... [164]

This turning point in Protestant-Catholic relations was
attributed by Protestants mainly to the actions and personality
of Pope John XXIII. What he did and what he was became the
touchstone of progress in ecumenical relations before and during
the Council.

The pope's actions were often the source and inspiration for
the new image of Catholicism in the Protestant mind. The editors
of *Lutheran Standard* held that Pope John would go down in
history as the first pontiff to make a genuine attempt to thrust
into the background the frustration and anger surrounding the
Council of Trent.[165] For the first time since the Reformation,
Catholic prelates returned from Rome anxious to talk with
their "separated brethren." Pope John was seen as chiefly
responsible for the noticeable change in Catholic attitudes
toward Protestants,[166] because of his "deep personal interest

in Christian unity."[167] According to James H. Nichols, the actions of Pope John were the prime factors in the new Catholic outlook: "There is no doubt that the initiative and leadership of Pope John has been far and away the most important factor in the revolution of recent months."[168] This accomplishment was possible because the pope, "a genuinely Christian man," was disposed to serve the inspirations of the Holy Spirit: "The Holy Spirit has found him, being who he is and what he is, ready and willing to serve the divine purpose."[169]

But beneath what John did was what he was: "a most benevolent and gracious person."[170] The main new quality that had entered the relationship of Catholic and Reformation churches was charity, which the Archbishop of Canterbury attributed to John: "Where there is charity, the results are incalculable."[171] A frequent correspondent of *Lutheran*, Albert P. Stauderman, spoke of Pope John as a man of wisdom, saintliness, and courage, while Jesse M. Bader was impressed by his humility, sincerity, and authentic love for people.[172] Douglas Horton remarked that in all the pomp of St. Peter's nothing truly reminded him of what the church really stood for, until his eyes rested on John. There, he found a kindness and humility that did not confuse the forms with the essence of Christianity.[173]

When the pope's last illness became known, it proved to be as much a concern for Protestants as for Catholics.[174] Kenneth S. Latourette felt that much of the progressive spirit of the Council depended for its continuance on the pope's health.[175] The same sentiment was expressed shortly after the adjournment of the first session by the editors of *Christian Century:* "Whether the Council reconvenes in the early fall of 1963 depends on the health of Pope John XXIII, who has had more non-Romans praying for him than any pope in the history of the church."[176] Although these editors thought the fate of conciliar renewal hung largely on the well-being of Pope John, they maintained that even without him, the liberalizing forces that he had released could not be suppressed.[177]

This chapter has shown something of the impact of Pope John and the first session of his Council on the Protestant mind, mainly in the United States. It seems reasonable to conclude that the events in Rome in the fall of 1962 so influenced the Protestant image of Roman Catholicism that they constituted a definite turning point in ecumenical relations between the Roman and non-Roman churches. Although there had been intimations in Protestant circles of important changes afoot in Catholicism in the years just previous to Vatican II, it took the Council itself to produce a conscious reorientation of the Catholic image in the Protestant mind.

It is true that evangelicals still called for radical changes in the Roman Church, and warned Protestants against falling prey to the absorbing ecumenism of the Vatican. But conservatives welcomed the new climate of charity in interchurch relations and hailed specific signs of Roman renewal: the new spirit of repentance, reform of worship, and cultivation of religious liberty. Central to all these changes for both conservatives and liberals was the winning personality of John XXIII, who shattered the Roman monolith image by his pronouncements and deeds. Among more progressive Protestants, the Council, through its free discussions on liturgy and revelation and its warm acceptance of non-Roman observers, marked a true turning point in Catholic-Protestant relations.

The next chapter, dealing with Protestant reactions to the death of Pope John, is a logical conclusion to the developments described in this chapter. For after the first session of the Council, the impact of Pope John was most clearly perceived when men asked themselves what his life had meant to them.

# 6

## *The Death of a Transition Pope*

It is revealing to study the reactions of American Protestants to the death of Pope John XXIII. Of course, the death of any important leader generally evokes a recounting of his virtues rather than an itemizing of his defects. But even when this tendency to speak well of the dead is taken into account, the passing of Pope John elicited much more than normal regret and praise in Protestant circles. Both the extent and the intensity of these reactions showed that a new dimension of Protestant interest in and concern for the Roman Catholic Church had been aroused, largely from the influence of this one occupant of the Roman see. These new attitudes will be studied in three phases: as compared with Protestant reactions at the death of Pius XII, as seen in the more conservative Protestant journals, and as portrayed in the generally more liberal Protestant press.

### THE DEATH OF PIUS XII

The death of Pius XII on October 9, 1958, certainly brought forth praise for the man and his work. Franklin Clark Fry, president of the Lutheran World Federation, found him a skillful leader and an impressive moral force, and Eugene Carson Blake, stated clerk of the United Presbyterian Church, commended the dedicated life of Pius XII, which had transcended

ecclesiastical boundaries.[1] The editors of *Christian Century*
praised him for his efforts toward European unity, toward peace,
social justice, and human freedom.[2] Although such statements
could be multiplied, it must be admitted that the death of Pius
XII occupied much less space in the Protestant press than the
passing of John XXIII. Some journals, such as *Witness*, made no
mention of Pius' death.

In other journals, writers were both laudatory and critical.
John C. Bennett recognized that this pontiff had transcended the
papacy and had made a significant impression on the non-
Catholic world. Despite the pomp and pretensions of the papacy,
which Bennett said gave offense to Protestants, Pius was a man
of dignity who had issued some splendid papal statements. But
Bennett also noted that Protestants saw Pius XII as having
favored a one-sided clericalism and alienated Protestants by his
strictures in *Humani Generis* and by his definition of the dogma of
the Assumption.[3] An editor of *Christian Herald* saw Pius XII as
devout and learned, but also as the inflexible ruler of the largest
"state" outside of Communist China, with 450 million Catholics
at his command. Amid the pomp and circumstance of his funeral,
the specter of Roman power was not hidden.[4] Another commentator felt that the world had lost a great humanitarian and
Christian leader, but the papacy Pius represented was seen as a
force to be reckoned with.[5] *Watchman-Examiner*, in underlining
Pius' political acumen, saw in his passing the loss of an outstanding world figure, rather than of a spiritual leader.[6]

Other judgments on Pius XII in the Protestant press were
more severe. Henry P. Van Dusen, then president of Union
Theological Seminary in New York, thought that history would
eventually find Pius XII a mighty influence for reactionary
Roman Catholic theology, despite his talents, his saintliness,
and his devotion to peace.[7] His death was also the occasion for
POAU to question the citizenship of American cardinals who
would vote in the papal conclave, and thus declare their fealty to
a foreign potentate.[8] Although this issue was not of great consequence in itself, it did reveal the image of political power
projected by the papacy.

Two reviews referred to the death of Pius XII by citing a statement of the Presbyterian Synod of Clydesdale which had disassociated itself from the expressions of sorrow by the Moderator of the Scotch Presbyterians. The Synod did not want to say that "he was a constant influence for good, especially in the cause of peace," because of his alleged relationships with Fascism and Nazism. The pope was also accused of urging the democracies of the West into a holy war against Soviet Russia, and of failure to end the persecution of Protestants in Spain and Colombia.[9] The most bitter criticism of Pius XII was to be found in *Eternity:*

> Can such a man be in heaven? We may thank God that we do not have to answer that question. But we must remark that according to the Bible the Pope was a blind leader of the blind, and that within Christendom he was the head of a system that disseminates theological error.[10]

## CONSERVATIVE REACTIONS AT POPE JOHN'S DEATH

If reactions to the death of Pius XII were mixed, the impact of Pope John's demise on American Protestants leaves little doubt that his pontificate had brought about a most vital change in Catholic-Protestant relations. Even among more conservative Protestants, admiration for the man and his work was almost universal.

As a person, Pope John was termed history's most universally loved pope because of his sincere compassion for all of mankind.[11] The sometimes violently anti-Catholic *United Evangelical Action* supported the opinion of a United Church of Canada editor who said that John was "the best pope the Protestants ever had." The editors of this evangelical review underscored Pope John's personal qualities: "His human warmth and genial good humor, combined with a humility and plain common sense, won universal respect and admiration."[12] Daniel A. Poling spoke of John XXIII as "a good and great man [who] had died as he lived, with peace on his lips and brotherhood in his heart. He will speak now to the ages."[13] The Southern Baptist *Biblical Recorder* editorialized on John's humanity, which both Catholics and Protestants might emulate. His simplicity made him approachable to all, and his genuine love for each human person drew to him men of different religious and intellectual commitments. Reflecting an evangelical orientation, the editors of *Biblical Recorder* maintained that John's love for the individual soul was far more important than theological or social movements or unity proposals: "The son of an Italian sharecropper who became Pope John XXIII proved that."[14]

It is particularly interesting to note the comments of *Lutheran Witness*, an organ of the conservative Missouri Synod. So favorable was its eulogy for Pope John that the editors felt an apology to readers was in order: "The death of any man who has influenced Christendom and the world as much as Angelo Giuseppe Roncalli calls for comment—even though he was a Roman Catholic pope and this is a Lutheran periodical."[15] Pope John was described as one of the "towering figures of his time," not only because of his accomplishments, but because of his personal warmth that made many non-Catholics throughout the world feel a personal loss at his death.[16]

In addition to Pope John's human qualities, his endeavor to better Protestant-Catholic relations left its mark in conservative Protestant circles. E. S. James, a frequent critic of the Roman Catholic Church, thought that John XXIII was one of the best men ever to occupy the papal throne. James further stated: "There is no doubt that through his efforts there has evolved a better understanding between Protestants and Catholics."[17] It was especially surprising to note the favorable attitude in *Eternity* towards the pope's ecumenical strivings. This monthly, as well as many other evangelical journals, emphasized the Ecumenical Council as the greatest accomplishment of Pope John, who was seen as the Council's driving, beneficent spirit. As his illness became more publicly known, the editors of *Eternity* announced:

Many Protestants join in prayer for the physical welfare of the present pope, for they realize that the course of the Vatican Council is dependent on the life of Pope John XXIII. If the Council takes the course he has outlined, great changes could come which might affect the whole Christian world.[18]

After John's death, *Eternity* ran his photo and commended him for thinking of non-Catholics as separated brethren, not as heretics. In his annual roundup of the religious scene, Ralph L. Keiper affirmed: "In June the entire world—Catholic and non-Catholic—was saddened by the death of Pope John XXIII . . . he will probably go down in the Church's history as one of the greatest popes of this century, if not in the entire history of the Roman Church."[19] Keiper also noted that Pope John would be remembered by history for summoning the Vatican Council, and thus throwing open the windows of his Church. He had begun trends which would be hard to reverse.[20] Just as surprising as these remarks in *Eternity* were those of Glenn L. Archer of the POAU shortly before the pope's death. The pontiff's hopes for the Council would dim, thought Archer, if Roman clericalism were to prevail, for Pope John had been trying to resurrect the message of Christian love from the grave of institutional absolutism.[21] It must be remembered here that these journals and writers had been among the most vociferous opponents of the Roman Church. The changed attitude toward Pope John and his Council indicates a most significant shift in the Protestant image of what the Catholic Church could become:

Now at his death the late Pope's reforms and council stand in abeyance. Whether the prevailing spirit of freedom and openness continues and the reforms of the council are completed and fully implemented will depend on his successor.[22]

Pope John's efforts for a just peace and an equitable social order were also praised by American Protestant evangelicals. Besides improving the universal religious climate of the world, commented an editorialist in *Lutheran Witness*, John XXIII "more than any other single figure in our time . . . focused the eyes and hearts of people on peace."[23] In this regard, his two major social encyclicals were widely hailed as being among his most notable achievements. E. S. James let it be clearly known in his editorial on Pope John's death that he was no believer in the office of the pope. Nevertheless, he believed that Pope John was indeed "a champion of peace; and that if he could have lived, he might have led the Catholic Church to alter its course and make peace possible in many areas where it does not now obtain."[24] It seems that James was thinking mainly of internal tensions in some countries where full religious liberty was denied, but he thought that history would credit Pope John with a major contribution in establishing such liberty. The president of the Southern Baptist Convention, K. Owen White, saw John as a man of wide vision and of peace;[25] White's comments contrasted the reactions of various Protestants to the pontiff's death with the attitudes of Luther and Calvin toward the papacy. From the antichrist who was guilty of suppressing the gospel, the pope had become "accessible and tradition-shattering, [a person who] embodied for many the deep-rooted longings of men of good will for the unity of mankind."[26]

## LIBERAL REACTIONS AT POPE JOHN'S DEATH

If the response to Pope John's death among more conservative Protestants was truly significant, the reaction among liberals was extraordinary for its great appreciation and intense feeling. Their sense of personal loss was keen. "I was concerned for him as for an old and honored friend,"[27] remarked Douglas Horton, who noted that Pope John's ill health filled him with an intimate and curiously personal sadness. Claud D. Nelson expressed gratitude for "the kindling warmth of his dedicated personality."[28] Frederick C. Grant spoke of Pope John as one "wholly committed in charity, with a profound understanding of human life, human needs, human hopes and fears, a deep trust in God . . . this one man changed the whole face of Christendom during the brief period of his richly fruitful pontificate."[29]

In an issue of *Living Church*, which printed a photograph of

Pope John on the cover, the Archbishop of Canterbury referred to the pontiff as "the great Christian of our time." On the same page, Bishop Arthur Lichtenberger's personal reflections were cited: "I feel a deep personal loss at his death." [30] From one brief meeting with John, Lichtenberger felt that they had been friends all their lives. Similarly, Chad Walsh, a Rome correspondent for *Episcopalian*, mentioned that he had heard Pope John speak only once, but that he had long before fallen under his benign and thoroughly Christian spell. [31] A high-ranking Episcopal lay leader, Clifford P. Morehouse, stressed the universal impact of Pope John's personality:

> Never in the history of the Christian Chrurch has a pope been so beloved by men and women outside of his particular household of faith, nor so universally mourned at his death. John XXIII was more than the Holy Father of the Roman Catholic Church; he was the elder brother in Christ of the faithful of every communion of the Church Universal. [32]

The editors of *Christian Century* spoke of Pope John as having "a spirit so compassionate that it bridged the widest religious and political gulfs of our time." The same journal also remarked that "if anyone had predicted five years ago that in 1963 most of the Protestant world would view the election of a Roman Catholic pope with prayerful concern and a strong sense of involvement, the prediction would have been subject to ridicule." [33] Yet such an unexpected turn of events was accredited to "the most beloved pope of the modern era," [34] who in five years had become a universal leader honored more for his humanity than for his office.

Franklin Clark Fry spoke for the majority of Lutherans when he said: "The hearts of Christians of every confession are united to a degree that is unique for many centuries at the death of the universally esteemed and beloved John XXIII." [35] The editors of a southern Presbyterian journal associated themselves with the statement of a Catholic woman: "This is the first pope I ever cared anything about." [36] In a glowing tribute to Pope John, Robert McAfee Brown pointed out that the "caretaker pope" had indeed taken more care of the church in four years than had any other person in four centuries. Brown noted that Karl Barth had once said of another pope that he could not hear the voice of the Good Shepherd from the see of Peter. But in reference to John, Brown wrote: "In him we have heard the voice of the Good Shepherd, solicitous for those outside as well as inside the sheepfold. Roman Catholics have lost a pope; we have lost a friend and brother."[37] These outpourings of esteem and affection for Pope John clearly transcended any routine tributes accorded by protocol to the great of this world. The person of John XXIII had succeeded in throwing the papal office into a new light, even for the sons of the Reformation. Historians can detect some of the many personal qualities subtly combined in this man, but ultimately, this personal dimension of Pope John was so unique that it escapes description.

As in the evangelical press, the voices in the liberal camp acclaimed the new ecumenical spirit that the pope's actions, especially his Council, had brought about. Frederick C. Grant looked upon the new attitude between Protestants and Catholics, effected in about a year, as a "modern miracle."[38] Similarly, the editors of *Living Church* commented on the amazing transformation of Roman Catholic attitudes toward the rest of the Christian world and "of the attitudes of the rest of us towards Rome." The papacy, asserted *Living Church*, had always claimed to be the center of unity, but only under Pope John's charismatic leadership had it actually become that. Pope John did not talk about papal claims; he simply was the central person in Christendom.[39] Indeed, for these observers, Rome had really changed, for it had entered into genuine dialogue with other Christians. Claud D. Nelson called this new Catholic approach to the separated brethren an "irreversible contribution" to ecumenism.[40]

Robert McAfee Brown observed that Pope John had not initiated Catholic concern for Christians outside their own church. Rather, he had given his blessing to the ecumenical forces already tentatively at work within the Roman Church, encouraging them so that ecumenical Catholics soon realized that they were not just being tolerated, but were articulating those emphases the Holy Father wished to have at the center of the church's life. The most important symbol of this new orientation was Pope John's creation of a permanent Secretariat for Unity.[41] And in another place, Brown pointed out that in John's thinking the emphasis in the term "separated brethren" fell on the noun rather than on the adjective:

> To him we were first of all "brethren" and only secondarily "separated." That so much has happened in so little time to improve the climate of understanding between Catholics and Protestants is something we must attribute to the initiative and leadership of Pope John—though to be totally accurate we would have to assign the reason for this, as he would have done, not to himself, but to the Holy Spirit.[42]

The editors of *Christian Century* also praised the Johannine gesture of reaching across the barriers of centuries to grasp the hands of separated brothers, whom the pope referred to as "all my sons."[43]

The Methodist editors of *Christian Advocate* commented favorably on the increase of fruitful dialogue on issues of tension between Protestants and Catholics in the United States. This progress was attributed to Pope John's *aggiornamento*, which had stimulated a vast movement toward Christian unity among Roman Catholics.[44] Dean Samuel H. Miller of Harvard University was reported in *Christian Advocate* as saying that Roman Catholicism had moved further in three years than Protestantism had moved in the past fifty years.[45] In the same vein, Douglas Horton affirmed that Pope John had set in motion a sequence of events that had done more than anything in the past 400 years to bring Christians together. In a graphic description, Horton maintained that John was an "interim pope" in the same way that Copernicus could be spoken of as an interim figure between the old and new astronomy, or Einstein as interim scientist between Newton and modernity. Pope John's updating of Catholicism made him a primary transition point in church history; the true interim consisted of the four centuries that preceded him.[46]

The main living memorial to Pope John in the Protestant mind was the Vatican Council. Everywhere, hopes were expressed for its continuance and for its successful completion.[47] Pope John had startled the whole Christian world by announcing plans for an ecumenical council to modernize the Roman Church and work toward the unity of all Christians.[48] The Council became the watershed dividing the scholastic and defensive church from newer orientations in Catholic theology and intellectual life, as well as newer, more positive approaches toward the world. The main credit for this achievement was undeniably due to John, who, because of his sensitivity and responsiveness to new needs and insights, unleashed the forces of renewal that had been building up for many years in Catholicism.[49] Pope John's Council meant "that issues only quietly mentioned in the past can be openly discussed, and . . . that as a result the last remnants of the 'monolith' image of Roman Catholicism are being shattered."[50] Pope John had thrust the Catholic Church into a long-overdue confrontation with the non-Catholic world, and especially with non-Catholic Christendom. The love and concern with which he had done this endeared his life and memory to Protestants.

Appreciations of the life and work of Pope John, in both the conservative and the liberal wings of American Protestantism, followed a similar pattern, which conformed closely to the three circles of Johannine concern mentioned earlier in this study. The first circle was that of internal Catholic reform; the second was the creating of new avenues of rapprochement with other Christian communions; the third, and in some ways the most important, was the establishment of positive dialogue with and service to the non-Christian world.

The third circle of Catholic renewal received wide acclaim among American Protestants, as has already been shown. After Pope John's death, his influence outside the Christian community was the focus of a significant portion of the commentaries on his influence. Through *Pacem in Terris* and *Mater et Magistra* he had brought the teaching of the Catholic Church on social, economic, and world affairs up to date. The encyclical on peace, addressed to all men, "was hailed on both sides of the Iron Curtain. And without compromising principles, he opened the lines of communication with Communist leaders."[51] In these encyclicals, John aligned the papacy with liberal and democratic forces in a way that had long been considered alien to the official Vatican mind.[52]

What the pope was to the Christians of the world, noted *Living Church*, he was also to a great degree to mankind as a whole. "He was loved by those who did not know Christ, and perhaps in loving him, they began to know Christ a little."[53] It was on the note of Pope John's dynamic involvement in the third circle of his concerns that the editors of *Presbyterian Outlook* concluded their statement on the occasion of his death:

> For his broad and understanding sympathies, his significant social concern and his personal identification with the deep needs and longings of mankind, we can thank God as we pray that his successor may be a worthy one of comparable spirit and influence.[54]

Finally, the depth of the influence of Pope John on the American Protestant mind can be envisioned in the following two selections, one poetic, the other prose. What this poem in *Christian Century* a few weeks after John's death may lack in artistry, it makes up for in understanding of the Johannine phenomenon:

> History with its reversals
> Cannot wreck this tomb.
> Here is no image to be disenthroned.
> Here is no myth to be destroyed.
> This life was too plain, too clear;
> Too many people saw the smiling truth
> For any future raid to steal such honor.
> No sentry need be posted,
> No watchman set to guard
> The tomb that is a hundred million hearts.[55]

Undoubtedly, it was the man himself and what he stood for that had the most profound and lasting influence in fashioning a new Protestant image of Catholicism. In the view of Robert McAfee Brown, the personal dimension of Pope John had penetrated and quickened all his other efforts:

> So we non-Catholics share with our Roman Catholic brethren in their sorrow, for it is also our sorrow. And it is assuaged only by the recognition that the forces Pope John unleashed within his brief pontificate will be the dominant forces in the future of the church he served, as the influence and impact of God are extended across the weeks, months, years and centuries in which his name will be accorded reverence and honor, and will be uttered with love.[56]

# 7

# *Continuing Issues and New Openings*

The Johannine impact on American Protestantism, traced through this study, has without doubt been one of the momentous religious events of this century. The image of the Catholic Church in the Protestant mind, as presented in the first chapter, was clearly one of monolithic uniformity dominated by Rome. The elevation of Pope John and the announcement of his Council began a very gradual reorientation of Protestant-Catholic attitudes, but the basic picture of Roman Catholicism remained largely the same. By a providential convergence of history, an American Catholic President was able to promote, both in speech and action, liberal views on church-state relations and on respect for religious liberty. John F. Kennedy thus added new thrust to the Johannine renewal that was beginning to sweep through the Catholic world. Pope John's major social encyclicals reflected a church that was anxious to help mankind build a more just and peaceful world. The first session of Vatican II threw new light on the possibilities for freedom and adaptation in Roman Catholicism. And finally, the death of Pope John was the occasion for an eloquent expression from American Protestants of what this Roman pontiff, through his personality and his works, had meant to them.

And yet, although Pope John and his revolution made a significant impact on American Protestantism, important questions of theology and practice continued to interfere with better relations between Catholics and Protestants in America. For it would be false and naive to so emphasize the Johannine influence as to gloss over persistent points of conflict. Both during and after the Council, many problems continued to beset the Protestant mind in reference to the Catholic Church. The new atmosphere created by Pope John did not carry with it the happy solution of all problems, but rather opened new perspectives in which perennial difficulties might be reconsidered and possibly resolved. The purpose of this summary chapter is to examine some of these continuing issues in the light of the new openings created by Pope John and his Council.

A continuing point of contention, especially for more conservative Protestants, was the nature and role of the papacy. Pope John had certainly done much to mitigate Protestant suspicions of the papacy. But no sooner was John laid to rest than the old misgivings about idolatrous and absolute power invested in one man began to stir again. The elevation of Paul VI was the catalyst for these sentiments, especially among American evangelicals. The pomp of his coronation ceremonies resurrected the charge of idolatry. The editors of *Christianity Today* noted that because of the friendlier climate engendered by Pope John and Vatican II, more prayers were offered by Protestants for Paul VI than for any previous pope since the Reformation, but the princely pomp of the coronation services made those same prayers choke in many Protestant throats.[1] Such glorification of a man could not be reconciled for these observers with the spirit of the gospel. The obeisances of medieval servility, the display of wealth, and the triumphal words addressed to Pope Paul constituted a "picture of shocking extravagance to a humble Christian."[2]

And yet, all this external pomp, however offensive to Protestant sensibilities, was but the sign of deeper antipathies to what was seen as papal dominance over the lives of individuals and societies. This deep-rooted fear, so evident in the early sections of this study, could not be easily allayed. A man was being elevated to a throne, and claims of power belonging only to Christ would be made for him.[3] But criticism of papal absolutism extended also to Vatican intentions in the temporal order. Were the formulas of the coronation, such as "ruler of kings," meant to signify designs for the dominance of statesmen and nations?[4]

These suspicions of the papacy were, however, less prevalent after Pope John, even in conservative periodicals. *Eternity*, which had been able to find nothing but evil and delusion in the office of the papacy at the time of Pope John's election, was at least willing in 1963 to entertain the possibility that a pope could reject worldly glory and temporal power. The editors wondered whether Pope Paul would incline toward the symbols of temporal power or toward the sign of burning flax, which reminded the pope of the transitoriness of all human glory.[5] One wonders whether such alternatives would even have been entertained in this sector of Protestant opinion, had it not been for the example of Pope John. The idea that the papacy could be exercised differently than was commonly believed among conservative Protestants was in itself a significant change. Had that "greatest of all popes" lived, E. S. James said of Pope John, a great reform might have taken place in the papacy and in the whole Catholic Church.[6]

In more progressive Protestant circles, difficulties with the papacy remained, but expressions of opinion before the election of Pope Paul were almost universally positive and hopeful. In itself, this fact marked a significant advance over the dimmer views widely held in 1958. But even more promising were the theological insights among Protestants concerning new possibilities for a papacy that would conform more fully to evangelical ideals. Some observers even felt that a future united church would look to the bishop of Rome as the center of leadership. But this demanded the relinquishing of dictatorial powers in the notion of primacy. It also implied a great papal respect for diversity within the church and for democratic and charismatic initiatives.[7]

Although the Reformation churches were forthright in their rejection of any narrow dictation from Curial Roman sources, the development of collegiality under Pope John was looked upon as a promise of decentralized authority. In a system of genuinely elaborated episcopal collegiality, Protestants looked hopefully for a larger role for the Catholic laity. Could Catholic clerical control, some Protestants were asking, gradually permit laymen to have an important voice in high policy-making synods and in the election of church leaders?[8] A new vision was growing of an international presiding bishop who would foster churchly communion by showing great respect for the diverse works of the Spirit in various Christian communities. Such a bishop would lead his brother bishops in mediating disputed questions, while at the same time promoting a maximum of freedom of religious expression within the limits of basic beliefs. This promotion of freedom became a Protestant expectation from the Johannine Council. It was hoped that those who mirrored the mind of Pope John would guard the right to freedom of speech for Catholic intellectuals such as those banned from speaking at Catholic University in 1963.[9]

It would be erroneous to give the impression that the thorny problems occasioned by the papal office were nearing a definitive solution because of the movements Pope John had instigated. The historical and theological claims of the papacy would surely continue to be contested by Protestant scholars. Nevertheless, because of the impetus given by the Johannine revolution, a number of Protestant and Catholic thinkers were resolving certain fundamental differences on the basis of a biblical understanding of the faith. As such a scriptural rapprochement continued, Catholics and Protestants would gain a deeper insight into the nature and purpose of authority in the church. In the resolution of this centuries-old problem, much would depend on the way authority was used. A papacy that could show itself to be the servant of faith and love in the Christian community and beyond it might someday become both credible and convincing to many Protestants. George Lindbeck thought that events were moving so fast "that the old dream of an evangelical pope may become a reality."[10] This was, indeed, a hope for the distant future, but the very fact that it could be voiced by such a knowledgeable student of Catholicism was a sign of new openings in Protestant-Catholic relations.

Undoubtedly, the whole concept of the papacy, especially in its Italianate mold, would continue to be a major stumbling block for the Protestant mind. This was particularly true of the Free-Church tradition with its congregational views of church polity. Added to this were the theological difficulties arising from different understandings of the nature of the church, its ministry, and worship. Thus, the problem of the papacy cannot be isolated from these wider concerns. But even on such a grave barrier as Catholic teaching on infallibility, the Johannine renewal had opened some new vistas previously closed to most Protestant thinkers. It was noted earlier that certain liberal Protestant scholars, well acquainted with Catholic thought, were encouraged that the notion of infallibility was being understood in the wider context of the whole believing and witnessing church. Among more conservative theologians, G. C. Berkouwer, in a brilliant study of the "New Catholicism," wrote:

> The bishops, it is urged, must take their place and exercise their powers in the church *with* the pope. The Council itself gained new significance through this vote. It saw itself as functioning with its own authority; and the question of infallibility was taken out of its confinement within the authority of the pope and set in the context of the entire *church*.[11]

It was a significant opening, indeed, that new aspects of the papacy question took shape at the Council, new because the papacy was being seen from the viewpoint of the church as a communion and a mystery rather than as a merely juridical-ecclesiastical institution. Berkouwer stressed the importance of the Council's emphasis on high churchly office as a service, not a dominance:

> The offices of the church are not positions of privilege or power which elevate their holders above the church, but are special positions of service *within* the body of Christ. The offices of papacy and of the episcopate have to be liberated from a complex of competitive claims of power over the church. This idea is not being pushed because of a devaluation of the papal office, but to

give this and other offices their true evangelical character and to protect them from power-conscious perversion.[12]

Such estimates do not mean that a union of Catholicism and Protestantism is nearing, but they do indicate important new openings toward a better understanding of the papal office. The image of absolute dominance associated with the papacy (see Chapter 1) has to some extent given place in the Protestant mind to one of service within the whole church.

The question of Catholic power and dominance, centered in the papal system, carries over to another continuing obstacle to improved Protestant-Catholic relations in the United States: the problem of Catholic efforts to exert pressure on public agencies for the benefit of Catholic schools or other church-affiliated institutions. Both during and after the first session of the Council, charges of Catholic power plays could be heard, especially among more conservative Protestants. When Monsignor William E. McManus of Chicago urged a shared-time program between Catholic and public high schools, it was termed a bold device to secure government funds for sectarian purposes.[13] The editors of *Missions* sided with Glenn Archer of POAU, who looked on the large federal subsidies for college-building construction, even in private schools, as a sad breach in the wall of separation between church and state.[14] After praising some of the achievements of Pope John and the Vatican Council, the editors of *Biblical Recorder* complained: "But in America the pressure is still on Congress to provide tax aid for sectarian schools. If the bishops want peace with Baptists, then let them call off the baying hounds which have had Congress up a tree."[15]

Among more liberal Protestant observers, the fears of Catholic power were somewhat diminished, but conflicts over public funds and lands were far from resolved. *Christian Century* voiced its strong disapproval of valuable public lands going to a Jesuit institution, Loyola University in Chicago. The editors hastened to add, however, that no church, Catholic or Protestant, should so benefit at the expense of the public; such actions were a violation of the principle of separation.[16] The same review rejoiced when the Supreme Court rejected an appeal of an Oregon court decision that state money could not be spent for textbooks in Roman Catholic schools.[17] A few months later, Catholic plans for a special urban program were criticized as a power play to protect church property in a time of rapid change.[18]

These examples illustrate a continuing Catholic-Protestant problem in the United States. As seen in Chapter 3, the traditional American stand on church-state separation, especially in matters of education, has perennially clashed with the Catholic under-standing of church-state cooperation, even under American constitutional principles. The impact of President Kennedy was, indeed, significant in demonstrating to Protestants that a Catholic in high office could uphold the traditional American conviction, even under opposition from the Catholic hierarchy. On the other hand, certain progressive Protestants were willing to allow fringe benefits to Catholic students, out of a sense of justice and peaceful accommodation. But the basic problem of an extensive Catholic system of institutions seeking public support remains unresolved on the American scene. Certain develop-ments in the Johannine revolution, however, could lay the groundwork for new openings and possible solutions.

On the part of Catholics, a deeper understanding and respect for institutions and convictions outside their religious heritage was represented in Chapter 3 by Kennedy's dedication to American ways. It was also indicated in Chapter 4 by the world-wide Johannine concern for the needs of men and nations outside the Catholic tradition.[19] Pope John's Council, as seen in Chapter 5, explicitly rejected the way of domination for the path of service to both the church and the world. Such a road would seem well calculated to awaken Catholics to their wider responsibil-ities toward the public schools and other institutions in America, whose welfare would have to enter more significantly into future Catholic decisions to support or oppose proposed legislation. From the Protestant point of view, the Johannine renewal in Catholicism would seem to have instilled a greater degree of trust in the honesty and ultimate purposes of Catholic intentions. Conflicts will continue, but their resolution could be facilitated by the new attitudes engendered by the Catholic reform now underway.

Another facet of the same basic difficulty—fear of Catholic domination—continued to show itself in the persistence of the charge of antidemocratic tendencies in the Roman Church. The fear that the Catholic Church intended to undermine and take over the United States government was generally absent from the more liberal Protestant press after the Johannine developments. This in itself represented a real change of attitude. But among the more evangelical spokesmen, fear of the Roman menace persisted. The Catholic position, James D. Mosteller maintained, was that the Roman Catholic Church should direct and control the state.[20] With a growing Roman Catholic population in the United States, there was grave danger that the Roman Church would become a perilously threatening political power.[21] And regardless of whether such a population expansion materialized or not, Daniel A. Poling voiced his misgivings about the increasing financial and political strength of the Roman Church in America.[22]

It is encouraging to note, however, that even among evangelicals, the number and intensity of such accusations were not nearly so great as those recorded in Chapter 1 or during the Kennedy electoral campaign (Chapter 3). John Kennedy had indirectly demonstrated that, contrary to long-standing fears of many Americans, a Catholic could hold the highest office in the land without sacrificing anything of its democratic heritage. The respect for democratic rights shown by Pope John in his social encyclicals also put the Catholic Church firmly on the side of political and economic freedom. But it was perhaps the first session of the Vatican Council which gave the most impressive manifestation of respect for democratic procedures and freedom of expression. For this gathering was not simply giving an exhortation on freedom of speech to those outside the Catholic Church; rather, the first session portrayed Catholic bishops themselves honestly disagreeing with one another in public, a sight that few Protestants, liberal or conservative, would have thought possible a few years earlier. In brief, a new wave of inner freedom was sweeping the Roman Church; this event could not help but diminish the classic charge of Catholic totalitarianism.

It would be naive, however, to suppose that to the Protestant mind all the ghosts of antidemocratic Rome had been laid. Nor would it be true to claim that the new freedom experienced in the Johannine revolution was yet clearly understood or orchestrated in the Catholic Church. The very sociology of institutional change would caution against such rapid assimilation and execution of the new spirit. Yet the seed had been sown for a new Catholic liberty within the Roman Church, toward other Christian groups, and toward a wholehearted appreciation of democratic values. This was a new opening for better relations with American Protestants, who were so closely identified with the genesis and evolution of a democratic republic. But if the new seed were to grow in Catholicism, it would be necessary for Catholic leaders to cultivate every sound expression of freedom and human rights within the church and within American society. The new openings toward democracy also imply a Protestant responsibility to desist from stereotyped denunciations of Catholic tyranny, although real abuses of human rights in Catholicism should be criticized by both Catholics and Protestants. The new spirit in the Catholic Church also challenges Protestants to enter with sympathy and candor into discussion of the unreconciled issues pertaining to church-state relations.

A closely related problem which continues to some degree to poison Catholic-Protestant encounters concerns religious liberty. This was a burning issue in the late fifties (Chapter 1) and again in the 1960 presidential elections (Chapter 3). Religious liberty was high on the list of Protestant hopes for Vatican II (Chapter 5). As the first session of the Council approached, Protestant journals continued their litany of reported abuses in Spain and Colombia. In the latter country, Protestants were protesting discrimination in the schools and the sending of American tax money to support what was termed a bitterly anti-

Protestant regime.[23] In Spain,[24] things were not much better. "Iberian Fascism" was pictured as doing all in its power to eradicate the evangelical witness of Protestants.[25]

In this area of religious liberty, a remarkable change took place during and after the first session of Vatican II, as already alluded to in Chapter 5. Because of the efforts of Pope John and Cardinal Bea, as well as the spirit of the Council, Protestants became conscious of new openings not only in Catholic theory on freedom of religious conscience, but also in Catholic practice, both in Spain and Latin America. There were hopeful reports from Colombia on the elimination of disabilities imposed on Protestants.[26] Friendly contacts between Protestants and Catholics in that country were attributed "largely to the change of climate in Rome because of Pope John XXIII's recognition of non-Roman Christians as separated brethren."[27] A new tone was also heard from *Eternity*, which in the past had needed little encouragement to excoriate Catholic activities. Pope John's liberal ideas "planted seeds of a new era of 'peaceful co-existence,' in contrast to the violent persecution which the evangelical church had often experienced at the hands of an all-powerful Roman hierarchy."[28]

The fact that Catholic attitudes on religious liberty were changing in high places, and not just among a few liberal theologians, had a very important effect on American Protestants. The editors of *World Call* noted that Spain was granting a greater measure of freedom for non-Catholic worship and education. If the "wise and loving" Pope John and Cardinal Bea had their way, Spain might emerge into the twentieth century.[29] When Cardinal Montini angered General Franco by seeking clemency for certain political prisoners, it was seen as a sign of a growing antidictatorial attitude in the Catholic Church.[30] The reform of Spanish law on matters of religious liberty seemed almost incredible to a writer in *Eternity*.[31] This modification of Spanish Catholic attitudes toward Protestants was attributed to Pope John's encyclical *Pacem in Terris* and to the Ecumenical Council. A new day was beginning to dawn for Protestants who could now run their own schools and seminaries;

they could also print and distribute their own Bibles, even though they were not allowed to "proselytize."[32] Something undeniably important had happened in the Catholic Church when age-old attitudes of suppressing heresy could be so altered in the direction of tolerance and even respect for other theological positions. The Counter-Reformation, with all its polemic animosity, was coming to an end, even in the traditionally "Catholic" countries.

A full explanation of the end of the Counter-Reformation mentality in the Roman Church is beyond the scope of this study, but it may be remarked that it also was influenced by factors not directly attributable to either Catholicism or Protestantism. The gradual autonomy of political and economic life in the West, the rise of science and technology, the independence of the laity, and the development of new learning in history and other disciplines— those were but some of the elements from outside the churches that fostered respect for pluralism of ideas and institutions. The positive aspects of modern democracies and the negative qualities of recent totalitarian regimes also underlined the need to uphold the rights of conscience. Theologians today seem more conscious of such pressures on the churches as the work of God in the world. Respect for religious liberty in contemporary Catholicism owes much to such extra-ecclesiastical factors, which stimulated Catholic thinkers to re-examine their own basic tenets. More immediately significant in promoting respect for religious liberty among American Catholics was the experience of generations of immigrants who lived in the religiously free and pluralistic environment of the United States.

And yet continuing problems concerning religious liberty remained on the American scene. The Catholic stand on birth control, seen in Chapter 1 to be such a sore point in Catholic-Protestant relations, continued to be viewed as an imposition of sectarian morality on the consciences of non-Catholics. Catholic pressures against freer birth-control legislation and practice were judged by Protestants as unwarranted interference with the convictions, often based on religious motives, of the majority of the American populace. The editors of *Churchman* noted that despite a few enlightened members, the Roman Catholic Church kept up its fight against adequate birth-control education and legislation.[33] The same commentators spoke for many Protestants when they regretted that Pope John in his "distinguished encyclical" *Pacem in Terris*, failed to add five more words: We approve of birth control.[34] Catholic opposition to various forms of birth control appeared to attack the common good of the poor and underprivileged.[35]

And yet, new openings for a resolution of the birth-control dilemma came to the fore with renewed vigor during the Johannine reformation. A new sensitivity to the rights of conscience was reflected in *Pacem in Terris* and in the Council itself. The liberal Catholic position on religious liberty was moving rapidly from the periphery of Catholicism to the center of the church; its movement, despite many attempts to arrest it, was irreversible. Positive tolerance of non-Catholic convictions about family limitation was a logical corollary of the discussions on religious liberty. This meant that in the future Catholics would have to refrain diligently from pressuring others, through laws, boycotts, or other disabilities, to conform to Catholic sexual tenets.

But an ever broader rethinking of Catholic sexual norms was in process, as a result of deep theological exploration in the Council and of an unprecedented atmosphere of open discussion.[36] The traditional position on contraceptives was challenged by some Catholics both on the basis of its reasoned arguments and of its ground in ecclesiastical authority. Newer insights into natural law from a more personalist and existential viewpoint suggested inadequacies in traditional arguments, and paved the way for a richer understanding of the relationship between sexual love and procreation. Similarly, a more biblical and sacramental theology in Catholicism tended to correct certain overly juridical and Jansenistic outlooks in Catholic sexual theory. Finally, the teaching authority of the church, seen in the biblical and historical context of a pilgrim People of God, was modifying its rigid view of its own infallibility. John Henry Newman's ideas on "development of dogma," which made much of historical conditioning, was also beginning to affect thinking on the development of moral knowledge. These new openings in Catholic thought on the subject of birth control would seem to call for a careful reappraisal among Protestants of their past attitudes toward the Roman stance on family limitation. Faulty understanding of the serious rethinking in the Catholic Church can only lead to the repetition of old accusations and disparagements. World population problems are too grave for the dubious comfort of easy recourse to old slogans.

A further realm of tension in Catholic-Protestant relations in the United States and abroad concerns the implications of religious liberty in mixed marriages. The editors of *Christian Century* remarked before the first session of Vatican II that if the Roman Catholic Church desired better ecumenical relations, it would have to revise its Canon Law on the subject of mixed marriage.[37] Similar admonitions were noted in Chapter 5. But among the new openings in the wake of the first session of the Council, progressive Catholics were calling for an ecumenically minded review of canonical legislation on mixed marriage, and Protestant commentators praised Cardinal Cushing and Hans Küng for their foresight and courage in supporting such reforms.[38]

In the ecumenical ferment of the Council, a new appreciation for the beliefs and practices of other Christian groups was making itself felt. Moreover, a more biblical understanding of "conversion" as a spiritual change of heart for all Christians was mitigating the proselytizing force of modern uses of the word. New probings into sacramental theology were also causing Catholic thinkers to question the requirement of ecclesiastical "form" for validity in a marriage between two Christians, even though one partner is not a Catholic. Such an insistence on liturgical form was seen as endangering what had always been accepted as the key element for validity in marriage, the mutual consent of the marriage partners. It became, therefore, more intolerable to consider illegitimate the children born of a marriage not contracted under proper ecclesiastical form. These new openings in Catholic views on mixed marriage, though not yet fully realized in official legislation, were much encouraged by the ecumenical-theological thrust of the Johannine renewal.

Another heartening development in Protestant-Catholic relations was that of mutual enrichment in theological scholarship. Pope John's revolution spelled the end of an anti-Protestant apologetic in Catholic teaching, which had seen little more than heretical dangers in Protestant theology. In the area of biblical study, the best Catholic scholars had long profited much from Protestant biblical scholarship. But when freedom of intellectual inquiry was jeopardized by ecclesiastical power techniques, as in the Biblical Institute–Lateran University controversy in Rome, Protestants wondered if the Roman Catholic Church could really be renewed.[39] But it gradually became clearer that the Catholic renewal was indeed based on a serious, scholarly return to sources. For Lindbeck, the rejection by the Council Fathers of the conservative scripture-tradition schema at the first session was a turning point in modern Catholic intellectual life. Pope John and the progressive bishops had given the biblical movement an important impetus.[40] This meant that Catholics would be speaking more and more to Protestant concerns. The new intellectual freedom and the scholarly return to sources implied a new openness to ideas from outside the Catholic Church, and an explicit recognition and acceptance of the modern world. The Catholic Church would have to be willing to learn from all sources.[41] Such an attitude could help to make the Christian message more relevant to the modern world.

Linked to the use of modern techniques in biblical studies was a renewed historical understanding of theology in the Catholic Church. The best of the liberal Roman theologies now avoided the shallowness of the largely unhistorical Modernism of the early twentieth century. Serious historical scholarship in Catholicism was effecting a new approach to the Reformation and its valuable religious insights.[42] This resulted in much greater Catholic-Protestant agreement on such disputed doctrines as faith and works, law and gospel, sanctification and the *simul justus et peccator*. Indicative of this new intellectual climate was the lifting of a ban on the motion picture *Martin Luther* by Catholic authorities in the province of Quebec.[43]

Even such a perennial obstacle to Catholic-Protestant theological relations as the doctrine of seven sacraments was beginning to crumble. Much depended on what one meant by seven and how one defined "sacrament." Catholic theology had largely abandoned the theory that Christ had explicitly and personally instituted all seven sacraments before his crucifixion. Also, four of the seven sacraments were coming to be seen in their relation to the two principal sacraments of baptism and the Eucharist.[44] Fundamental to such rethinking was a widely developing understanding of the church itself as a sacramental communion prior to any juridical or monarchical developments. Externalizing, rubrical, and reifying concerns in Catholic sacramentology were giving place to a deeper understanding of the symbolic meaning of the sacraments. They were being seen more and more as the graced gestures of Christ, living in his church-community, calling to faith and charity.[45]

These and other intellectual questions were discussed in a very significant colloquium held at Harvard University in March 1963. A distinguished gathering of Protestant and Catholic scholars met to engage in dialogue on issues of theology, scripture, worship, and morality. Important differences of theology continued to separate the participants, but, in the words of the editors of the conference proceedings, "that with such diversity of opinion we could begin to see the common ground in Christ on which we were all striving to stand, brought an inner joy that obviously lends itself to no report. The truth is that we were conscious of having broken out of our schismatic separation and of having found in such freedom food for our souls."[46] Commenting on this conference, the editors of *United Church Herald* noted that although the unexpected Catholic plunge into ecumenism had as yet failed to dissolve the enigma that the Holy See presented to Protestants, Cardinal Bea's appearance at Harvard showed an "authentic love for truth."[47] He portrayed the Catholic Church not as the controller of truth, but as its servant. The agreements achieved at Harvard on scriptural points and on a common doctrine of baptism provided a basis for future discussions.

After four hundred years of estranged separation, it is to be expected that misgivings about the new Roman ecumenical orientation will persist among American Protestants.[48] But within the short period of Pope John's pontificate, so great a change has come about in Catholic-Protestant attitudes that the future can be large with promise for constructive relations between these two branches of Western Christianity. In the months following the death of Pope John, hope was high in all shades of Protestant opinion for at least an easing of tensions with Roman Catholics, for the simple reason that that "man of broad sympathies,"[49] Pope John, had spurred an unprecedented development in the ecumenical movement. The editors of *Eternity* urged evangelicals to welcome the new Roman steps in the right direction,[50] even to the extent of studying the Bible with Catholics. Protestants and Catholics now needed a long period of getting to know one another on many levels, before any form of real organizational merger could even be contemplated.[51] But continued theological dialogue and cooperation in social and political areas, when serious moral questions were at stake, constituted important steps in bettering relations.[52]

The fact that the Secretariat for Promoting Christian Unity would probably become a permanent agency was also a cause for rejoicing; in itself this organization would settle no significant ecclesiastical or theological problems, but it could foster the climate necessary for their solution.[53] The General Assembly of the United Presbyterian Church (U.S.A.) acknowledged this new climate in an official statement. The Assembly encouraged biblical study and theological dialogues with Catholics. It also advocated cooperation in social action according to the spirit of the papal encyclicals and the statements of the National and World Council of Churches.[54]

The Johannine renewal in Roman Catholicism not only provoked such favorable reaction among Protestants toward Catholicism, but it also encouraged a reappraisal among

Protestants of their own heritage. Even in the pages of the conservative *Eternity*, evangelicals were exhorted to rethink their stance toward the Roman Church. They were urged to observe and study the new developments with an open mind, for the late pope, his Council, and its spirit of dialogue had created a "tremendous thaw" in relations with Catholics. The writer found this change both "amazing and gratifying."[55] If Protestants were to respond adequately to the challenge of the Roman renewal, they would face a huge theological task of re-examining their own heritage in the light of the new trends.[56]

Among progressive Protestant thinkers, the Catholic reforms of the Johannine epoch were seen as strong reminders that Protestantism, which was especially devoted to the principle *ecclesia semper reformanda*, could not allow itself to stand still. Reflecting on the meaning of the Catholic changes for Protestantism, John C. Bennett remarked: "My first suggestion is that we have here an example of reformation which we might well follow—perhaps we will benefit by contagion."[57] After criticizing some of his fellow Protestants for their "implacable anti-Roman bias" against the Council, Albert C. Outler, the noted Methodist theologian, asked what it would mean for Protestantism if the Council succeeded. He answered that "it would change the conventional posture of every Christian communion in the world." It would mean "reform in Protestantism or else."[58] In a somewhat more specific way, Robert McAfee Brown thought that the changes in Catholic theology and practice would tend to undermine the polemical nature of much Protestant theology. It would also motivate Protestants to take a much wider view of ecumenism, now that the Roman Church had entered the unity movement. Moreover, Protestants would be forced to re-examine portions of their heritage which they often tended to neglect, and thus rediscover authoritative elements in their own tradition.[59]

In concluding this study of the influence of Pope John on American Protestantism, some continuing problems and new openings have been considered. It seems particularly fitting to end on this note of unfinished business, and to underline some of the tensions that could in the future retard or even corrupt the ecumenical movement. Although the conclusions of this study have been generally optimistic, there is no guarantee that interchurch progress will continue in an ever rising curve. Such misplaced optimism could bring about a failure to deal seriously with the deeper theoretical and practical tensions that still divide Christians. The result would be complacency, apathy, and eventual disillusionment.

The entrance of the Roman Catholic Church into the ecumenical movement has injected a new spirit of enthusiasm into the church-unity movement. But a hard look at the fifty-year ecumenical experience of Protestant churches since the Edinburgh Conference in 1910 would temper enthusiasm for church unity with an awareness of the difficulties involved. It is true that impressive church mergers have occurred since then, and important interchurch agencies have been erected. But have the mergers always been based on profound theological and religious renewal of the uniting communities, or have the unions often enough been motivated mainly by a desire for organizational efficiency and growth? Moreover, the attitude of many Protestants toward national and international councils of churches has ranged from suspicious to hostile. A searching critique about the nature and purpose of the World Council of Churches itself was published in 1963 by churchmen committed to the ecumenical movement.[60] They questioned whether the movement toward Christian unity could survive as a living force or whether it was headed for premature senility.

The appearance of modern Catholic ecumenism has also tended to exacerbate tensions that already existed among Protestant churches. This study has shown the bitterness and resentment expressed by Protestants of more conservative tendencies toward their brethren who engaged in the new dialogue with Rome. Bilateral talks between Catholics and Anglicans or Catholics and Orthodox run the same risk of setting these non-Roman Catholics apart from their fellow ecumenists of Protestant persuasion. Direct efforts toward union between particular churches should be encouraged. But the delicate task of keeping doors open to those not directly involved in the discussions must also accompany such efforts. Moreover, both Catholic and Protestant churches of ecumenical inclinations must begin to make special attempts to understand the reasons for the anti-ecumenical positions of their more conservative-evangelical brothers.

Still another area of possible ecumenical tension today is that of church renewal which would not leave room for sufficient Christian diversity. As seen in the preceding chapters, significant renewal has taken place in Catholic theology, polity, and worship. But there can be a danger of so solidifying the new developments in the Catholic Church that they cease to be open to different emphases from other Christian bodies. The liturgy, for example, can now tend to become fixed in a relatively satisfactory way. The temptation might then arise to ignore other more spontaneous and less ritualistic Christian traditions as having nothing to contribute to the Catholic understanding of worship. The same kind of rejection of diversity and its educative role could apply to the renewed Catholic appreciation of collegiality. To canonize the gains in collegiality, out of some mistaken sense of having arrived at the *aggiornamento*, could alienate the Catholic Church from other communions whose polity relationships differ from those in the Roman Church. Ecumenical tensions can become salutary polarities when all the churches realize that they must remain open to further developments in their understanding of theology, polity, and worship.

Perhaps the greatest peril to the church-unity movement today is its lack of a truly dynamic popular base. Unless ecumenism becomes a vital part of the life of the local congregations, it could fade considerably in the years to come. The unity movement today is still almost completely the concern of professionals, be they theologians or church leaders. Fortunately, there is a growing awareness of this top-heavy situation in ecumenism, as expressed by a Protestant active in ecumenical work:

> The ecumenical movement has yet to evoke a significant response in the life of most local congregations. It is a disturbing fact to

note that, in spite of rapid development of great ecumenical institutions of Christian co-operation on the world and national levels and the widespread growth of local councils of churches, little reflection of this concern for Christian unity has actually permeated the total life of First Church on Main Street.[61]

Some encouraging efforts are afoot to bring the meaning of ecumenical Christianity to bear on the life of the local parish. A significant example of this attempt is the widely used *Living Room Dialogues*,[62] a paperback for ecumenical discussion groups. It contains essays by Catholic, Protestant, and Orthodox authors, who provide material for neighborhood groups to deepen their appreciation of common prayer, theological dialogue, and joint service.

Finally, ecumenism could create new tensions with non-Christian and secular groups in a pluralistic society. Jewish organizations, for instance, might be inclined to fear the centralized growth of Christian churches through efforts at unity. History could well support this Jewish uneasiness about Christian bodies gaining greater power and control in society, for the Jewish community has often suffered in the past at the hands of Christians in church and civil roles. The ecumenical movement among Christian churches, therefore, must take very special precautions to avoid any coercive methods on those outside the Christian family. Strivings toward Christian unity must be accompanied at every step of the way by efforts to understand and sympathize with the beliefs and aspirations of non-Christian groups in a pluralistic society. Without such measures, Christian ecumenism will only become a new and oppressive sectarianism within the larger context of human brotherhood.

These real tensions at the heart of the church-unity movement should provide a safeguard against starry-eyed enthusiasm in the wake of the Johannine renewal. What seems clear from this modest study is that Pope John, by what he was and by what he did, had a significant impact on American Protestants. His conciliar renewal gradually changed attitudes and opened new vistas for Protestant-Catholic cooperation and unity in this country. But in the light of the ecumenical complexities just reviewed, Pope John's main legacy to the church and to the world might best be described as one of new and challenging beginnings.

# *Notes*

## INTRODUCTION

1. For an excellent brief treatment of Puritanism, see Alan Simpson, *Puritanism in Old and New England* (Chicago, 1955); see also the brilliant work of Perry Miller, *Errand into the Wilderness* (Cambridge, 1956). A competent and perceptive general study of religion in America with selected documents and commentary is H. Shelton Smith, Robert T. Handy and Lefferts & A. Loetscher, *American Christianity* (2 vols.; New York, 1960). See also Winthrop S. Hudson, *Religion in America* (New York, 1965). For a remarkable series of interpretative essays on American Christianity, see Sidney E. Mead, *The Lively Experiment* (New York, 1963). John Tracy Ellis, *American Catholicism* (Chicago, 1956) presents a broad survey of Catholic developments in America.

2. "The Ideologists and the Missing Dialogue," *Christianity and Crisis*, XIX (June 8, 1959), 81–84.

3. *Ibid.*, p. 84.

## CHAPTER 1

1. (New York, 1953), pp. 116, 123. The vision of Catholicism as an authoritarian monolith has a long history in Protestant writing in America: Winfred E. Garrison, *Catholicism and the American Mind* (Chicago, 1928). See also Claris Edwin Silcox and Galen M. Fisher, *Catholics, Jews and Protestants* (New York, 1934), pp. 355 ff. For charges of Fascist tendencies in Catholicism, see George Seldes, *The Catholic Crisis* (New York, 1939). Another book by Charles C. Morrison, *Can Protestantism Win America?* (New York, 1948), pp. 60–77, is a sharp

criticism of monolithic Catholicism. More a political-secular than a religious-Christian attack on Roman authoritarianism is Paul Blanshard's *American Freedom and Catholic Power* (Boston, 1948). See also the best Catholic answer at that time to Blanshard: James M. O'Neill, *Catholicism and American Freedom* (New York, 1952). Criticisms of Roman Catholicism from Anglican writers are: Richard Hanson and Reginald Fuller, *The Church of Rome: A Dissuasive* (London, 1948), and William Shaw Kerr, *A Handbook on the Papacy* (New York, 1951). More recently, similar criticisms of the Roman Church can be found in Stanley I. Stuber, *A Primer on Roman Catholicism for Protestants* (New York, 1960); James Hastings Nichols, *A Short Primer for Protestants* (New York, 1957); Ilion T. Jones, *A Protestant Speaks His Mind* (Philadelphia, 1960); Winthrop S. Hudson, *Understanding Roman Catholocism* (Philadelphia, 1959). Again, these criticisms can be found, but in a more conciliatory context, in Robert McAfee Brown and Gustave Weigel, *An American Dialogue* (New York, 1961); Jaroslav Pelikan, *The Riddle of Roman Catholicism* (New York, 1959).

2. *Primer on Roman Catholicism*, p. 246.

3. XLVII (Jan. 22, 1959), 69. See also Donald Grey Barnhouse, "The Roman Empire Is Revived," *Eternity*, X (April, 1959), 13 ff.

4. XLIX (Feb. 23, 1961), 146.

5. L (Feb. 8, 1962), 106.

6. LXX (Nov. 5, 1958), 2.

7. LXXI (Aug. 5, 1959), 5.

8. LXXI (Oct. 7, 1959), 4–5.

9. Don Hillis, "Will Rome Rule the World?" *United Evangelical Action*, XVIII (April, 1959), 6.

10. The term "conservative" is ambiguous, indeed. It is worth repeating that it is being used in this study as a general working category for a class of journals which tend to be opposed to re-interpretation of Christian doctrine, organizational ecumenicity, and ecclesiastical involvement in the change of social structures in national and international affairs. They tend to follow rather closely, and at times with vehement approval, the views of POAU (Protestants and Other Americans United for the Separation of Church and State) on the dangers of Catholic power in a democracy. The more "liberal" reviews would tend in an opposite direction, although often agreeing with POAU opinions. These categories of liberal and conservative, though useful tools of analysis, should not be too rigidly distinguished. Rather, they form part of a continuum of Protestant opinions from radically conservative on one side to strongly liberal on the other.

11. (Boston, 1958), p. x. There is a similar genre of book, more theoretical than Blanshard's for the most part, that is dedicated to a point-by-point refutation of Roman Catholic doctrine as an evil perversion of the gospel of Jesus Christ. Two such books, whose authors term themselves evangelical Protestants, are *Roman Catholicism* by Loraine Boettner (Philadelphia, 1962) and *Roman Catholicism in the Light of Scripture* by F. C. H. Dreyer and E. Weller (Chicago, 1960). Many of their themes will be reflected in the evangelical literature reviewed in this study. These *summas* of anti-Catholicism do not really seem interested in trying to understand before they reject. Also, their arguments are often superficial and they are almost totally devoid of self-criticism. They pertain, however, to this study inasmuch as they reveal an evangelical mentality about Catholicism that was significantly widespread during the period dealt with in this chapter. The oversimplification and stridency of these books tend, unfortunately, to make one question their value.

12. LXXI (July 15, 1959), 3. See also C. Stanley Lowell, "The Pope and Our Freedom," *Eternity*, X (July, 1959), 24 ff.

13. LXXII (Aug. 10, 1960), 4–5.

14. Morrison, *The Unfinished Reformation,* p. 126.

15. *Lutheran*, XLI (April 15, 1959), 50.

16. "Catholic Bishops on Communism," *Christianity and Crisis*, XIX (Dec. 14, 1959), 179.

17. "The Issues Which Divide Us," *American Catholics: A Protestant-Jewish View*, ed. Philip Scharper (New York, 1959), p. 92.

18. *Understanding Roman Catholicism* (Philadelphia, 1959), pp. 148–150.

19. LXXV (Mar. 5, 1958), 269–70.

20. "Blanshard's 'Power' After Ten Years," *Missions*, CLVI (May, 1958), 13–14. The antidemocratic aspects of Catholicism have been a recurrent theme in Protestant writing, especially in this century when the Catholic community has grown in size and influence. Most of the books mentioned in footnote 1 (p. 223) also deal with this topic. But in a more specific way, Charles C. Marshall, *Governor Smith's American Catholicism* (New York, 1928) offered telling arguments, drawn from Catholic documents and history, to substantiate the antidemocratic bias in the Roman Church. The controversy came to a head within the American Catholic Church in the late 1940's and early 1950's. For a good résumé of the many articles that appeared in this debate, see Thomas T. Love, *John Courtney Murray: Contemporary Church-State Theory* (New York, 1965). The background of liberal Catholicism in America can be traced in Robert D. Cross, *The*

*Emergence of Liberal Catholicism in America* (Cambridge, 1958). The main reference for the conservative Catholic position on church-state matters can be found in the 1940 edition of John A. Ryan and Francis J. Boland, *Catholic Principles of Politics* (New York, 1940). A strong criticism of undemocratic tendencies in Catholicism is found in James Hastings Nichols, *Democracy and the Churches* (Philadelphia, 1951). A more moderate appraisal is seen in John C. Bennett, *Christians and the State* (New York, 1958). Bennett is in the tradition of another moderate (especially for its time) treatment of Roman Catholic church-state views: William Adams Brown, *Church and State in Contemporary America* (New York, 1936), pp. 183–207. Important background and documentation on this topic can be found in Anson Phelps Stokes, *Church and State in the United States*, 3 vols. (New York, 1950). Various criticisms of undemocratic elements appear in George N. Shuster (ed.), *Catholicism in America* (New York, 1953); Philip Scharper (ed.), *American Catholics: A Protestant-Jewish View* (New York, 1959); Wayne H. Cowan (ed.), *Facing Protestant-Roman Catholic Tensions* (New York, 1960).

21. "If the U.S. Becomes 51% Catholic," *Christianity Today*, III (Oct. 27, 1958), 8–12.

22. "Needed, A Revitalized Protestantism," *United Evangelical Action*, XVII (April 1, 1958), 5–6.

23. *Baptist Standard*, LXXI (April 1, 1959), 3.

24. *Democracy and the Churches* (Philadelphia, 1951), pp. 245–46.

25. *A Protestant Speaks His Mind* (Philadelphia, 1960), pp. 162 ff.

26. *Ibid.*, p. 203.

27. "'Bigotry' in Politics," *Christian Century*, LXXV (June 25, 1958), 746.

28. "A Protestant View of Roman Catholic Power," *Christianity and Crisis*, XVIII (Aug. 4, 1958), 114. See also Winthrop S. Hudson, *Understanding Roman Catholicism*, p. 155; John C. Bennett, *Christians and the State* (New York, 1958), pp. 252 ff.

29. "A Dialogue of Histories," *American Catholicism: A Protestant-Jewish View*, ed. Philip Scharper (New York, 1959), p. 53. See also Martin E. Marty, *The New Shape of American Religion* (New York, 1958), p. 165.

30. LXX (April 19, 1958), 3.

31. LXX (Feb. 15, 1958), 3.

32. XLVII (Jan. 29, 1959), 89.

33. XL (April, 1958), 9.

34. II (May, 1958), 99–100.

35. LXXV (Mar. 19, 1958), 334.

36. *Watchman-Examiner*, XLVI (Nov. 6, 1958), 907.

37. "The Papal Election and American Law," *Christian Century*, LXXV (Nov. 19, 1958), 1331.

38. XLVII (Mar. 26, 1959), 258.

39. *Christian Century*, LXXVI (Mar. 4, 1959), 253.

40. Carl S. Meyer, *Lutheran Witness*, LXXVII (Aug. 26, 1958), 20.

41. "Church and State," *Baptist Standard*, LXXIII (July 12, 1961), 6–7.

42. XLVI (July 3, 1958), 569.

43. XLVI (Jan. 9, 1958), 29. See also E. S. James, "Are Catholics Pulling Their Weight?" *Baptist Program*, March, 1959, p. 51.

44. Victor B. Harris, "An Unhallowed Perversion," *Christian Century*, LXXVI (Oct. 7, 1959), 1143–45.

45. *Christian Century*, LXXV (Jan. 15, 1958), 67–68.

46. XL (October, 1958), 9.

47. LXXV (July 9, 1958), 798.

48. John W. Dykstra, "Parochial Divisions in American Life," *Christian Century*, LXXV (April 15, 1958), 464–67.

49. *Watchman-Examiner*, XLVI (July 5, 1958), 479.

50. XLVI (July 17, 1958), 615. See also *Baptist Standard*, LXX (July 9, 1958), 2.

51. *Watchman-Examiner*, XLVI (July 19, 1958), 529.

52. Glenn L. Archer, "Freedom's Golden Strands," *Watchman-Examiner*, XLIX (June 22–29, 1961), 504.

53. *Watchman-Examiner*, XLVII (Sept. 17, 1959), 754–55.

54. Jack Click, "We Heretics Called Baptists," *Baptist Standard*, LXXII (Nov. 30, 1960), 7. See also Don Hillis, "Does Rome Still Persecute?" *United Evangelical Action*, XVIII (June, 1959), 7, 16, 26. The long history of Protestant criticism of Catholic views on religious liberty can be found in many of the books cited in earlier footnotes. Another important work on this subject is M. Searle Bates, *Religious Liberty: An Inquiry* (New York, 1945).

55. XLVI (April 17, 1958), 329.

56. CLVII (October, 1959), 13–14.

57. Theodore F. Adams, "Religious Liberty in Colombia," *Watchman-Examiner*, XLVI (May 29, 1958), 464–65. *Christianity Today*, IV (June 6, 1960), 751–52. C. W. Scudder, "The Catholic Church and Religious Liberty," *Baptist Standard*, LXXII (June 8, 1960), 7.

Eugene L. Madeira, "The Janus-Face of Roman Catholic Diplomacy," *Eternity*, XII (September, 1961), 22–23.

58. "New Troubles for Colombian Protestants," *Presbyterian Life*, XI (Mar. 22, 1958), 24.

59. XI (May 3, 1958), 17.

60. *Presbyterian Life*, XIII (July 1, 1960), 29–30.

61. *Presbyterian Life*, XII (Nov. 15, 1959), 22–23.

62. LXXVI (July 15, 1959), 820.

63. LXXV (Oct. 8, 1958), 1133–34.

64. William R. Estep, Jr., "Struggle for Religious Freedom—1960," *Baptist Standard*, LXXII (Sept. 21, 1960), 8–9.

65. *Baptist Standard*, LXXI (May 27, 1959), 3; LXXIII (Nov. 22, 1961), 4; LXXII (Sept. 14, 1960), 4–5. The last reference is to the government white paper.

66. *United Evangelical Action*, XVIII (August, 1959), 9.

67. Frank Pickett, "Protestantism Is Needed in Paraguay," *World Call*, XLI (March, 1960), 29.

68. *Watchman-Examiner*, XLVII (Nov. 12, 1959), 921; XLVIII (Oct. 27, 1960), 837.

69. "Shocking Intolerance in Spain," *Biblical Recorder*, CXXV (Dec. 19, 1959), 4.

70. E. S. James, *Baptist Standard*, LXX (Feb. 1, 1958), 2–3.

71. "Religious Freedom, Spanish Style," *Christian Herald*, December, 1959, p. 19.

72. "Human Rights in Spain," *Watchman-Examiner*, XLVII (Jan. 8, 1959), 27–28. See also XLVII (May 21, 1959), 433.

73. "Ecclesiastical Justice in Spain—I," *Christian Century*, LXXVI (Sept. 23, 1959), 1080–81.

74. February, 1961, p. 35.

75. "The Secret Life of Spanish Protestants," *Presbyterian Life*, XII (June 1, 1959), 28–30. See also *Christian Century*, LXXV (Aug. 6, 1958), 894.

76. "In the Name of Freedom," *United Church Herald*, II (Jan. 15, 1959), 11.

77. *Presbyterian Life*, XIII (July 15, 1960), 19.

78. *Christian Century*, LXXVII (June 29, 1960), 766.

79. *Presbyterian Life*, XII (Nov. 15, 1959), 23–24.

80. Howard Schomer, "Christian Unity in Spain," *Christian Century*, LXXV (Dec. 17, 1958), 1456–58.

81. *Baptist Standard*, LXXII (June 22, 1960), 4.

82. *New Christian Advocate*, II (November, 1958), 100.

83. LXXVII (Aug. 10, 1960), 917.

84. *Christian Century*, LXXV (Aug. 27, 1958), 964–65.

85. *Lutheran*, XLIII (Nov. 23, 1960), 50; XLIII (Mar. 2, 1960), 12–15.

86. *Christian Century*, LXXVII (April 20, 1960), 461.

87. *Christian Century*, LXXV (Sept. 10, 1958), 1012.

88. *Christian Herald*, November, 1958, p. 21.

89. *Watchman-Examiner*, XLVI (Sept. 25, 1958), 784. See also XLVI (Sept. 11, 1958), 743.

90. *Lutheran*, XL (Aug. 20, 1958), 50.

91. LXXV (June 18, 1958), 710.

92. XLIX (Aug. 3, 1961), 602; XLIX (Dec. 14, 1961), 970. See also *Christian Herald*, December, 1960, p. 15.

93. LXXV (Oct. 1, 1958), 1100–1101.

94. James H. Nichols, *A Short Primer for Protestants* (New York, 1957), pp. 33 ff. Stanley I. Stuber, *How Protestants Differ from Roman Catholics* (New York, 1961), pp. 14 ff. Most of the books mentioned in earlier footnotes deal with these and other theological obstacles between Protestantism and Catholicism. See also Mario Colacci, *The Doctrinal Conflict Between Roman Catholic and Protestant Christianity* (Minneapolis, 1962).

95. Jones, *A Protestant Speaks His Mind*, pp. 118 ff.

96. *Lutheran Witness*, LXXVIII (Mar. 10, 1959), 8–9.

97. *Lutheran Witness*, LXXIX (Dec. 29, 1959), 10, 20.

98. Richard S. Beal, Sr., "Peter's Fallibility," *Watchman-Examiner*, XLVI (Jan. 9, 1958), 34–36.

99. LXXII (Feb. 24, 1960), 4.

100. *Baptist Standard*, LXXI (July 22, 1959), 5.

101. *A Short Primer*, p. 97.

102. J. Philip Pulliam, Jr., "Roman Catholic—Catholic or Roman?" *Witness*, XLVII (Oct. 20, 1960), 12–14.

103. Philip Edgcumbe Hughes, "Modern Roman Catholicism," *Christianity Today*, IV (June 6, 1960), 40.

104. Robert McAfee Brown, *The Significance of the Church* (Philadelphia, 1956), p. 63. See also O. Walter Wagner, "Our Hallowed Preoccupation," *Christian Century*, LXXVI (Nov. 11, 1959), 1303–4.

105. *Christian*, XCIX (Mar. 26, 1961), 8.

106. It is interesting to contrast older and more rigid views of the papacy with the more subtle and developed thought by Catholic authors during the time of conciliar renewal: Karl Rahner and Joseph Ratzinger, *The Episcopate and the Primacy* (New York, 1963); Hans Küng, *Structures of the Church* (New York, 1964).

107. *The Quest and Character of a United Church* (New York, 1957), p. 205. Protestant-Catholic relations in the U.S. from the mid-19th century to the 1920's can, for the most part, be understood as the relationship between foreign immigrants and Reformation churches that saw themselves as intrinsically linked to American democratic life. For the 19th century, Protestant hostility toward Catholicism is chronicled and interpreted in Ray Allen Billington, *The Protestant Crusade: 1800–1860* (Chicago, 1964); see also John Tracy Ellis, *American Catholicism* (Chicago, 1956), III. For an excellent description of different Catholic attitudes, liberal and conservative, toward Protestantism in the 19th century, see Robert D. Cross, *The Emergence of Liberal Catholicism*, III. After World War I, Protestant-Catholic relations entered a more overt period of proselytizing. After the "Americanism" and Modernism scares, the Catholic community became especially defensive and protective of its own flock: see Gerald Shaughnessy, *Has the Immigrant Kept the Faith?* (New York, 1925). Another goal was to convert Protestants to Catholicism: John A. O'Brien (ed.), *The White Harvest* (New York, 1927). A similar purpose was pursued on the Protestant side: Theodore Abel, *Protestant Home Missions to Catholic Immigrants* (New York, 1933). During the period of our study, many Protestant churches had already entered an era of ecumenicity among themselves, but their hopes for reconciliation with Roman Catholicism were slight. This can be seen from the books already cited of Hudson, Jones, Morrison, Van Dusen, and Spinka. A sociological analysis of Protestant-Catholic relations in a small town, indicating the general lack of dialogue, is Kenneth W. Underwood, *Protestant and Catholic* (Boston, 1957). A very new look in recent Catholic ecumenism can be found in Gregory Baum, *Progress and Perspectives* (New York, 1962), and Augustin Cardinal Bea, *The Unity of Christians* (New York, 1963).

108. LXX (Feb. 8, 1958), 3.

109. *Baptist Standard*, LXX (Mar. 8, 1959), 2–3.

110. *A Protestant Speaks*, p. 47.

111. XLIII (Jan. 25, 1961), 50.

112. *Christian-Evangelist*, XCVII (Jan. 25, 1959), 5.

113. *Christian-Evangelist*, XCVI (Mar. 10, 1959), 6.

114. *Christian Century*, LXXVI (Sept. 16, 1959), 1044.

115. *Democracy and the Churches*, p. 14.

116. *The Riddle of Roman Catholicism*, p. 212.

117. It is important to understand that hidden forces quietly at work in Catholicism over the years also contributed to the Johannine ecumenical orientation. There were the influences in the career of Angelo Roncalli that opened him to world views beyond the Catholic Church. Nor can one overlook the social factors urging Christians to resolve their animosities in order to face together the challenges of the time. Furthermore, the theological, biblical, liturgical, and historical advances in shcolarship within Catholicism gradually helped to break through the confinement of the narrow and xenophobic mentality of religious ghettoism. But more specifically, the spirit of the French priest Paul Couturier made itself felt in Catholic quarters. In the days when the official Catholic attitude toward the ecumenical movement was cool and at times complacent, Couturier encouraged work and prayer for Christian unity in God's way and in his good time. See Maurice Villain, *L'Abbé Paul Couturier, apôtre de l'unité chrétienne* (Tournai, 1957); Geoffrey W. S. Curtis, *Paul Couturier and Unity in Christ* (Westminster, Md., 1964). Developments for unity with the Eastern churches, such as the monastery of Chevetogne in Belgium and the publication *Istina*, had long been active. But relations with the Protestant world had been tainted for Catholics by fears of religious indifferentism and doctrinal compromise.

On the more scholarly level, two books by French authors especially stand out as milestones for their time: Yves M-J Congar, *Chrétiens désunis* (Paris, 1937), and Louis Bouyer, *Du Protestantisme à l'Eglise* (Paris, 1954). The historical works of the German Catholic scholar Josef Lortz also fostered a more honest appraisal of the Reformation. Although Catholic ecumenists have moved beyond these books, they remain important landmarks of scholarly breakthroughs. Another Catholic ecumenist of long standing is Christophe J. Dumont, *Approaches to Christian Unity*, trans., Henry St. John (Baltimore, 1959).

In the United States, except for a few exceptions in social cooperation, there was little or no formal Catholic-Protestant dialogue until the 1950's. As far back as 1942, however, John Courtney Murray, writing in *Theological Studies*, was arguing for collaboration with non-Catholics. But this attitude was by no means common in the American Catholic Church. In the 1950's new developments in Catholic theology in Europe were increasingly felt in America, and the stage was being set for the appearance of the Johannine era. A few early books on ecumenism were: George Tavard, *The Catholic Approach to Protestantism* (New York, 1955); Gustave Weigel, *A Catholic Primer on the Ecumenical Movement* (Westminster, 1957); Gustave Weigel and Robert McAfee Brown, *An American Dialogue* (New York, 1960).

118. *Democracy and the Churches*, p. 121.

119. Jones, *A Protestant Speaks*, pp. 136 ff.

120. Morrison, *Can Protestantism Win?*, pp. 113 ff.

121. Hudson, *Understanding*, pp. 152 ff. Perhaps the best single volume on the history of the laity in American Catholicism is Daniel Callahan, *The Mind of the Catholic Layman* (New York, 1963). The most influential and searching Catholic work on the laity in modern times is Yves M-J Congar, *Jalons pour une théologie du laïcat* (Paris, 1961).

122. *Baptist Standard*, LXXIV (April 11, 1962), 4.

123. *Baptist Standard*, LXXIII (March 8, 1961), 5.

124. IV (Jan. 4, 1960), 22–23.

125. Don Hillis, "Is Romanism Christian?" *United Evangelical Action*, XVIII (May, 1959), p. 6.

126. *Baptist Standard*, LXX (July 2, 1958), 2.

127. LXXVI (Aug. 26, 1959), 964.

128. LXXVI (Sept. 2, 1959), 989. See also *Baptist Standard*, LXXV (Jan. 23, 1963), 4.

129. CXXXIX (Nov. 8, 1959), 17. See also *Christian Century*, LXXV (Jan. 15, 1958), 69.

130. CXXXVI (Feb. 23, 1958), 17.

131. CXXXIX (Nov. 8, 1959), 17.

132. *The Riddle*, p. 126. For a contemporary Catholic sacramental theology which takes account of past defects and develops a more personalist, communal and dynamic approach, see E. Schillebeeckx, *Christ the Sacrament of the Encounter with God* (New York, 1963), and Karl Rahner, *The Church and the Sacraments* (New York, 1963). For recent Catholic developments in liturgy, see Josef A. Jungmann, *Pastoral Liturgy* (New York, 1962); an excellent current bibliography can be found in C. J. McNaspy, *Our Changing Liturgy* (New York, 1966); and an ecumenical effort in liturgical renewal is described in Romey P. Marshall and Michael Taylor, *Liturgy and Christian Unity* (Englewood Cliffs, N. J., 1965).

133. *Watchman-Examiner*, XLVII (April 2, 1959), 279.

134. *Watchman-Examiner*, XLVI (Mar. 27, 1958), 263.

135. *United Evangelical Action*, XVII (April 15, 1958), 11.

136. Pelikan, pp. 126–27. See also *Lutheran Witness*, LXXVII (Nov. 4, 1958), 20.

137. Pelikan, pp. 140 ff.

138. *Lutheran Witness*, LXXVIII (Feb. 24, 1959), 10.

139. Ernest Samuels, "Henry Adams' Twentieth Century Virgin," *Christian Century*, LXXVII (Oct. 5, 1960), 1143–46.

140. *Watchman-Examiner*, XLVIII (May 12, 1960), 389.

141. *Living Church* CXLI (July 3, 1960), 14.

142. Pelikan, p. 142.

143. p. 71.

144. "A Protestant View of Roman Catholic Power—II," *Christianity and Crisis*, XVIII (Sept. 15, 1958), 120–23. See also John C. Bennett, *Christians and the State* (New York, 1958), pp. 258 ff.

145. II (December, 1958), 2–3.

146. *The Vatican Revolution* (Boston, 1957), pp. 128 ff.

147. *The Riddle*, pp. 108–9.

148. "The Issues Which Divide Us," *American Catholics: A Protestant-Jewish View*, ed. Philip Scharper (New York, 1959), pp. 102ff.

149. *The Emergence of Liberal Catholicism in America* (Cambridge, Mass., 1958), pp. 223–24.

150. Martin E. Marty, "A Dialogue of Conspirators," *Christian Century*, LXXV (May 28, 1958), 638–39.

151. Carl Umhau Wolf, "Reform in Roman Catholicism," *Lutheran Quarterly*, XIII (February, 1961), 66. Serious works by Catholics critical of their own church were rather few before Vatican II. One of the first was Joseph H. Fichter, *Dynamics of a City Parish* (Chicago, 1951). This book, which spoke with the frankness of sociological observation and interpretation, was not well received in certain hierarchical circles. Other critical books were John Tracy Ellis, *American Catholics and the Intellectual Life* (Chicago, 1956); Walter J. Ong, *Frontiers in American Catholicism* (New York, 1957); Thomas F. O'Dea, *American Catholic Dilemma* (New York, 1958); Walter J. Ong, *American Catholic Crossroads* (New York, 1959). For a criticism of Catholic historical scholarship by a Catholic, see Henry J. Browne, "Catholicism," *The Shaping of American Religion*, ed. J. W. Smith and A. L. Jamison (Princeton, 1961), I, 72–121. It is interesting to contrast this more critical Catholic literature with such laudatory books of an earlier period, such as Frederick J. Kinsman, *Americanism and Catholicism* (New York, 1924), and George N. Shuster, *The Catholic Spirit in America* (New York, 1927). The contrast is even greater when these books are compared to a very recent volume dealing with candor in the church: Daniel Callahan, *Honesty in the Church* (New York, 1965).

152. XIX (Nov. 20, 1959), 171. See also LXXVI (Nov. 11, 1959), 1300–01.

153. *New Christian Advocate*, II (July, 1958), 112–13. *Presbyterian*

*Life*, XII (Dec. 1, 1959), 21–22. *Christian Century*, LXXVII (Oct. 19, 1960), 1204. See also Ernest B. Koenker, "The New Role of the Scriptures in Roman Catholicism," *Lutheran Quarterly*, X (August, 1958), 248–54; Samuel J. Wylie, "Reformation and Roman Catholics in Dialogue," *Religion in Life*, XXIX (Spring, 1960), 220–27.

154. "The Evangelical Possibilities of Roman Catholic Theology," *Lutheran World*, VII (September, 1960), 142–52.

155. Wolf, "Reform," *Lutheran Quarterly*, XIII (February, 1961), 60. See Joseph Lortz, *The Reformation: A Problem for Today*, trans., John C. Dwyer (Westminster, Md., 1964). Louis Bouyer, *The Spirit and Forms of Protestantism*, trans., A. V. Littledale (Cleveland, 1964). Gustave Weigel, *A Catholic Primer on the Ecumenical Movement* (Westminster, Md., 1957).

156. "Catholic Views on Karl Barth," *Christian Century*, LXXVI (Feb. 4, 1959), 133.

157. *Christian Century*, LXXV (Nov. 26, 1958), 1356.

158. Myron W. Fowell, "Catholic Protestant Co-operation," *Christian Century*, LXXVI (Jan. 21, 1959), 76–78.

159. *United Church Herald*, II (Sept. 3, 1959), 29.

160. *Christian Century*, LXXV (July 16, 1958), 820.

161. *Christian Century*, LXXVII (April 6, 1960), 406.

162. *United Church Herald*, II (Oct. 1, 1959), 35.

163. LXXVII (Feb. 10, 1960), 157.

164. LXXVII (Feb. 17, 1960), 183–85. See also Robert McAfee Brown and Gustave Weigel, *An American Dialogue* (New York, 1961), p. 34.

165. Martin E. Marty, *The New Shape of American Religion* (New York, 1958), p.165.

166. Pelikan, *The Riddle*, pp. 216 ff.

167. Pelikan, pp. 227 ff.

168. "The Ecumenical Responsibility of Baptists," *Foundations*, I (April, 1958), 76.

169. "Protestant-Catholic Tensions and Human Relations," *Foundations*, IV (July 1961), 282 ff.

170. "The Ecumenical Task Today," *Foundations*, IV (April, 1961), 102–11.

171. *The Riddle*, p. 210.

## CHAPTER 2

1. "American Catholicism: Grounds for Misgivings," *Christianity and Crisis*, XIX (Aug. 3, 1959), 116.

2. *Religion in Life*, XXIX (Spring, 1960), 292.

3. *Ibid.*, p. 294.

4. *The Quest for Church Unity* (New York, 1960), p. 67.

5. CXXXIX (Sept. 13, 1959), 10.

6. *Witness*, XLVI (Feb. 5, 1959), 3–4. See also XLVI (Feb. 12, 1959), 7–8. It should also be noted that Catholics themselves did not have a very clear idea about the purpose of the proposed Council. It was seen as an attempt to "dramatize the international, interracial, and timeless character of the Church of Christ," *America*, C (Feb. 7, 1959), 536. Thus, the whole notion of a searching internal reform of Catholicism was missed. In its stead, the Council was projected as some kind of Catholic spectacle of already achieved unity. The notion of a reunion conference for separated Christians was also strong in the Catholic mind, but the whole approach to Christian unity was predicated on the narrow basis of return of dissidents to an unchanging and uncompromising Catholic Church. See Robert A. Graham, "Will Christians Come Together?" *America*, C (Feb. 28, 1959), 626–28.

7. XII (Feb. 15, 1959), 29.

8. XLVI (Feb. 19, 1959), 7–8.

9. XLI (Feb. 11, 1959), 50.

10. III (April, 1959), 98.

11. V (Dec. 21, 1961), 20.

12. *United Church Herald*, II (Feb. 26, 1959), 29.

13. LXXVI (Feb. 18, 1959), 189.

14. *Ibid.*, p. 189.

15. LXXVI (Feb. 4, 1959), 124–25.

16. "The Pope's Ecumenical Council," *Christian Century*, LXXVI (Feb. 25, 1959), 224–25.

17. LXXVII (Feb. 4, 1960), 156–57.

18. *Ibid.*, p. 157.

19. *Christianity and Crisis*, XIX (Feb. 16, 1959), 11.

20. *One Great Ground of Hope* (Philadelphia, 1961), pp. 146–47.

21. *Christianity and Crisis*, XIX (June 8, 1959), 77.

22. *Witness*, XLVI (Feb. 5, 1959), 3.

23. *Witness*, XLVI (Feb. 5, 1959), 4; XLVII (May 12, 1960), 3–6.

*Presbyterian Survey*, L (February, 1960), 56. *Christian Century*, LXXVII (May 18, 1960), 599.

24. CXXXVIII (April 19, 1959), 9–10.

25. CXXXIX (Nov. 22, 1959), 16.

26. LXXVIII (Jan. 4, 1961), 4–5. See also *United Evangelical Action*, XIX (December, 1960), 13.

27. *The Riddle*, p. 176.

28. "What's Behind the Pope's Ecumenical Council?" *Eternity*, X (December, 1959), 47.

29. *Ibid.*, p. 49.

30. *Ibid.*, p. 47.

31. Ralph L. Keiper, "Pope John Calls a Council," *Eternity*, X (April, 1959), 27.

32. Robert J. St. Clair, "A Protestant Council on Roman Catholicism—Talks and Talks and Talks," *United Evangelical Action*, XIX (June, 1960), 17.

33. *Christian Herald*, January, 1960, p. 50. This family journal is a good example of the difficulty of classifying too rigorously into liberal and conservative categories. Although the magazine tended to be conservative in its theological and political orientations, it published articles by such men as Latourette, a scholar respected in liberal quarters also.

34. *Ibid.*, p. 52.

35. *Christian Herald,* April, 1960, p. 21.

36. III (Feb. 16, 1959), 28.

37. *Ibid.*, p. 28.

38. III (July 20, 1959), 20–21. See also V (Oct. 10, 1960), 29 ff.

39. "The Protestant-Catholic Dialogue," *Christianity Today*, V (Oct. 24, 1960), 3 ff.

40. *Lutheran Standard*, CXVII (Feb. 14, 1959), 23, 24.

41. *Ibid.*, CXVII (April 25, 1959), 8–10.

42. XLI (December, 1959), 10.

43. *Baptist Standard*, LXXI (Feb. 4, 1959), 3.

44. *Ibid.*, p. 3.

45. *Watchman-Examiner*, XLVII (Feb. 12, 1959), 131.

46. *Ibid.*, XLVII (Mar. 12, 1959), 213–14.

47. *Ibid.*, XLVII (Aug. 13, 1959), 665.

48. "Pope John's Ecumenical Council," *Watchman-Examiner*, XLVII (Dec. 10, 1959), 1013–14.

49. CLVII (April, 1959), 14.

50. CLVII (November, 1959), 15.

51. LXXV (Nov. 26, 1958), 1357–58.

52. LXXV (Nov. 12, 1958), 1293.

53. XLVI (Nov. 20, 1958), 952.

54. William R. Estep, Jr., "John XXIII and the Papacy," *Baptist Standard*, LXX (Dec. 10, 1958), 4–5 ff.; LXX (Dec. 17, 1958), 6–7.

55. *Watchman-Examiner*, XLVI (Dec. 25, 1958), 1061.

56. III (Sept. 28, 1959), 33.

57. *Christian Century*, LXXVII (Jan. 20, 1960), 75.

58. *Ibid.*, LXXVI (Dec. 23, 1959), 1496.

59. *Ibid.*, LXXVI (Sept. 30, 1959), 1108–9.

60. LXXVI (Dec. 23, 1959), 1491.

61. "Italian Liberals and John XXIII," *Christian Century*, LXXVII (Mar. 16, 1960), 314–15.

62. Pp. 128–29. These lines were written in criticism of Pius IX, whom the author described as lacking in open-minded and open-hearted simplicity. The rightness or falsity of the author's judgment of Pio Nono is beside the point of this study. What is significant is the description of qualities in a pope that proved to be particularly meaningful to Protestants.

63. Joseph Wittkofski, "Violent Hands," *Living Church*, CXLII (Mar. 19, 1961), 14–15.

64. LXXVI (Nov. 4, 1959), 1267.

65. *Ibid.*, p. 1268.

66. *Christian Century*, LXXVII (Jan. 27, 1960), 102.

67. *Ibid.*, LXXVII (Aug. 31, 1960), 989.

68. CXLI (Aug. 21, 1960), 10.

69. LXXIII (May 24, 1961), 4–5.

70. *Missions*, CLIX (March, 1961), 13–14.

71. *Ibid.*, p. 13.

72. L (Mar. 22, 1962), 226.

73. *Christianity Today*, V (Nov. 21, 1960), 161–62. See also Ralph L. Keiper, "Roman Catholicism," *Eternity*, XIII (January, 1962), 30.

74. *Watchman-Examiner*, XLVIII (Dec. 22, 1960), 1003.

75. LXXII (Mar. 9, 1960), 5.

76. *Ibid.*, p. 5.

77. *Christianity Today*, IV (Dec. 7, 1959), 22.

78. *Watchman-Examiner*, XLVII (Nov. 26, 1959), 965. See also *Baptist Standard*, LXXII (Jan. 13, 1960), 5.

79. LXXIV (Jan. 17, 1962), 4.

80. LXXIV (June 6, 1962), 4–5.

81. *United Church Herald*, III (Dec. 1, 1960), 29.

82. *Witness*, XLVII (Nov. 17, 1960), 6. See also XLVII (Dec. 15, 1960), 3–4.

83. *Living Church*, CXLIII (Nov. 26, 1961), 15.

84. *Christian Century*, LXXVII (Nov. 16, 1960), 1333.

85. XLIII (Dec. 14, 1960), 50.

86. *Witness*, XLVI (Nov. 23, 1961), 3.

87. *Christian Century*, LXXVIII (Nov. 29, 1961), 1420–21.

88. LXIX (May 2, 1962), 580.

89. "Reflections on the Division of Christians," *Christianity and Crisis*, XXI (Oct. 30, 1961), 181–84.

90. *Presbyterian Life*, XV (Feb. 1, 1962), 31.

91. *Christian Century*, LXXVIII (Sept. 27, 1961), 1133–34.

92. *Witness*, XLVI (Dec. 28, 1961), 3–4.

## CHAPTER 3

1. It is interesting to compare the religious polemic that surrounded the 1928 presidential campaign with the religious issue as confronted by Kennedy in 1960. The well-documented charges against the Catholic Church's attitude toward democracy, as expressed in papal statements, provided potent arguments against Alfred E. Smith's candidacy in Charles C. Marshall's *Governor Smith's American Catholicism* and in his *The Roman Catholic Church in the Modern State* (New York, 1928). In the same year, the first editor of *Commonweal*, Michael Williams, attempted to answer Marshall's arguments in an essay in *Catholicism and the Modern Mind* (New York, 1928), pp. 129–42. From the present vantage point in history, Williams' response seems weak indeed, resting as it largely did on appeals to *de facto* Catholic loyalty. For a picture of the intense campaign of religious bigotry and bitterness, see Michael Williams, *The Shadow of the Pope* (New York, 1932). For a good survey of the religious issues in the 1928 campaign, see Edmund A. Moore, *A Catholic Runs for President* (New York, 1956). Ruth C. Silva's *Rum, Religion and Votes* (University Park, Pa., 1962) emphasizes aspects other than religion that contributed to the defeat of Smith. A searching Catholic appraisal of official Vatican church-state theory would have to await a John Courtney Murray in the late 1940's. For a discussion of this relatively new understanding of

Catholic church-state teaching, in addition to the work by Thomas T. Love mentioned earlier, see Thomas G. Sanders, "A Comparison of Two Current American Roman Catholic Theories of the American Political System with Particular Reference to the Problem of Religious Liberty," unpublished Ph.D. dissertation (Columbia University Library). The books by White, Pike, Sorensen, and Schlesinger cited in the course of this chapter reflect a more liberal Catholic stance that was widespread and well articulated by the time Kennedy faced the religious question in his presidential campaign. For a good general survey of Catholic thought on political questions, see Jerome G. Kerwin, *Catholic Viewpoint on Church and State* (New York, 1960). For a good collection of references to anti-Kennedy leaflets, see Patricia Barrett, *Religious Liberty and the American Presidency* (New York, 1963).

2. John Wicklein, "John Kennedy and the Catholic Issue: 1960–1964," *Religion and Contemporary Society*, ed. Harold Stahmer (New York, 1963), p. 219.

3. *Ibid.*, p. 222. See also Theodore H. White, *The Making of the President: 1960* (New York, 1961), pp. 126 ff.

4. *Lutheran Witness*, LXXVII (Feb. 11, 1958), 11.

5. Don Hillis, "If We Elect A Roman Catholic as President," *United Evangelical Action*, XVII (Mar. 15, 1958), 3.

6. Clyde W. Taylor, "Needed: A Revitalized Protestantism," *United Evangelical Action*, XVII (April 1, 1958), 8.

7. November, 1958, 22.

8. *United Evangelical Action*, XVII (January, 1959), 3–4.

9. Wicklein, in Stahmer, p. 224.

10. LXXII (Feb. 3, 1960), 4.

11. LXXII (Feb. 17, 1960), 4–5. A similar theme of foreign domination was voiced the following month by L. R. Elliott, "The President's Church Affiliation," *Baptist Standard*, LXXII (Mar. 2, 1960), 22.

12. LXXII (April 20, 1960), 5.

13. LXXII (May 25, 1960), 5. See also George L. Ford, "A Catholic President: How Free from Church Control?" *United Eangelical Action*, XIX (May, 1960), 7.

14. *Baptist Standard*, LXXII (July 27, 1960), 4.

15. *Ibid.*

16. "The Presidency and the Catholic Church," *Baptist Standard*, LXXII (Oct. 12, 1960), 6–7.

17. W. R. Estep, Jr., "Fact Sheet on Roman Catholicism," *Baptist Standard*, LXXII (Oct. 19, 1960), 12–13.

18. CXXVI (Mar. 5, 1960), 3.

19. White, *The Making*, p. 312.

20. *Ibid.*, pp. 312–13.

21. C. Stanley Lowell, "Protestants, Catholics and Politics," *Christianity Today*, III (July 20, 1959), 5–8.

22. James Curry, "Politics, the Pope and the Presidency," *Eternity*, X (February, 1959), 14.

23. *Christianity Today*, IV (Feb. 1, 1960), 20–21.

24. *Ibid.*

25. George L. Ford, "A Catholic President: How Free From Church Control?" *United Evangelical Action*, XIX (May, 1960), 6.

26. *Watchman-Examiner*, XLVIII (Mar. 24, 1960), 234–35. See also Jackson Wilcox, "Religion and Your Vote," *Watchman-Examiner*, XLVIII (May 5, 1960), 368–69.

27. *Ibid.*, XLVIII (July 28, 1960), 594.

28. W. O. Vought, Sr., "Temporal Power," *Watchman-Examiner*, XLVIII (Aug. 18, 1960), 655–56.

29. (New York, 1960), pp. 99 ff.

30. Howard Johnson, "Are American Catholics Different?" *Watchman-Examiner*, XLVIII (Sept. 1, 1960), 687–88. See also Wicklein, in Stahmer, p. 218.

31. Pike, *A Roman Catholic*, p. 133.

32. Gordon Palmer, "Religion and the United States' Presidency," *Watchman-Examiner*, XLVIII (Sept. 15, 1960), 720–21.

33. Sterling L. Price, "The Catholic-Protestant Dilemma," *Watchman-Examiner*, XLVIII (Sept. 29, 1960), 762–64.

34. XLVIII (Oct. 6, 1960), 778.

35. Gordon Palmer, "Look Ahead!" *Watchman-Examiner*, LXVIII (Oct. 20, 1960), 821–22.

36. CLVIII (November, 1960), 13–14.

37. LXXII (June 15, 1960), 4.

38. IV (June 20, 1960), 31.

39. XLVIII (June 23, 1960), 498.

40. LXXII (June 29, 1960), 4.

41. October, 1960, 24–27.

42. Pike, *A Roman Catholic*, p. 128.

43. Donald Grey Barnhouse, "The Peril Over the Presidency," *Eternity*, XI (October, 1960), 8–10.

44. John W. Dykstra, "Catholics as a Pluralistic Minority," *Christian Century*, LXXVII (Oct. 19, 1960), 1214.

45. Robert A. Baker, "The Presidency and the Roman Catholic Church," *Journal of Church and State*, II (November, 1960), 112–16.

46. CXXVI (Oct. 29, 1960), 3.

47. *Ibid.*, CXXVI (Nov. 5, 1960), 3.

48. *Watchman-Examiner*, XLVIII (Sept. 29, 1960), p. 757.

49. *Baptist Standard*, LXXII (Aug. 31, 1960), 4.

50. White, *The Making*, pp. 468–69.

51. *Ibid.*, p. 313.

52. *Ibid.*, pp. 313–14.

53. Theodore C. Sorensen, *Kennedy* (New York, 1965), p. 193.

54. *Ibid.*, p. 190.

55. V (Nov. 21, 1960), 21–22. For an interesting review of last minute efforts to stop Kennedy on religious grounds, see Wicklein, in Stahmer, pp. 237 ff. On Reformation Sunday, October 30, a special anti-Kennedy effort was launched in many pulpits by the National Association of Evangelicals, a number of Southern Baptist ministers, and other conservative preachers. "Anti-Catholicism seemed to be the major reason for Kennedy's loss of Oklahoma, Tennessee, and Kentucky. It was a contributing factor in Florida and Virginia, and it came very close to costing him South Carolina. The inroads of the Republicans in the traditionally Democratic southern and border states seemed directly attributable to the Catholic question" (Wicklein, *op. cit.*, pp. 243–44).

56. XLVIII (Nov. 24, 1960), 921.

57. James G. Harris, "Presidential Election as Viewed by a Pastor," *Baptist Standard*, LXXII (Dec. 14, 1960), 9.

58. *Baptist Standard*, LXXII (Nov. 16, 1960), 4–5.

59. James G. Manz, "The Religious Significance of the 1960 Presidential Election," *Lutheran Witness*, LXXIX (Nov. 29, 1960), 10 ff.

60. XCIII (June 5, 1960), 6–7.

61. *World Call*, XLI (April, 1959), 10.

62. *Churchman*, CLXXIV (February, 1960), 5.

63. Joseph Wittkofski, "Can a Roman Catholic Be President?" *Witness*, XLVII (June 23, 1960), 7–9.

64. *Witness*, XLVII (Sept. 29, 1960), 3.

65. John Baiz, "Can a Roman Catholic Be President?" *Witness*, XLVII (Aug. 18, 1960), 7–9. See also *Christian Century*, LXXVII (Oct. 26, 1960), 1235–36.

66. *Witness*, XLVII (June 2, 1960), 3–4.

67. Roy Pearson, "Reservations About a Roman Catholic President," *United Church Herald*, III (Feb. 4, 1960), 22.

68. Richard C. Rainer, "Stones Are Falling from the Wall of Separation," *Christian Advocate*, IV (Sept. 29, 1960), 11-12.

69. Harold A. Bosley, "Inconsistencies on Church and State," *Christian Advocate*, IV (May 26, 1960), 20–21.

70. LXXVII (Sept. 21, 1960), 1108.

71. LXXVII (Sept. 7, 1960), 1011–12.

72. LXXVI (Mar. 4, 1959), 251–53.

73. LXXVII (May 4, 1960), 533.

74. "A Catholic President: Con," *Christian Century*, LXXVII Oct. 26, 1960), 1244–47. Although this seemed to express the general tenor of *Christian Century's* mind on Kennedy's election, this review did run an important article supporting a Catholic President: Charles R. Andrews, "A Catholic President: Pro," LXXVII (Oct. 26, 1960), 1241–43. Andrews held that a liberal Catholic President would help to oppose the very things Protestants feared: Catholic political power, exclusivism, and anti-Protestantism. He cited the liberal movement in Roman Catholic thought on religious liberty, etc., and he hoped that both John XXIII in his Council and John Kennedy as President might further these trends in Catholicism.

75. Sorensen, *Kennedy*, p. 144.

76. Wicklein, in Stahmer, pp. 231–32.

77. *Lutheran*, XLII (Dec. 16, 1959), 50; XLII (May 18, 1960), 50.

78. *Ibid.*, XLII (July 27, 1960), 50.

79. *Ibid.*, XLIII (Oct. 5, 1960), 50.

80. *Lutheran Quarterly*, XII (November, 1960), 357–58.

81. *Presbyterian Life*, XIII (June 1, 1960), 18–19.

82. Kenneth G. Phifer, "A Roman Catholic for President," *Presbyterian Outlook*, CXLII (June 20, 1960), 5; CXLII (Sept. 12, 1960), 8; CXLII (Sept. 19, 1960), 8.

83. John Sutherland Bonnell, "Religion and the Presidency," *Presbyterian Life*, XIII (May 1, 1960), 8–10.

84. III (July, 1959), 5–6.

85. *Ibid.*, IV (June 23, 1960), 3.

86. *Ibid.*, IV (Oct. 13, 1960), 24; IV (Oct 27, 1960), 21. In a symposium about how Methodists should preach concerning the candidates, considerable variety of opinion was expressed: IV (Oct. 13, 1960), 11–13.

87. Kenneth R. Forbes, "Separation of Church and State," *Witness*, XLVII (June 2, 1960),7–8.

88. CXL (May 8, 1960), 15.

89. CXXXVIII (June 14, 1959), 18–19.

90. CXLI (Sept. 25, 1960), 16–17.

91. Howard R. Burkle, "Ought a Protestant Vote for a Roman Catholic?" *United Church Herald*, III (Jan. 21, 1960), 8–10 ff. See also III (Oct. 6, 1960), 7.

92. "A Roman Catholic for President?" *Christianity and Crisis*, XX (Mar. 7, 1960), 17–19.

93. "Catholics in America," *New Republic*, CXLII (Mar. 21, 1960), 12.

94. "The Dangers of Religious Solidarity," *Christianity and Crisis*, XX (May 2, 1960), 54.

95. "The Roman Catholic 'Issue' Again," *Christianity and Crisis*, XX (Sept. 19, 1960), 125–26.

96. "Triumph for American Democracy," *Christianity and Crisis*, XX (Nov. 28, 1960), 170–71.

97. Wicklein, in Stahmer, p. 248.

98. John C. Bennett, *Christians and the State* (New York, 1958), p. 246. Though opposing direct aid to parochial schools, Bennett held that "fringe benefits," such as transportation, health services, school lunches, and textbooks, were justified (p. 248). A similar view can be found in Nevin C. Harner, "A Protestant Educator's View," *American Education and Religion*, ed. F. E. Johnson (New York, 1952), pp. 77–92. Another important viewpoint, admitting certain auxiliary benefits to Catholic schools, but firmly opposed to direct tax help, is expressed in George R. La Noue, *Public Funds for Parochial Schools*? (New York, 1963). Much background on the aid-to-education issue can be found in Leo Pfeffer, *Church, State and Freedom* (Boston, 1953). For the position that opposes any public money for parochial schools, see Paul Blanshard, *Religion and the Schools* (Boston, 1963). The same conclusion is reached after a broad historical interpretation by Freeman R. Butts, *The American Tradition in Religion and Education* (Boston, 1950). A similar argument from historical documents of colonial days is seen in Joseph L. Blau, *Cornerstones of Religious Freedom in America* (Boston, 1949). For the Catholic viewpoint on governmental aid to nonpublic schools, see Neil G. McCluskey, *The Catholic Viewpoint on Education* (New York, 1959), chap. 7. For an historical interpretation from the Catholic perspective, see J. M. O'Neill, *Religion and Education Under the Constitution* (New York, 1949).

99. *Christianity Today*, IV (Feb. 29, 1960), 27.

100. *Ibid.*

101. V (Mar. 27, 1961), 21–22.

102. *Ibid.*; see also VI (Feb. 16, 1962), 30.

103. April, 1961, p. 19; May, 1961, p. 23. In the issue of September, 1961, p. 25, Poling claimed that indirect pressure was being exerted on the President by the charge that he was not loyal to his faith.

104. *Christian Herald*, July, 1962, p. 25. See also *Baptist Standard*, LXXII (Oct. 19, 1960), 4–5, praising the statement of 100 Catholic laymen on religious liberty.

105. *Missions*, CLIX (March, 1961), 13; CLIX (May, 1961), 13–14.

106. *Missions*, CLX (April, 1962), 14.

107. *Watchman-Examiner*, XLIX (April 13, 1961), 286.

108. *Lutheran Witness*, LXXXI (Mar. 6, 1962), 21. Also *Watchman-Examiner*, XLIX (April 6, 1961), 267.

109. James G. Manz, "Federal Aid to Parochial Schools," *Lutheran Witness*, LXXX (Oct. 31, 1961), 516–18.

110. C. C. Meeden, "Our Public Schools," *Watchman-Examiner*, XLIX (June 8, 1961), 458–60.

111. *Ibid.*

112. *Watchman-Examiner*, XLIX (July 20, 1961), 570; L (Oct. 11, 1962), 721.

113. Ralph L. Keiper, "Roman Catholicism," *Eternity*, XII (January, 1962), 30–31.

114. *Watchman-Examiner*, LIX (July 27, 1961), 570.

115. L (Mar. 29, 1962), 247.

116. LXXIII (April 5, 1961), 4–5.

117. *Biblical Recorder*, CXXVI (Sept. 10, 1960), 3.

118. *Ibid.*, CXXVII (Feb. 25, 1961), 3.

119. *Biblical Recorder*, CXXVII (July 29, 1961), 3. *Baptist Standard*, LXXIII (Nov. 29, 1961), 4–5.

120. Wicklein, in Stahmer, p. 249.

121. Sorensen, *Kennedy*, pp. 362–63.

122. *Lutheran*, XLIII (Jan. 18, 1961), 50; *Lutheran Standard*, I (Mar. 28, 1961), 20–21.

123. *Lutheran*, XLIII (April 12, 1961), 54; *Lutheran Standard*, I (May 9, 1961), 14.

124. *Lutheran*, XLIII (Aug. 30, 1961), 50.

125. *Christian Advocate*, V (April 27, 1961), 21–22. *Presbyterian Life*, XIV (April 15, 1961), 24–26.

126. *Christian Advocate*, V (Nov. 9, 1961), 11.

127. "What Do the Catholics Want?" *Churchman*, CLXXIII (November, 1959), 6–7.

128. Robert L. Gildea, "A Watchdog Worth Watching," *Christian Advocate*, V (Mar. 30, 1961), 7–8. This article was answered by C. Stanley Lowell, reiterating POAU's opposition to hierarchical pressures that were destructive of American democracy: *Christian Advocate*, V (May 11, 1961), 9.

129. *Christian Advocate*, V (May 11, 1961), 7–8.

130. IV (April 6, 1961), 11.

131. LXXVIII (Feb. 1, 1961), 131–32; (Mar. 8, 1961), 291; (Mar. 15, 1961), 317; (April 5, 1961), 411–12; (April 12, 1961), 466; (April 19, 1961), 482; (April 26, 1961), 508.

132. LXXVIII (May 17, 1961), 613.

133. LXXIX (Jan. 24, 1962), 99–100. Even more noteworthy was the *Baptist Standard's* defense of President Kennedy against the *America* criticism. The editor affirmed that *America* was "hitting below the belt" in impugning the President's motives. He felt that JFK couldn't be intimidated, even by the powers of Rome: LXXIV (Jan. 24, 1962), 4.

134. VI (Mar. 1, 1962), 2.

135. XXI (May 1, 1961), 61–62. This more creative grasp of the problem was later reflected in an editorial in *Dialog*, a Lutheran ecumenical review, I (Summer, 1962), 6. The "Shared Time" solution was also proposed in other Protestant journals: Dean M. Kelley, "Shared Time: A Solution to the Education Dilemma," *Christian Advocate*, VI (Mar. 15, 1962), 7–8.

136. *Christianity and Crisis*, XXII (May 28, 1962), 79.

137. XXIII (Oct. 28, 1962), 189–91.

138. IV (Oct. 26, 1962), 22–23.

139. CLXXV (January, 1961), 15.

140. *Ibid.*, LXXVII (Nov. 16, 1960), 1331.

141. *Lutheran*, XLIII (Nov. 30, 1960), 50.

142. David O. Moberg, "A Victory for Religious Liberty?" *Eternity*, XII (February, 1961), 20.

143. *Ibid.*, p. 30.

144. LXXIII (Feb. 22, 1961), 5.

145. *Baptist Standard*, LXXIII (April 12, 1961), 5; LXXIV (Sept. 26, 1962), 4.

146. Richard C. C. Kim, "A Roman Catholic President in the

American Schema," *Journal of Church and State*, III (May,1961), 33–40.

147. "Roman Catholic Clericalism," *Journal of Church and State*, III (November, 1961), 182.

148. "Proposal on the School-Aid Impasse," *Christian Century*, LXXVIII (April 12, 1961), 448.

149. *United Church Herald*, V (Mar. 22, 1962), 29. See also *Lutheran Witness*, LXXX (Jan. 24, 1961), 5.

150. *A Thousand Days: John F. Kennedy in the White House* (Boston, 1965), p. 108.

151. *Ibid.*

152. "He Was a Man of Only One Season," *The New York Times Magazine*, Nov. 21, 1965, p. 29.

153. *Kennedy*, p. 365.

154. "The President's Untimely Death," *Baptist Standard*, LXXV (Nov. 27, 1963), 1.

155. "Forty Minutes with President Kennedy," *Baptist Standard*, LXXV (Feb. 27, 1963), 4–5. See also LXXV (Aug. 7, 1963), 4, on Kennedy's visit to Pope Paul VI.

156. *Biblical Recorder*, CXXVIII (Dec. 7, 1963), 4.

157. VIII (Dec. 6, 1963), 24.

158. VI (Winter, 1964), 5–11.

159. *The Making*, p. 427.

160. *Kennedy*, p. 364.

161. *A Thousand Days*, p. 108.

# CHAPTER 4

1. The best theoretical discussion of papal social teaching is Jean-Yves Calvez and Jacques Perrin, *The Church and Social Justice*, trans. J. R. Kirwan (Chicago, 1961). Two other important works on Catholic social doctrine are John F. Cronin, *Social Principles and Economic Life* (Milwaukee, 1959), and Benjamin L. Masse, *Justice for All* (Milwaukee, 1964). A brief historical perspective of Catholic social developments can be found in A. R. Vidler, *A Century of Social Catholicism 1820–1920* (London, 1964). For the American scene, see Aaron I. Abell, *American Catholicism and Social Action* (New York, 1960). For commentaries on *Mater et Magistra*, see Jean-Yves Calvez, *The Social Thought of John XXIII*, trans. George J. M. McKenzie (Chicago, 1964); Joseph N. Moody and George J. Lawler (eds.), *The*

*Challenge of Mater et Magistra* (New York, 1963); Donald R. Campion and Eugene K. Culhane (eds.), *Mater et Magistra* (New York, 1961).

2. LXXIII (Oct. 11, 1961), 5.

3. V (Sept. 11, 1961), 26–27.

4. XIII (January, 1962), 31.

5. *Witness*, XLVI (Aug. 10, 1961), 3–4.

6. LXXIX (Jan. 10, 1962), 43.

7. *Christianity and Crisis*, XXI (Aug. 7, 1961), 142.

8. *Ibid*. See also *Christian Century*, LXXVIII (Sept. 20, 1961), 1105–8.

9. *Christian Century*, LXXVIII (Sept. 6, 1961), 1047–50.

10. *Ibid*., p. 1049.

11. XXI (Jan. 8, 1962), 236–38.

12. *Christian Century*, LXXVIII (Sept. 20, 1961), 1105–8.

13. The over-all comment of the noted Catholic historian E. E. Y. Hales on the agricultural aspect of Pope John's letter is especially pertinent: "After more than a thousand years of relative indifference to the agricultural backwardness of the papal states, and a hundred years of only small concern for the hideous problem of agricultural poverty in Naples and Sicily, the Holy See was now taking her place, with Pope John, in the van of the movement for agricultural reform" (*Pope John and His Revolution* [New York, 1965], p. 51).

14. Ramsey, *Christian Century*, LXXVIII (Sept. 6, 1961), 1047–50. Jaroslav Pelikan's views were recorded in "Mother Church and Mother Earth," *Catholic Messenger*, Jan. 25, 1962, p. 9.

15. "A Protestant Views the Encyclical and Catholic Social Action" (mimeographed). Paper delivered at the Sixth Annual National Catholic Social Action Conference, Aug. 24, 1962.

16. As quoted by Hiley H. Ward in "Detroit Pastors Hail Pope's Labor Letter," *Detroit Free Press*, July 17, 1961.

17. *Christian Century*, LXXVIII (Sept. 20, 1961), p. 1105.

18. *Christianity and Crisis*, XXI (Aug. 7, 1961), 142–43.

19. LXXVIII (Sept. 20, 1961), 1107.

20. LXXVIII (Aug. 16, 1961), 792–93.

21. Jo-Ann Price, "Clerics Take Issue with Pope," *San Francisco Examiner*, July 17, 1961, p. 9. In this article, Bishop James A. Pike also voiced his disagreement with Pope John's birth-control policy. Pike gives a clear and brief presentation of the Protestant viewpoint on birth control in *If You Marry Outside Your Faith* (New York, 1954).

22. *Christian Century*, LXXVIII (Sept. 6, 1961), 1078.

23. *Christianity and Crisis*, XXI (Aug. 7, 1961), 142–43. See also *Living Church*, 143 (July 30, 1961), 10.

24. *Christian Century*, LXXVIII (Sept. 6, 1961), 1079.

25. *Christian Century*, LXXVIII (Sept. 20, 1961), 1108.

26. I (Winter, 1962), 69–70.

27. I (Aug. 29, 1961), 20–21.

28. 143 (July 30, 1961), 10.

29. Right-wing Catholic reactions to *Mater et Magistra* were also in evidence. An editorial in *National Review* by its Catholic editor, William F. Buckley, Jr., called the encyclical "a venture in triviality," and quipped: "Mater, sí; Magistra, no." This was criticized in *America*, CV (Sept. 30, 1961), pp. 820–21. Another article on the rather widespread right-wing attitude among American Catholics against the encyclical was by Philip S. Land, "Pope John XXIII: Teacher," *America*, CVI (Nov. 4, 1961), 149–51.

30. Jo-Ann Price, "Clerics Take Issue," p. 9.

31. *Witness*, XLVI (Nov. 9, 1961), 3.

32. *Christian Century*, LXXVIII (Sept. 5, 1961), 1078. It should be noted that Pope John's concern for social issues and also his universalist outlook had been fostered by various experiences in his long life. As secretary to Bishop Radini-Tedeschi of Bergamo from 1904 to 1914, Roncalli was in close contact with a pioneer in Italian social action. Radini-Tedeschi was a leader of progressive social Catholicism in Italy, and is thought to have influenced *Rerum Novarum* of Leo XIII (Hales, *Pope John*, p. 13). Roncalli's experience in Bulgaria as a capable and well-liked diplomat also put him into important contacts with the Orthodox and the non-Catholic worlds. His next assignment was in Istanbul, where he encountered a cosmopolitan atmosphere and came to a deeper understanding of Eastern Christianity and of Islamic religion. His high post as Nuncio in Paris after World War II gave him first-hand appreciation of French Catholic efforts to reach and serve the religiously disaffected proletariat in such ministries as the priest-worker movement. In France, Roncalli also learned to deal successfully with politically hostile groups as well as with such leading figures as the Socialist President Auriol and the radical Edouard Herriot (Leone Algisi, *John the Twenty-Third*, trans. Peter Ryde [Westminster, 1963], p. 176). In the delicate post-war relations with Germany, Roncalli saw the need to make the important distinction between the German people and the government of the Third Reich (Andrea Lazzarini, *Pope John XXIII*, trans. Michael Hatwell [New York, 1959], p. 76). This distinction would have important consequences in *Pacem in Terris*, where Pope John would distinguish between ideologies and human movements in history. Another biography, which reviews some of these points, is

Zsolt Aradi, James I. Tucek, and James C. O' Neill, *Pope John XXIII* (New York, 1959). An intimate view of Pope John by a close associate during his pontificate is Loris Capovilla, *The Heart and Mind of John XXIII*, trans. Patrick Riley (New York, 1964). Pope John's own journal and interior autobiography is *Journal of a Soul*, trans. Dorothy White (New York, 1965). One of the most complete collections of his writings in English is *The Encyclicals and Other Messages of John XXIII* (Washington, D.C., 1964). See also Ernesto Balducci, *John "The Transitional Pope"* (New York, 1965).

33. John C. Bennett welcomed the fact that *Pacem in Terris* avoided the overly involved language of earlier papal natural-law statements, and that it kept to a minimum the pious phrases that bothered Protestants: "*Pacem in Terris*, Two Views," *Christianity and Crisis*, XXIII (May 13, 1963), 81.

34. A good translation of the encyclical is *Pacem in Terris: Peace on Earth* (New York, 1963). In a short commentary, John Courtney Murray points out the significance of freedom in the thought of Pope John. A more extended commentary is Peter Riga, *Peace on Earth* (New York, 1964). Another commentary on significant issues in the encyclical can be found in four essays in *Social Order*, XIII (September, 1963). An extensive bibliography on the encyclical is published in Everett J. Morgan, *The Social Conscience of a Catholic* (Milwaukee, 1964), pp. 274–76. A helpful collection of public pronouncements by the Holy See on topics treated in *Pacem in Terris* is Harry W. Flannery (ed.), *Patterns for Peace: Catholic Statements on International Order* (Westminster, 1962).

35. XLV (June, 1963), 9.

36. XLVIII (April 25, 1963), 3–6.

37. CLXXVII (June, 1963), 5.

38. VI (May 16, 1963), 6.

39. LXXX (April 24, 1963), 517.

40. "Toward Peace and Justice," *Christian Century*, LXXX (May 29, 1963), 705–6.

41. *United Evangelical Action*, XXII (June, 1963), 28–29.

42. LXIII (June, 1963), 12–13.

43. *Christianity and Crisis*, XXIII (May 13, 1963), 81, 83. The historian Hales also sees John's advocacy of natural rights as an important change from the papal attitude of the 19th century, which condemned the "modern liberties": "Yet what was wrong in the days of Mazzini was now declared to be a God-given natural right" (*Pope John*, p. 74).

44. "The Problems That Beset the Human Family Today,"

*United Church Herald*, VI (May 30, 1963), 32–33. Hales also makes much of this new emphasis on democracy in the writings of Pope John (pp. 56 ff.)

45. In *Therefore Choose Life* (Santa Barbara, 1965), p. 22.

46. In *To Live as Men: An Anatomy of Peace* (Santa Barbara, 1965), p. 13.

47. *Christianity and Crisis*, XXIII (May 13, 1963).

48. Brown, in *Therefore*, p. 23.

49. VII (April 26, 1963), 25.

50. In *To Live*, pp. 18–19.

51. *"Pacem in Terris," Religion in Life*, XXXIII (Winter, 1963/64), 117.

52. *Christianity and Crisis*, XXIII (May 13, 1963), p. 83.

53. Brown, in *Therefore*, p. 21.

54. Niebuhr, *Christianity and Crisis*, XXIII (May 13, 1963), p. 83. At the time *Pacem in Terris* appeared, the morality of nuclear weapons had been more seriously studied by Protestants than by Catholics. Two books on the nuclear dilemma by Protestant moralists are John C. Bennett (ed.), *Nuclear Weapons and the Conflict of Conscience* (New York, 1962), and Paul Ramsey, *The Limits of Nuclear War* (New York, 1963). A discussion of this subject by two Catholic thinkers is found in William Clancy (ed.), *The Moral Dilemma of Nuclear War* (New York, 1961).

55. In *Therefore*, p. 23.

56. *Christianity and Crisis*, XXIII (May 13, 1963), p. 83.

57. *Religion in Life*, XXXIII (Winter, 1963/64), 118. See also *Living Church*, CXLVI (April 28, 1963), 20–21; *Presbyterian Life*, XVI (May 15, 1963), 26–28.

58. *Christianity and Crisis*, XXIII (May 13, 1963), p. 83. See also *Christian Century*, LXXX (June 5, 1963), 734.

59. *Presbyterian Life*, XVI (May 15, 1963), 26–28.

60. In *Therefore*, p. 16.

61. *Ibid.*, p. 24.

62. *"Pacem in Terris*, Two Views," *Christianity and Crisis*, XXIII (May 13, 1963), 82.

63. Reissig, *United Church Herald*, VI (May 30, 1963), p. 34.

64. III (May 7, 1963), 6.

65. *Churchman*, CLXXVII (June, 1963), 5. In a very perceptive article, Michael Novak, a Catholic lay author, described the sense of panic in some conservative Catholic circles over the changes under

Pope John. The pope, Novak maintained, was breaking with the abstract and essentially moralistic perspective of Latin scholasticism. Pope John was returning the church to a more historical and empirical view by which men learned the natural law only gradually under the conditioning of history ("Break with the Past," *Commonweal*, LXXVIII [June 28, 1963], 372–75).

66. In *To Live*, p. 14.

67. Brown, in *Therefore*, p. 18.

68. *Presbyterian Life*, XVI (May 15, 1963), 26.

69. It should be noted that Johannine universalism, although it gave a special impetus to Catholic social consciousness, was building on a considerable background of teaching and action in Europe and in the United States. *Rerum Novarum* and *Quadragesimo Anno* spoke to the social upheavals of the late 19th century and the Great Depression, respectively. After World War II, the *Mission de Paris* and the priest-worker movements attempted to bring the church to the religiously estranged worker (Pierre Andreu, *Histoire des prêtres-ouvriers* [Paris, 1960]). Similar efforts to cope with social problems can be seen in Jacques Loew, *Mission to the Poorest*, trans. Pamela Carswell (New York, 1950), and Abbé G. Michonneau, *Revolution in a City Parish* (Westminster, Md., 1950). Also noteworthy among the many movements since World War II were the various Catholic centers of socio-religious research which were formed in the larger cities of Europe, and which extended their influence into Latin America and Africa. In his early encyclicals and messages, Pius XII showed great concern for social and political problems (Guido Gonella, *A World to Reconstruct: Pius XII on Peace and Reconstruction*, trans. T. Lincoln Bouscaren [Milwaukee, 1944]).

In the United States, the problems of a church of poor immigrants and the crisis of the Great Depression produced significant social thinkers and movements. Although Pope John's social views met with some opposition in America, many American Catholics had been prepared by their own experiences to welcome the pope's words. In addition to Aaron I. Abell's survey of American Catholic social involvements, the life of the outstanding social-gospel pioneer, John A. Ryan, provides insights into the Catholic commitment to social reform in America (Francis L. Broderick, *Right Reverend New Dealer: John A. Ryan* [New York, 1963]). Ryan's long life of social involvement grew out of a native American, Midwestern populist tradition, and flourished within the National Catholic Welfare Conference. Peter E. Dietz represented another tradition of Catholic social concern rising out of the German Central Verein (Mary Harrita Fox, *Peter E. Dietz, Labor Priest* [Notre Dame, Ind., 1953]).

Important movements in American social Catholicism were the

National Catholic Rural Life Conference, Catholic interracial councils, the labor school movement, the Christian Family Movement, and other social action groups, especially in the Chicago area whence issued journals like *Today, Work,* and *Act.* In the 1930's an influential book on the racial dilemma appeared: John LaFarge, *Interracial Justice* (New York, 1937). Some of the earliest Catholic-Protestant ecumenical encounters stemmed from joint social action through the National Conference of Christians and Jews, and through the publication of joint social statements: "Economic Justice," *Catholic Mind,* XLV (February, 1947), 102–5. In this statement, the Federal Council of Churches collaborated with the National Catholic Welfare Conference. Earlier joint social statements were issued in 1919 and 1932: see Broderick, *Right Reverend,* p. 197.

After World War II, Catholic Relief Services assumed a greater role, and the newer aspects of racial, poverty, and peace problems confronted the American church. The increased Catholic appreciation for democratic values, already seen in previous references, was strikingly manifested in John Courtney Murray, *We Hold These Truths* (New York, 1960). Publications like *Commonweal, Catholic World,* and *America* also contributed over the years to the formation of social consciousness among American Catholics. It should also be noted, however, that despite these social and democratic advances in American Catholicism, considerable Protestant-Catholic animosity was building up in the post-World War II years (Samuel Lubell, *The Future of American Politics* [New York, 1956], pp. 235 ff.). This deterioration of Protestant-Catholic relations was also described in Chapter 1. The Johannine impact of universalism, therefore, appeared at a time when it could foster the positive social and democratic trends in American Catholicism toward new ecumenical relationships.

## CHAPTER 5

1. The most important book by a Catholic author prior to Vatican II was Hans Küng, *The Council, Reform and Reunion* (New York, 1961). This book had a far-reaching influence, and many of its topics on renewal and reform were echoed by the Protestants studied in this chapter. An earlier book that gave considerable background on the coming Council was Lorenz Jaeger, *The Ecumenical Council, the Church and Christendom* (London, 1961). Among Protestant books on the Council before its opening, one of the most searching was a collection of essays by Lutheran thinkers, Kristen E. Skydsgaard (ed.), *The Papal Council and the Gospel* (Minneapolis, 1961). Other books dealing with the background of and hopes for the Council were Claud D. Nelson, *The Vatican Council and All Christians* (New York, 1962);

Eugene R. Fairweather & Edward R. Hardy, *The Voice of the Church: The Ecumenical Council* (Greenwich, Conn., 1962); and Bernard Pawley, *Looking at the Vatican Council* (London, 1962).

2. *Baptist Standard*, LXXIV (June 13, 1962), 4.

3. CLX (February, 1962), 13.

4. CLX (October, 1962), 13–14.

5. L (June 14, 1962), 451.

6. L (Oct. 4, 1962), 705.

7. XXI (November, 1962), 20–21.

8. Philip E. Hughes, "Review of Current Religious Thought," *Christianity Today*, VI (July 6, 1962), 52. *Christianity Today* manifested some interesting changes as the Council approached: much more space was devoted to the affairs of the Catholic Church, and a variety of views about the Council were expressed, some very conservative and negative, others more friendly and open.

9. Don Francisco Lacueva, "Should We Return to Rome?" *Christianity Today*, VII (Oct. 12, 1962), 12–13.

10. *Christianity Today*, VI (July 6, 1962), 27.

11. *Christianity Today*, VI (Sept. 14, 1962), 47.

12. C. Gregg Singer, "Agreements and Differences," *Christianity Today*, VII (Oct. 12, 1962), 14.

13. *Ibid.*, p. 18.

14. *Christianity Today*, VII (Oct. 26, 1962), 100–101.

15. Herbert H. Ehrenstein, "Peter, the Pope and the Vatican," *Eternity*, XIII (November, 1962), 17–20.

16. Harold O. Brown, "The Second Vatican Council," *United Evangelical Action*, XXI (December, 1962), 25.

17. "Papacy as a Force in History," *Christianity Today*, VIII (Oct. 12, 1962), 8–12.

18. *Christianity Today*, VII (Nov. 9, 1962), 55.

19. Daniel L. Eckert, "The Answer is 'No'," *Watchman-Examiner*, L (Sept. 6, 1962), 636–37.

20. "The Vatican Council—1962," *Watchman-Examiner*, L (May 17, 1962), 388–89.

21. *Baptist Standard*, LXXIV (Oct. 10, 1962), 4.

22. VI (July 6, 1962), 52.

23. *Christianity Today*, VII (Oct. 12, 1962), 16.

24. *Lutheran Witness*, LXXXI (Feb. 6, 1962), 54. Manz' articles continued in each issue to June 26, 1962.

25. II (Oct. 23, 1962), 18.

26. L (Oct. 18, 1962), 743.

27. "Protestant-Catholic Tensions," *Christianity Today*, VII (Oct. 12, 1962), 20.

28. "Evangelicals and Roman Catholics," *Christianity Today*, V (July 3, 1961), 3–5.

29. Walter G. Tillmanns, "Popes and Councils," *Lutheran Standard*, II (Sept. 25, 1962), 3 ff. By way of brief explanation, neither *Lutheran Standard*, representative of the American Lutheran Church, nor *Lutheran Witness*, an organ of the Missouri Synod Lutherans, should be strictly classified as conservative-evangelical reviews. But because their attitude toward the Council since its announcement tended to be negative, they are included in this section.

30. "Rethinking Protestant-Catholic Relations," *Lutheran Standard*, II (Sept. 25, 1962), 11.

31. LXXXI (Oct. 16, 1962), 19.

32. V (Feb. 27, 1961), 52.

33. LXXIV (Oct. 17, 1962), 4–5.

34. Arthur A. Rouner, Jr., "Gathered Church, Great Church," *Christianity Today*, VI (May 25, 1962), 9–11. A second article in the same issue, A. Dale Ihrie, "The Free Churches and Ecumenism," pp. 12–14, conveys a similar message.

35. VII (Oct. 12, 1962), 4–7.

36. *Ibid.*, p. 30.

37. C (Aug. 26, 1962), 7.

38. *Ibid.*, C (Oct. 21, 1962), 7.

39. *World Call*, XLIII (March, 1962), 9–10.

40. *Christian Herald*, June, 1962, p. 61.

41. *Dialog*, I (Autumn, 1962), 67.

42. *Lutheran*, XLIV (Aug. 1, 1962), 18–21.

43. VI (Aug. 16, 1962), 2.

44. *United Church Herald*, V (Nov. 1, 1962), 7.

45. *Christianity and Crisis*, XXII (Oct. 1, 1962), 157–59.

46. *Presbyterian Life*, XV (Mar. 15, 1962), 23.

47. *Christianity and Crisis*, XXII (Oct. 1, 1962), 159.

48. V (Sept. 20, 1962), 29.

49. LXXIX (Oct. 3, 1962), 1186.

50. Claud D. Nelson, "The Second Vatican Council," *Religion in Life*, XXXII (Winter, 1962/63), 72.

51. *Christian Century*, LXXIX (Oct. 31, 1962), 1315.

52. CXXVII (September, 1962), 58–59.

53. J. Rodman Williams, "Can Protestants and Roman Catholics Get Together?" *Presbyterian Survey*, LII (October, 1962), 10.

54. *United Church Herald*, IV (Mar. 8, 1962), 29.

55. *Christianity and Crisis*, XXII (Oct. 1, 1962), 159.

56. *Witness*, XLVI (July 27, 1961), 3.

57. *Looking at the Vatican Council* (London, 1962), p. 120.

58. *Christian Advocate*, VI (Oct. 11, 1962), 13.

59. CLXXVI (November, 1962), 4.

60. *Lutheran*, XLIV (Mar. 28, 1962), 50. See also *Christian Herald*, June, 1962, p. 61.

61. I (Summer, 1962), 53.

62. Claud D. Nelson, "The Pope Calls a Council—II," *Christian Century*, LXXVIII (Oct. 4, 1961), 1172–74.

63. "The Second Vatican Council," *Presbyterian Life*, XV (Oct. 1, 1962), 42.

64. Robert McAfee Brown, "An American Protestant View," *Cross Currents*, XII (Spring, 1962), 234.

65. "Reform and Infallibility," *Cross Currents*, XI (Fall, 1961), 356. The theological renewal manifested in most of the documents of Vatican II was mainly built on the work of creative and progressive Catholic thinkers of the first half of this century. These men fed into schools and movements the material from which the conciliar breakthrough could be realized. Although it is beyond the scope of this study to adequately summarize progressive Catholic theology in the 20th century, a few developments should be noted. In general, a more historical, scientific, and developmental approach to theological disciplines began to be in evidence in Catholic circles in the late 19th century. Johann Adam Moehler and John Henry Newman could be cited as early pioneers in this movement. The Catholic Modernist controversy in the first decade of this century caused ecclesiastical authorities to impose more rigid strictures on Catholic theological research and education: see Emile Poulat, *Histoire, dogme et critique dans la crise moderniste* (Paris, 1962). Although Catholic seminary and college theology long remained statically orthodox, northern European thinkers continued to explore patristic and biblical sources for a deeper and more relevant theology. A great name in the Tübingen school was Karl Adam, who first published *The Spirit of Catholicism* in 1924. His return to sources, in the tradition of Moehler and others, allowed him to develop a theology of the church as the Mystical Body of Christ and the Communion of Saints. See Karl Adam, *The Spirit of Catholicism*, trans. Justin McCann (New York, 1954). The Mystical

Body doctrine, developed by scholars like Emile Mersch and Henri de Lubac, eventuated in the famous letter of Pius XII in 1943, *Mystici Corporis Christi.* One of the greatest Catholic minds in this century has been Karl Rahner; his work, influenced by solid traditional studies and modern philosophies, has had a most significant effect on renewal in Vatican II. See Karl Rahner, *Theological Investigations* (2 vols.; Baltimore, 1961/62): *Inquiries* (New York, 1964).

A number of important European Catholic thinkers were associated with the "New Theology," which received a temporary setback with the publication of Pius XII's *Humani Generis* in 1950. Two outstanding French theologians, whose work was later to be honored by Vatican II and Pope Paul VI, were Yves M-J Congar, *Vraie et fausse réforme dans l'Eglise* (Paris, 1950) and *The Mystery of the Church*, trans, A.V. Littledale (Baltimore, 1960); and Henri de Lubac, *The Splendor of the Church*, trans. Michael Mason (New York, 1956) and *The Drama of Atheistic Humanism*, trans. Edith M. Riley (New York, 1947). The renewal-oriented thinking of French progressives was captured in Cardinal Emmanuel Suhard, *Growth or Decline?* trans. James A. Corbett (South Bend, 1948). An important ecumenical work was Henri Bouillard's three-volume study *Karl Barth* (Paris, 1957). Among the important figures in European Catholic theology, one would have to mention such names as Léopold Malevez, M.D. Chenu, Jean Daniélou, Jean Mouroux, Josef R. Geiselmann, Otto Semmelroth, Henri Rondet, and Hans Urs von Balthasar. Nor can one overlook the great influence of Teilhard de Chardin; see Claude Cuénot, *Teilhard de Chardin*, trans, Vincent Colimore (London, 1965). Among a number of scholarly and semi-scholarly publications, the French journal *Esprit* was in the forefront of progressive Catholic thought.

In the United States it is difficult to point to original scholarly publications that opened the way to the Johannine breakthrough. After the scares of "Americanism" (Thomas T. McAvoy, *The Great Crisis in American Church History, 1895–1900* [Chicago, 1957]) and Modernism, Catholic theological formation in the U.S. went into an especially deep freeze. But movements like the Catholic Commission on Intellectual and Cultural Affairs managed to keep in touch with progressive thought. Catholic publishing houses like Sheed and Ward, Fides, and Herder and Herder performed the important function of making European thought available to American Catholics. The journal *Theological Studies*, which began in 1939, brought considerable scholarship to the American scene, including that of the Woodstock theologians. Periodicals such as *Thought* and *Cross Currents* also contributed much to theological ferment in American Catholicism.

66. John Henry Cardinal Newman, *An Essay on the Development of Christian Doctrine* (London, 1897).

67. George A. Lindbeck. "Roman Catholicism on the Eve of the Council," *The Papal Council and the Gospel*, ed. Kristen E. Skydsgaard (Minneapolis, 1961), pp. 61 ff.

68. *Looking at the Vatican Council*, p. 123.

69. *Christianity and Crisis*, XXII (Oct. 1, 1962), 166. *Episcopalian*, CXXVII (September, 1962), 58–59.

70. Eugene R. Fairweather and Edward R. Hardy, *The Voice of the Church: the Ecumenical Council* (Greenwich, Conn., 1962), p. 56.

71. Stephen Neill, "An Anglican Plea for Clear Answers," *Cross Currents*, XII (Spring, 1962), 221. *Also Christian Century*, LXXIX (Jan. 17, 1962), 76.

72. "An American Protestant View," *Cross Currents*, XII (Spring, 1962), 237. *Presbyterian Life*, XV (Oct. 1, 1962), 42. *Christian*, C (Aug. 26, 1962), 7.

73. CXLIV (June 17, 1962), 21.

74. *The Papal Council and the Gospel*, p. 167.

75. Father Leonard Feeney, S.J., maintained that a man's desire to belong to the church must be explicit, if he was to be saved. For teaching this doctrine and especially for his refusal to accept ecclesiastical authority, Feeney was excommunicated.

76. George A. Lindbeck, "The Second Vatican Council," *Christianity and Crisis*, XXII (Oct. 1, 1962), 166.

77. I (Autumn, 1962), 67.

78. Pawley, *Looking*, p. 124. Also Neill, *Cross Currents* (Spring, 1962), 222.

79. Nelson, *The Vatican Council and All Christians*, p. 117.

80. Skydsgaard, *The Papal Council and the Gospel*, p. 122.

81. *Christian Century*, LXXIX (Oct. 31, 1962), 1314–15. See also *Episcopalian*, CXXVII (September, 1962), 58–59.

82. George A. Lindbeck, "Reform and the Council," *Lutheran World*, IX (October, 1962), 315.

83. *Ibid.*, p. 316.

84. *Lutheran*, XLIV (Aug. 29, 1962), 50.

85. "The Permanent Significance of the Catholic Church for Protestants," *Dialog*, I (Summer, 1962), 25.

86. *Christian*, C (Aug. 26, 1962), 7. *Presbyterian Life*, XV (Oct. 1, 1962), 42.

87. Robert McAfee Brown, "An American Protestant View," *Cross Currents*, XII (Spring, 1962), 233.

88. *Christian Century*, LXXVIII (Oct. 4, 1961), 1172–74.

89. *Christianity and Crisis*, XXII (Oct. 1, 1962), 164–67.

90. *Lutheran World*, IX (October, 1962), 312.

91. *Cross Currents*, XII (Spring, 1962), 222.

92. *Looking*, p. 125.

93. *Ibid.*, p. 126. *Cross Currents*, XII (Spring, 1962), 228. *Dialog*, I (Autumn, 1962), 67. *Presbyterian Life*, XV (Mar. 15, 1962), 23. *Lutheran*, XLIV (Mar. 28, 1962), 50.

94. *Christianity and Crisis*, XXII (Oct. 1, 1962), 167.

95. Pawley, p. 126.

96. *Christianity and Crisis*, XXII (Oct. 1, 1962), 164–67. *Lutheran World*, IX (October, 1962), 315.

97. *Churchman*, CLXXVI (October, 1962), 4.

98. Claud D. Nelson, "The Second Vatican Council," *Religion in Life*, XXXII (Winter, 1962/63), 79.

99. Robert McAfee Brown, "An American Protestant View," *Cross Currents*, XII (Spring, 1962), 236.

100. Pawley, p. 133.

101. *Witness*, XLVII (July 26, 1962), 7.

102. Hales, p. 139. *Acta Apostolicae Sedis*, LIV, pp. 788–89.

103. One of the best descriptive interpretations of the first session of the Council is Xavier Rynne, *Letters From Vatican City* (New York, 1963). Another journalistic if more partisan book is Robert B. Kaiser, *Pope, Council and World* (New York, 1963). Vincent A. Yzermans, *A New Pentecost* (Westminster, Md., 1963) is a collection of interviews and documentation giving a general, though haphazard, impression of the 1962 session. Theological reflections on the first session and other relevant essays are found in Hans Küng, *The Council in Action*, trans. Cecily Hastings (New York, 1963). An important compilation of speeches by Council Fathers, which reveal the progressive direction of the Council, is Hans Küng, Yves Congar & Daniel O'Hanlon (eds.), *Council Speeches of Vatican II* (Glen Rock, N.J., 1964). Michael Novak's *The Open Church* (New York, 1964), though dealing mainly with the second session of the Council, is one of the most perceptive books on developments of thought at Vatican II. An early chapter in this book deals with the first session. The fifth chapter on non-historical orthodoxy helps in understanding the theological reorientation that was at work in the Council. Bernard Häring, *The Johannine Council* (New York, 1963) is a theological-pastoral reflection on some of the new directions initiated by Pope John's Council. Two books by Protestant authors on the first session are Douglas Horton, *Vatican Diary 1962* (Philadelphia,

1964), and Presbyter Anglicanus, *The Second Vatican Council* (New York, 1963).

104. "Vatican II, Thus Far, How Far?" LI (May 2, 1963), 344–45.

105. L (Dec. 27, 1962), 946–47; L (Nov. 1, 1962), 782.

106. Milton Regier, "Special Report: Vatican II," XXII (March, 1963), 36.

107. LXXIV (Dec. 12, 1962), 4.

108. CI (Jan. 20, 1963), 7.

109. *Watchman-Examiner*, L (Nov. 1, 1962), 783.

110. L (Dec. 6, 1962), 885.

111. *Christianity Today*, VII (Nov. 23, 1962), 51.

112. Clyde W. Taylor, "Evangelicals, Ecumenical Councils and Eternity," *The Dynamics of Christian Unity*, ed. W. Stanley Mooneyham (Grand Rapids, 1963), p. 82.

113. LXXIV (Nov. 28, 1962), 4.

114. *Ibid.*, p. 5.

115. *Lutheran Witness*, LXXXII (Nov. 26, 1963), 548–49.

116. Leslie R. Keylock, "An Evangelical View of Vatican II," *Christianity Today*, VII (April 12, 1963), 31.

117. Gilbert A. Thiele, "The Vatican Council," *Lutheran Witness*, LXXXII (Jan. 8, 1963), 9. Despite the strictures on the Council from the editor of *Baptist Standard*, it is worth noting that this journal began to run regular articles by a Baptist reporter, W. Barry Garrett, who was covering the Council.

118. Stanley I. Stuber, "Baptists at the Second Vatican Council," *Missions*, CLX (December, 1962), 9.

119. LXXXII (Nov. 26, 1963), 549.

120. *Christianity Today*, VII (Jan. 4, 1963), 48.

121. *Ibid.*, VII (April 12, 1963), 32. Also *Lutheran Witness*, LXXXII (Jan. 8, 1963), 22.

122. *Lutheran Witness*, LXXXII (Jan. 8, 1963), 9.

123. *Christianity Today*, VII (April 12, 1963), 30.

124. C. E. Huber, "The Challenge of Rome's Council," *Lutheran Witness*, LXXXI (Nov. 27, 1962), 15.

125. Leslie R. Keylock, "The Bible Controversy in American Catholicism," *Christianity Today*, VII (Mar. 1, 1963), 22.

126. *Christianity Today*, VII (Mar. 15, 1963), 47.

127. *Missions*, CLX (December, 1962), 9.

128. VII (Feb. 14, 1963), 21.

129. LXXX (Feb. 27, 1963), 261; LXXX (Mar. 6, 1963), 294.

130. In *Dynamics*, ed. Mooneyman, p. 82. The impression should not be given, however, that respect among Catholics for universal religious liberty was an entirely new phenomenon created by Pope John. Rather, he unleashed forces long at work in liberal Catholic circles. The work of John Courtney Murray has already been referred to. In Europe, some important writings on religious liberty and separation of church and state were Jacques Maritain, *The Rights of Man and Natural Law*, trans. Doris C. Anson (New York, 1949); Joseph Lecler, *L'Eglise et la souveraineté de l'Etat* (Paris, 1946); Augustin Léonard. ed., *Tolérance et communauté humaine* (Tournai-Paris, 1952); Albert Hartmann, *Toleranz und christlicher Glaube* (Frankfurt a/M, 1955). Written against the background of a long history of religious strife, these modern European works reflect a Christian appreciation for the values of democratic societies.

131. Leslie R. Keylock, "An Evangelical View of Vatican II," *Christianity Today*, VII (April 12, 1963), 30.

132. *Christianity Today*, VII (Oct. 26, 1962), 34.

133. LI (Mar. 7, 1963), 173.

134. "Vatican II," March, 1963, p. 3.

135. LXXXII (Nov. 26, 1963), 548.

136. *Christianity Today*, VII (April 12, 1963), 31.

137. XXII (Jan. 7, 1963), 240.

138. *Missions*, CLX (December, 1962), 9.

139. CXLV (Jan. 7, 1963), 5.

140. *Living Church*, CXLV (Oct. 28, 1962), 15.

141. CXXVIII (January, 1963), 6.

142. "Vatican Council Desires 'Unity'," *World Call*, XLV (January, 1963), 29.

143. *United Church Herald*, V (Nov. 15, 1962), 16.

144. LXXX (Mar. 20, 1963), 359.

145. "Liturgical Reform in the Second Vatican Council," *Lutheran World*, X (April, 1963), 161–71. Again, it is important to see the Johannine breakthrough in liturgical matters in the light of earlier thinkers and movements which the Council was allowing to come to the center of Catholic consciousness. Half a century before Vatican II, a farsighted Benedictine in Louvain, Belgium, Dom Lambert Beauduin, was sowing the seeds of the modern liturgical movement. See Dom Lambert Beauduin, *Liturgy, the Life of the Church* (Collegeville, Minn., 1926). A newer appreciation of liturgical life was also present in Romano Guardini, *The Catholic Church and the Spirit of the Liturgy*,

trans. Ada Lane (New York, 1940). The quiet labors of the liturgists bore fruit in Pius XII's *Mediator Dei* in 1947, an encyclical that opened the way for further research among scholars. Perhaps the greatest name among Catholic liturgists in our time is that of Joseph A. Jungmann of Innsbruck, Austria. His classic work on the Roman mass can be found in a one-volume edition, prepared by Charles K. Riepe, *The Mass of the Roman Rite* (New York, 1959). The liturgical renewal was closely related to biblical developments among Catholic scholars: see Jean Daniélou, *The Bible and the Liturgy* (Notre Dame, Ind., 1956). Broad theological implications of worship are discussed in Cipriano Vagaggini, *The Theological Dimensions of the Liturgy* (Collegeville, Minn., 1959).

A pioneer of liturgical renewal in the United States was the Benedictine Dom Virgil Michel, who began publishing *Orate Fratres* in 1926. Later, this review became the excellent liturgical journal, *Worship*. From the time of Michel, St. John's Abbey in Collegeville, Minn., became a wellspring of liturgical progress. See Paul B. Marx, *The Life and Work of Virgil Michel* (Washington, D.C., 1957). Another liturgical pioneer in America was Gerald Ellard, *The Mass of the Future* (Milwaukee, 1948). In recent years, Notre Dame University has become a hub of theological renewal. A series of lectures given at Notre Dame by Louis Bouyer became something of a minor classic when published: *Liturgical Piety* (Notre Dame, Ind., 1955). The thought of leading contemporary liturgists, such as H. A. Reinhold, Godfrey Diekmann, and others, can be found in these two collections: Frederick R. McManus (ed.), *The Revival of the Liturgy* (New York, 1963); William J. Leonard (ed.), *Liturgy for the People* (Milwaukee, 1963). For a Protestant appreciation of Catholic liturgical renewal, see Ernest B. Koenker, *The Liturgical Renaissance in the Roman Catholic Church* (Chicago, 1954).

146. *Witness*, XLVIII (April 11, 1963), 3. Also *Christian Century*, LXXIX (Dec. 5, 1962), 1472. Had it not been for the biblical renewal in Catholicism, dating from the late 19th century, many of the conciliar advances would hardly have been possible. The biblical renewal, which owed much to the earlier work of non-Catholic scholars, generated new insights in such areas as catechetics, liturgy, sacraments, spirituality, and moral theology which had long been in the grip of scholastic immobilism, rigid juridicism, and individualistic devotionalism. Among Catholics, one of the greatest names in early scientific biblical research was that of Marie-Joseph Lagrange: see Richard T. A. Murphy, *The Work of Père Lagrange* (Milwaukee, 1963). Many modern Catholic scripture scholars have been trained in one of two schools, both highly respected in their field: the Biblical Institute in Rome and in Jerusalem. The work of these institutions was given new impetus by the publication of Pius XII's encyclical *Divino Afflante*

*Spiritu* in 1943. Augustin Bea as a Jesuit professor at the Biblical Institute in Rome is said to have been influential in the formulation of Pius XII's letter, which became the *magna carta* for contemporary Catholic biblical study. An important book for understanding the background of biblical developments in Catholicism is Jean Levie, *The Bible, Word of God in Words of Men*, trans. S. H. Treman (New York, 1961). A small volume reviewing the scripture-tradition controversy is Gabriel Moran, *Scripture and Tradition* (New York, 1963).

Biblical scholarship among Catholics in the United States, with the exception of a few men, was largely dependent on European research until the 1950's, when younger American scholars, formed mostly in Europe, began to make important contributions of their own. Two early popularizations of modern biblical research were Bruce Vawter, *A Path Through Genesis* (New York, 1954), and John L. McKenzie, *The Two-Edged Sword* (Milwaukee, 1957). The Catholic Biblical Association fostered scholarly contributions, inspired the Confraternity translation of the Bible, and has encouraged popular biblical commentaries and journals.

Closely related to developments in biblical theology has been the advance in catechetics and moral theology. The Lumen Vitae center in Brussels and the school of kerygmatic theology at Innsbruck pointed out new ways to understand and present the gospel message. See Johannes Hofinger, *The Art of Teaching Christian Doctrine* (Notre Dame, Ind., 1957); Gerald Sloyan (ed.), *Shaping the Christian Message* (New York, 1958). In Washington, D.C., the department of religious education at Catholic University has been a key center for the improvement of religion teaching. Important names in a Catholic rethinking of moral teaching in the light of greater freedom and charity are Gérard Gilleman, *The Primacy of Charity in Moral Theology*, trans. William F. Ryan and André Vachon (Westminster, Md., 1961); Bernard Häring, *The Law of Christ*, trans. Edwin G. Kaiser (2 vols.; Westminster, Md., 1963). New developments in religious-psychological education are represented in Marc Oraison, *Love or Constraint?* trans. Una Morissey (New York, 1961).

147. "Roman Catholicism in the Pangs of Rebirth," *Presbyterian Outlook*, CXLV (Feb. 11, 1963), 6–7.

148. *Witness*, XLVIII (April 11, 1963), 4. One of the most important books written by an observer on the Vatican Council was Robert McAfee Brown, *Observer in Rome* (New York, 1964). Although this book describes the second session, its spirit and general interpretation would also be applicable to the first session.

149. Oswald C. J. Hoffman, "Vatican II and the Reformation," *Lutheran Standard*, III (Oct. 22, 1963), 9. *United Church Herald*, V (Nov. 29, 1962), 12. *Christian Century*, LXXX (Jan. 2, 1963), 3–4.

150. Alden Hatch, *A Man Named John* (New York, 1963), p. 264.

151. James H. Nichols, "Report on Vatican II," *Presbyterian Life*, XVI (Jan. 1, 1963), 22. *Lutheran Standard*, III (Jan. 15, 1963), 7–8.

152. *Lutheran*, XLV (Nov. 7, 1962), 50.

153. V (Dec. 13, 1962), 12 ff; VI (Jan. 10, 1963), 16–17; VI (Jan. 24, 1963), 18–19; VI (Feb. 21, 1963), 20–21.

154. XLIV (December, 1962), 10.

155. LXXIX (Oct. 24, 1962), 1282–83.

156. LXXIX (Dec. 26, 1962), 1576; LXXX (Jan. 2, 1963), 3–4.

157. VII (Jan. 17, 1963), 2.

158. *Christian Advocate*, VI (Oct. 25, 1962), 24.

159. "A Protestant Theologian Looks at Ecumenism," *Ecumenism and Vatican II*, ed. Charles O'Neill (Milwaukee, 1964), p. 21.

160. *Living Church*, CXLV (Oct. 21, 1962), 13.

161. CXLV (Nov. 4, 1962), 25.

162. *Episcopalian*, CXXVIII (July, 1963), 36.

163. *Witness*, XLVIII (Oct. 3, 1963), 7. More unidentified comments of observers at Vatican II can be found in Rock Caporale, *Vatican II: Last of the Councils* (Baltimore, 1964). This book is particularly noteworthy as a sociological study of the advantages and disadvantages of communication patterns in the structure of the Council.

164. *The Second Vatican Council* (New York, 1963), pp. 27–28.

165. III (Oct. 22, 1963), 10.

166. Jesse M. Bader, "Vatican Council Makes History," *World Call*, XLIV (December, 1962), 31.

167. *Christian*, C (Dec. 2, 1962), 10.

168. *Presbyterian Life*, XVI (Jan. 1, 1963), 21.

169. Burke Rivers, "Brothers in Christ," *Witness*, XLVII (Dec. 27, 1962), 10.

170. Frederick C. Grant, "Heritage of the Anglican Communion," *Witness*, XLVII (Nov. 1, 1962), 11.

171. *Living Church*, CXLV (Oct. 7, 1962), 16.

172. *Lutheran*, XLV (Oct. 31, 1962), 50. *World Call*, XLV (January, 1963), 29.

173. *United Church Herald*, V (Nov. 29, 1962), 12.

174. *Episcopalian*, CXXVIII (January, 1963), 6.

175. *Christian Herald*, May, 1963, p. 49.

176. LXXIX (Dec. 26, 1962), 1576.

177. LXXX (Jan. 2, 1963), 3; LXXIX (Dec. 12, 1962), 1505.

## CHAPTER 6

1. *Presbyterian Life*, XI (Nov. 1, 1958), 22.
2. LXXV (Oct. 22, 1958), 1196.
3. *Christianity and Crisis*, XVIII (Nov. 10, 1958), 154–55.
4. December, 1958, pp. 16–17.
5. *Living Church*, CXXXVII (Oct. 19, 1958), 22.
6. XLVI (Oct. 30, 1958), 889.
7. *Christianity and Crisis*, XIX (Aug. 3, 1959), 116.
8. *Christian Century*, LXXV (Nov. 5, 1958), 1261. *Presbyterian Outlook*, CXL (Oct. 27, 1958), 11.
9. *Churchman*, CLXXIII (January, 1959), 16. *Presbyterian Outlook*, CXL (Oct. 27, 1958), 11.
10. X (January, 1959), 4.
11. *Christianity Today*, VII (June 21, 1963), 27.
12. XXII (July, 1963), 17.
13. *Christian Herald*, July, 1963, p. 25.
14. CXXVIII (June 15, 1963), 3.
15. LXXXII (June 25, 1963), 4.
16. *Ibid.*, p. 5.
17. *Baptist Standard*, LXXV (June 12, 1963), 5.
18. XIV (February, 1963), 6.
19. XV (January, 1964), 24.
20. *Ibid.*, 24.
21. "The Issue We Face—II," *Watchman-Examiner*, LI (May 16, 1963), 390.
22. *United Evangelical Action*, XXII (July, 1963), 17.
23. LXXXII (June 25, 1963), 3.
24. *Baptist Standard*, LXXV (June 12, 1963), 5.
25. *Christianity Today*, VII (June 21, 1963), 47.
26. *Ibid.*, p. 27. See also *United Evangelical Action*, XXII (July, 1963), 17.
27. "A Harvard Dean's Tribute," *America*, CVIII (June 15, 1963), 859.
28. "A Protestant's Tribute," *America*, CVIII (June 15, 1963), 856.
29. *Episcopalian*, CXXVIII (July, 1963), 36.
30. CXLVI (June 9, 1963), 4.
31. CXXVIII (August, 1963), 33.

32. *Living Church*, CXLVI (June 16, 1963), 9. See also CXLVI (Jan. 13, 1963), 15.

33. LXXX (June 19, 1963), 795.

34. LXXX (June 12, 1963), 763.

35. *Lutheran Standard*, III (June 18, 1963), 7–8.

36. *Presbyterian Outlook*, CXLV (June 17, 1963), 8.

37. *Christianity and Crisis*, XXIII (June 24, 1963), 115.

38. *Witness*, XLVIII (Oct. 3, 1963), 7.

39. CXLVI (June 16, 1963), 25.

40. *America*, CVIII (June 15, 1963), 855.

41. "Voice of the Good Shepherd," *Commonweal*, LXXVIII (June 28, 1963), 369–70. Another sign of the Johannine breakthrough in American Protestant-Catholic relations was the growing phenomenon of Protestant writers appearing in Roman Catholic journals.

42. "Pope John XXIII," *Presbyterian Life*, XVI (July 1, 1963), 25.

43. LXXX (June 12, 1963), 763.

44. VII (June 20, 1963), 2.

45. VII (July 4, 1963), 3.

46. *America*, CVIII (June 15, 1963), 860.

47. *Living Church*, CXLVI (June 16, 1963), 9; *Christian Century*, LXXX (June 12, 1963), 763.

48. *United Church Herald*, VI (July 4, 1963), 6.

49. *Presbyterian Outlook*, CXLV (June 17, 1963), 8.

50. Robert McAfee Brown, "Voice of the Good Shepherd," *Commonweal*, LXXVIII (June 28, 1963), 370.

51. *United Church Herald*, VI (July 4, 1963), 6; *America*, CVIII (June 15, 1963), 856.

52. *Christian Century*, LXXX (June 12, 1963), 763.

53. CXLVI (June 16, 1963), 25.

54. CXLV (June 17, 1963), 8.

55. Edith Lovejoy Pierce, "Pope John XXIII—In Memoriam," LXXX (June 26, 1963), 823.

56. *Commonweal*, LXXVIII (June 28, 1963), 371.


## CHAPTER 7

1. VII (July 19, 1963), 26.

2. *Watchman-Examiner*, LI (July 25, 1963), 573.

3. *Ibid.*, LI (June 27, 1963), 511.

4. *Ibid.*, LI (July 25, 1963), 573.

5. XIV (September, 1963), 9–10.

6. *Baptist Standard*, LXXVI (Dec. 9, 1964), 4.

7. Howard C. Olsen, "The Octave of Unity," *Living Church*, CXLVI (Jan. 13, 1963), 19.

8. *Christian Century*, LXXIX (June 6, 1962), 707; CI (Dec. 15, 1963), 8.

9. *Churchman*, CLXXVII (April, 1963), 4–5.

10. "The Future of Roman Catholic Theology in the Light of the First Session of the Second Vatican Council," *Dialog*, II (Summer, 1963), 251.

11. *The Second Vatican Council and the New Catholicism* (Grand Rapids, 1965), p. 157. This book, though written after the general period of this study, is an enlightening discussion of the theological polarities within Catholicism, brought to a sharp focus by Vatican II.

12. *Ibid.*, pp. 158–59.

13. *Watchman-Examiner*, LI (Feb. 21, 1963), 133.

14. CLXI (October, 1963), 14.

15. CXXVIII (Nov. 30, 1963), 8.

16. LXXIX (Sept. 5, 1962), 1057.

17. LXXIX (Oct. 24, 1962), 1281.

18. *Christian Century*, LXXX (April 3, 1963), 420.

19. See Hales, *Pope John*, pp. 163–92 for a stimulating discussion of how Pope John was willing to risk narrower Italian concerns for larger benefits on the world scene.

20. "Basic Baptist Principles and the Contemporary Scene," *Southwestern Journal of Theology*, VI (April, 1964), 75.

21. *Baptist Standard*, LXXIV (Aug. 29, 1962), 4.

22. *Christian Herald*, June, 1962, p. 21.

23. *Presbyterian Life*, XV (July 1, 1962), 26–27. *Christian Century*, LXXIX (June 20, 1962), 767.

24. *Baptist Standard*, LXXIV (May 2, 1962), 4. *Watchman-Examiner*, L (June 7, 1962), 427. *Christianity Today*, VI (April 27, 1962), 34.

25. *Churchman*, CLXXVI (August, 1962), 5. *Christian Century*, LXXIX (Jan. 3, 1962), 10–12. *Baptist Standard*, LXXIV (Feb. 21, 1962), 4–5. *Christian Century*, LXXIX (July 18, 1962), 881.

26. *Christian Century*, LXXIX (Dec. 19, 1962), 1561.

27. *Lutheran Standard*, III (June 18, 1963), 10.

28. Dayton Robert and Lois Thiessen, "Latin America," XV (January, 1964), 26.

29. XLV (May, 1963), 10.

30. *Christian Century*, LXXIX (Dec. 5, 1962), 1472–73.

31. Sidney Correll, "There's a Change in Spain," XIV (December, 1963), 22.

32. *Missions*, CLXI (April, 1963), 13.

33. CLXXVII (March, 1963), 4.

34. CLXXVII (June, 1963), 4.

35. *Christian Century*, LXXX (Mar. 27, 1963), 389.

36. Two examples of the Catholic discussion on birth control are Thomas D. Roberts, ed., *Contraception and Holiness* (New York, 1965), and John T. Noonan, *Contraception* (Cambridge, Mass., 1965). The latter book is an important scholarly history of the treatment of contraception by Catholic theologians and canonists.

37. LXXIX (Mar. 14, 1962), 318.

38. *Christian Century*, LXXX (June 26, 1963), 820–21; LXXX (April 10, 1963), 453. On March 18, 1966, the Holy See, in a document entitled *Matrimonii Sacramentum*, issued new rules on mixed marriage. The penalty of excommunication for Catholics who are married by a non-Catholic minister was dropped. But the document said nothing that would validate such marriages outside the Catholic Church. Some new concessions toward non-Catholics included a less strict stand on the written promises, permission to hold a mixed marriage in a Catholic church with mass and a nuptial blessing, and the allowing of a non-Catholic minister to assist at the ceremony.

39. *Christian Century*, LXXIX (Nov. 28, 1962), 1449–50. Shortly before the Ecumenical Council opened in Rome, A. Romeo, a conservative professor at the Lateran University, accused more progressive biblical scholars at the Biblical Institute of dangerous and unorthodox teachings. The ensuing controversy underlined the points of difference between the old and the new in Catholic biblical scholarship. See J. A. Fitzmyer, "A Recent Roman Scriptural Controversy," *Theological Studies*, 23 (1961), 426–44.

40. *Living Church*, CXLVI (May 26, 1963), 14–15.

41. Lindbeck, *Dialog*, II (Summer, 1963), 250.

42. Per Erik Persson, "The Reformation in Recent Roman Catholic Theology," *Dialog*, II (Winter, 1963), 24–31.

43. *Christian Century*, LXXIX (Aug. 15, 1962), 977.

44. Lindbeck, *Dialog*, II (Summer, 1963), 250.

45. Lindbeck, "Ecclesiology and Roman Catholic Renewal," *Religion in Life,* XXXIII (Summer, 1964), 383–94.

46. "Editors' Introduction," *Ecumenical Dialogue at Harvard,* ed. Samuel H. Miller and G. Ernest Wright (Cambridge, Mass., 1964), p. ix. This volume is an eloquent indication of how much the climate of Catholic-Protestant relations had been improved in the short time of Pope John's pontificate.

47. VI (May 2, 1963), 6. See Scott F. Brenner, "Catholic-Protestant Colloquium at Harvard," *Presbyterian Life,* XVI (May 1, 1963), 28–29.

48. *Watchman-Examiner,* LI (Feb. 21, 1963), 133.

49. *Missions,* CLXI (September, 1963), 13–14.

50. XIV (November, 1963), 6–7.

51. *Christian Century,* LXXIX (Aug. 22, 1963), 1000.

52. *Presbyterian Life,* XVI (Nov. 1, 1963), 11.

53. *Christian Century,* LXXX (April 17, 1963), 484.

54. *Presbyterian Life,* XVI (June 15, 1963), 21–22.

55. Wilton M. Nelson, "Is the Roman Church Changing?" XIV (October, 1963), 19–22.

56. Iain Wilson, "Dialog with Roman Catholics," *Presbyterian Outlook,* CXLV (May 6, 1963), 8.

57. "The Reformation of the Church," *Union Seminary Quarterly Review,* XIX (January, 1964), 102.

58. "What If Vatican II Succeeds?" *Motive,* XXIV (May, 1964), 8.

59. "The Emerging Ecumenical Complex," *Theology Today,* XX (January, 1964), 535 ff.

60. Keith R. Bridston and Walter D. Wagoner (eds.), *Unity in Mid-Career* (New York, 1963).

61. William B. Cate, *The Ecumenical Scandal on Main Street* (New York, 1965), p. 17.

62. William B. Greenspun and William A. Norgren (eds.), (Glen Rock, N.J., 1965).

# Bibliography

Abel, Theodore. *Protestant Home Missions to Catholic Immigrants.* New York, 1963.

Abell, Aaron I. *American Catholicism and Social Action.* New York, 1960.

Adam, Karl. *The Spirit of Catholicism.* Translated by Dom Justin McCann. New York, 1954.

Albornoz, A. F. Carrillo de. *Roman Catholicism and Religious Liberty.* Geneva, 1959.

Algisi, Leone. *John the Twenty-Third.* Translated by Peter Ryde. Westminster, 1963.

Andreu, Pierre. *Histoire des prêtres-ouvriers.* Paris, 1960.

Aradi, Zsolt, Tucek, James I., and O'Neill, James C. *Pope John XXIII.* New York, 1959.

Balducci, Ernesto. *John, "The Transitional Pope."* New York, 1965.

Barrett, Patricia. *Religious Liberty and the American Presidency.* New York, 1963.

Bates, M. Searle. *Religious Liberty: An Inquiry.* New York, 1945.

Baum, Gregory. *Progress and Perspectives: The Catholic Quest for Christian Unity.* New York, 1962.

Bea, Augustin. *The Unity of Christians,* ed. Bernard Leeming. New York, 1963.

Beauduin, Dom Lambert. *Liturgy, the Life of the Church.* Collegeville, Minn., 1926.

Bennett, John C. *Christians and the State.* New York, 1958.

────── (ed.). *Nuclear Weapons and the Conflict of Conscience.* New York. 1962.

Berkouwer, G. C. *The Second Vatican Council and the New Catholicism.* Grand Rapids, 1965.

Billington, Ray Allen. *The Protestant Crusade 1800–1860.* Chicago, 1964.

Blanshard, Paul. *American Freedom and Catholic Power*. Boston, 1958.
———— *Religion and the Schools*. Boston, 1963.
Blau, Joseph L. *Cornerstones of Religious Freedom in America*. Boston, 1949.
Boettner, Loraine. *Roman Catholicism*. Philadelphia, 1962.
Bouillard, Henri. *Karl Barth*. 3 vols. Paris, 1957.
Bouyer, Louis. *Liturgical Piety*. Notre Dame, Ind., 1955.
———— *Du Protestantisme à l'Eglise*. Paris, 1954.
Bridston, Keith R., and Wagoner, Walter D. (eds.). *Unity in Mid-Career*. New York, 1963.
Broderick, Francis L. *Right Reverend New Dealer: John A. Ryan*. New York, 1963.
Brown, Robert McAfee. *Observer in Rome*. New York, 1964.
———— *The Significance of the Church*. Philadelphia, 1956.
———— *The Spirit of Protestantism*. New York, 1961.
————, and Gustave Weigel. *An American Dialogue*. New York, 1961.
Brown, William Adams. *Church and State in Contemporary America*. New York, 1936.
Butts, Freeman R. *The American Tradition in Religion and Education*. Boston, 1950.
Callahan, Daniel. *Honesty in the Church*. New York, 1965.
————. *The Mind of the Catholic Layman*. New York, 1963.
Calvez, Jean-Yves and Perrin, Jacques. *The Church and Social Justice*. Translated by J. R. Kirwan. Chicago, 1961.
————. *The Social Thought of John XXIII*. Translated by J. M. McKenzie. Chicago, 1964.
Campion, Donald R., and Culhane, Eugene K. (eds.). *Mater et Magistra*. New York, 1961.
Caporale, Rock. *Vatican II: Last of the Councils*. Baltimore, 1964.
Capovilla, Loris. *The Heart and Mind of John XXIII*. Translated by Patrick Riley. New York, 1964.
Cate, William B. *The Ecumenical Scandal on Main Street*. New York, 1965.
Clancy, William (ed.). *The Moral Dilemma of Nuclear War*. New York, 1961.
Colacci, Mario. *The Doctrinal Conflict Between Roman Catholic and Protestant Christianity*. Minneapolis, 1962.
Congar, Yves M-J. *Chrétiens désunis*. Paris, 1937.
————. *Jalons pour une théologie du laïcat*. Paris, 1961.
————. *The Mystery of the Church*. Translated by A. V. Littledale. Baltimore, 1960.
————. *Vraie et fausse réforme dans l'Eglise*. Paris, 1950.
Cowan, Wayne H. (ed.). *Facing Protestant-Roman Catholic Tensions*. New York, 1960.

Cronin, John F. *Social Principles and Economic Life.* Milwaukee, 1959.

Cross, Robert D. *The Emergence of Liberal Catholicism in America.* Cambridge, 1958.

Cuénot, Claude. *Teilhard de Chardin.* Translated by Vincent Colimore. Baltimore, 1965.

Curtis, Geoffrey W. S. *Paul Couturier and Unity in Christ.* Westminster, Md., 1964.

Daniélou, Jean. *The Bible and the Liturgy.* Notre Dame, Ind., 1956.

Dreyer, F. C. H., and Weller, E. *Roman Catholicism in the Light of Scripture.* Chicago, 1960.

Dumont, Christophe. J. *Approaches to Christian Unity.* Translated by Henry St. John. Baltimore, 1959.

Ellard, Gerald. *The Mass of the Future.* Milwaukee, 1948.

Ellis, John Tracy. *American Catholicism.* Chicago, 1956.

——. *American Catholics and the Intellectual Life.* Chicago, 1956.

Fichter, Joseph H. *Dynamics of a City Church.* Chicago, 1951.

Fairweather, Eugene R., and Hardy, Edward R. *The Voice of the Church: The Ecumenical Council.* Greenwich, Conn., 1962.

Fox, Mary Harrita. *Peter E. Dietz, Labor Priest.* Notre Dame, Ind., 1953.

Garrison, Winfred E. *Catholicism and the American Mind.* Chicago, 1928.

——. *The Quest and Character of a United Church.* New York, 1957.

Gilleman, Gérard. *The Primacy of Charity in Moral Theology.* Translated by William F. Ryan and André Vachon. Westminster, Md., 1961.

Gonella, Guido. *A World to Reconstruct: Pius XII on Peace and Reconstruction.* Translated by T. Lincoln Bouscaren. Milwaukee, 1944.

Greenspun, William B., and Norgren, William A. (eds.). *Living Room Dialogues.* Glen Rock, N. J., 1965.

Guardini, Romano. *The Catholic Church and the Spirit of the Liturgy.* Translated by Ada Lane. New York, 1940.

Hales, E. E. Y. *Pope John and His Revolution.* New York, 1965.

Hanson, Richard, and Fuller, Reginald. *The Church of Rome: A Dissuasive.* London, 1948.

Häring, Bernard. *The Johannine Council.* Translated by Edwin G. Kaiser. New York, 1963.

——. *The Law of Christ.* Translated by Edwin G. Kaiser. 2 vols. Westminster, Md., 1963.

Hartmann, Albert. *Toleranz und christlicher Glaube.* Frankfurt a/M, 1955.

Hatch, Alden. *A Man Named John: The Life of Pope John XXIII.* New York, 1963.

Hofinger, Johannes. *The Art of Teaching Christian Doctrine.* Notre Dame, Ind., 1957.

Horton, Douglas. *Vatican Diary 1962.* Philadelphia, 1964.

Hudson, Winthrop S. *Religion in America.* New York, 1965.

———. *Understanding Roman Catholicism: A Guide to Papal Teaching for Protestants.* Philadelphia, 1959.

Jaeger, Lorenz. *The Ecumenical Council, the Church and Christendom.* Translated by A. V. Littledale. London, 1961.

John XXIII, Pope. *Journal of a Soul.* Translated by Dorothy White. New York, 1965.

Johnson, F. E. (ed.). *American Education and Religion.* New York, 1952.

Jones, Ilion T. *A Protestant Speaks His Mind.* Philadelphia, 1960.

Jungmann, Joseph A. *The Mass of the Roman Rite.* Translated by Charles K. Riepe. New York, 1959.

———. *Pastoral Liturgy.* Translated by Challoner Publications. New York, 1962.

Kaiser, Robert Blair. *Pope, Council and World.* New York, 1963.

Kerr, William Shaw. *A Handbook on the Papacy.* New York, 1951.

Kerwin, Jerome G. *Catholic Viewpoint on Church and State.* New York, 1960.

Kinsman, Frederick J. *Americanism and Catholicism.* New York, 1924.

Koenker, Ernest B. *The Liturgical Renaissance in the Roman Catholic Church.* Chicago, 1954.

Küng, Hans. *The Council, Reform and Reunion.* Translated by Cecily Hastings. New York, 1961.

———. *The Council in Action: Theological Reflections on the Second Vatican Council.* Translated by Cecily Hastings. New York, 1963.

———. *Structures of the Church.* Translated by Salvator Attanasio. New York, 1964.

———. Congar, Yves M-J, and O'Hanlon, Daniel (eds.). *Council Speeches of Vatican II.* Glen Rock, N.J., 1964.

La Farge, John. *Interracial Justice.* New York, 1937.

La Noue, George R. *Public Funds for Parochial Schools?* New York, 1963.

Lazzarini, Andrea. *Pope John XXIII.* Translated by Michael Hatwell. New York, 1959.

Lecler, Joseph. *L'Eglise et la souveraineté de l'état.* Paris, 1946.

Léonard, Augustin (ed.). *Tolérance et communauté humaine.* Tournai-Paris, 1952.

Leonard, William J. (ed.). *Liturgy for the People.* Milwaukee, 1963.

Levie, Jean. *The Bible, Word of God in Words of Men.* Translated by S. H. Tremen. New York, 1961.

Lindbeck, George A. (ed.). *Dialogue on the Way.* Minneapolis, 1965.

Loew, Jacques. *Mission to the Poorest*. Translated by Pamela Carswell. New York, 1950.

Lortz, Joseph. *The Reformation: A Problem for Today*. Translated by John C. Dwyer. Westminster, Md., 1964.

Love, Thomas T. *John Courtney Murray: Contemporary Church-State Theory*. New York, 1965.

Lubac, Henri de. *The Drama of Atheistic Humanism*. Translated by Edith M. Riley. New York, 1947.

———. *The Splendor of the Church*. Translated by Michael Mason. New York, 1956.

Lubell, Samuel. *The Future of American Politics*. New York, 1952.

MacGregor, Geddes. *The Vatican Revolution*. Boston, 1957.

Marshall, Charles C. *Governor Smith's American Catholicism*. New York, 1928.

———. *The Roman Catholic Church in the Modern State*. New York, 1928.

Marshall, Romey P., and Taylor, Michael J. *Liturgy and Christian Unity*. Englewood Cliffs, N.J., 1965.

Marty, Martin E. *The New Shape of American Religion*. New York, 1958.

Marx, Paul B. *The Life and Work of Virgil Michel*. Washington, 1957.

Masse, Benjamin L. *Justice for All*. Milwaukee, 1964.

McAvoy, Thomas T. *The Great Crisis in American Church History 1895–1900*. Chicago, 1957.

McCluskey, Neil G. *Catholic Viewpoint on Education*. New York, 1959.

McKenzie, John L. *The Two Edged Sword*. Milwaukee, 1957.

McManus, Frederick R. (ed.). *The Revival of the Liturgy*. New York, 1963.

McNaspy, C. J. *Our Changing Liturgy*. New York, 1966.

Mead, Sidney E. *The Lively Experiment*. New York, 1963.

Michonneau, Georges. *Revolution in a City Parish*. Westminster, Md., 1950.

Miller, Perry. *Errand into the Wilderness*. Cambridge, 1956.

Miller, Samuel H., and Wright, G. Ernest (eds.). *Ecumenical Dialogue at Harvard: The Roman Catholic-Protestant Colloquium*. Cambridge. 1964.

Moody, Joseph N., and Lawler, Justus George (eds.). *The Challenge of Mater et Magistra*. New York, 1963.

Mooneyham, W. Stanley (ed.). *The Dynamics of Christian Unity*. Grand Rapids, 1963.

Moore, Edmund A. *A Catholic Runs for President: The Campaign of 1928*. New York, 1956.

Moran, Gabriel. *Scripture and Tradition: A Survey of the Controversy*. New York, 1963.

Morgan, Everett J. *The Social Conscience of a Catholic.* Milwaukee. 1964.

Morrison, Charles C. *Can Protestantism Win America?* New York, 1948.

———. *The Unfinished Reformation.* New York, 1953.

Murphy, Richard T. A. *The Work of Père Lagrange.* Milwaukee, 1963.

Murray, John Courtney. *We Hold These Truths.* New York, 1960.

Nelson, Claud D. *The Vatican Council and All Christians.* New York, 1962.

Newman, John Henry Cardinal. *An Essay on the Development of Christian Doctrine.* London, 1897.

Nichols, James Hastings. *Democracy and the Churches.* Philadelphia, 1951.

———. *A Short Primer for Protestants.* New York, 1957.

Noonan, John T. *Contraception: A History of Its Treatment by Catholic Theologians and Canonists.* Cambridge, 1965.

Novak, Michael. *The Open Church: Vatican II, Act II.* New York, 1964.

O'Brien, John A. (ed.). *The White Harvest: A Symposium on Methods of Convert Making.* New York, 1927.

O'Dea, Thomas F. *American Catholic Dilemma.* New York, 1958.

O'Neill, Charles (ed.). *Ecumenism and Vatican II.* Milwaukee, 1964.

O'Neill, James M. *Catholicism and American Freedom.* New York, 1952.

———. *Religion and Education Under the Constitution.* New York, 1949.

Ong, Walter J. *American Catholic Crossroads.* New York, 1959.

———. *Frontiers in American Catholicism.* New York, 1957.

Oraison, Marc. *Love or Constraint?* Translated by Una Morissey, New York, 1961.

*Pacem in Terris.* New York, 1963.

Pawley, Bernard. *Looking at the Vatican Council.* London, 1962.

Pelikan, Jaroslav. *The Riddle of Roman Catholicism.* New York, 1959.

Pfeffer, Leo. *Church, State and Freedom.* Boston, 1953.

Pike, James A. *If You Marry Outside Your Faith.* New York, 1954.

———. *A Roman Catholic in the White House.* New York, 1960.

Poulat, Emile. *Histoire, dogme et critique dans la crise moderniste.* Paris, 1962.

Presbyter Anglicanus. *The Second Vatican Council.* New York, 1963.

Rahner, Karl. *The Church and the Sacraments.* Translated by William J. O'Hara. New York, 1963.

———. *Inquiries.* New York, 1964.

———. *Theological Investigations.* Translated by Cornelius Ernst and Karl H. Kruger. 2 vols. Baltimore, 1961–63.

———. and Ratzinger, Joseph. *The Episcopate and the Primacy.* Translated by Kenneth Barker and others. New York, 1963.

Ramsey, Paul. *The Limits of Nuclear War.* New York, 1963.

Riga, Peter. *Peace on Earth: A Commentary.* New York, 1964.

Roberts, Thomas D. *Contraception and Holiness.* New York, 1964.

Ryan, John A., and Boland, Francis J. *Catholic Principles of Politics.* New York, 1940.

Rynne, Xavier. *Letters from Vatican City.* New York, 1963.

Sanders, Thomas G. "A Comparison of Two Current American Roman Catholic Theories of the American Political System with Particular Reference to the Problem of Religious Liberty. Unpublished Ph.D. thesis (Columbia University Library).

Scharper, Philip (ed.). *American Catholics: A Protestant-Jewish View.* New York, 1959.

Schillebeeckx, Edward. *Christ, the Sacrament of the Encounter with God.* Translated by Paul Barrett. New York, 1963.

Schlesinger, Arthur M., Jr. *A Thousand Days: John F. Kennedy in the White House.* Boston, 1965.

Seldes, George. *The Catholic Crisis.* New York, 1939.

Shaughnessy, Gerald. *Has the Immigrant Kept the Faith?* New York, 1925.

Shields, Currin. *Democracy and Catholicism in America.* New York, 1958.

Shuster, George N. *The Catholic Spirit in America.* New York, 1928.

——— (ed.). *Catholicism in America.* New York, 1953.

Silcox, Claris Edwin, and Fisher, Galen M. *Catholics, Jews and Protestants.* New York, 1934.

Simpson, Alan. *Puritanism in Old and New England.* Chicago, 1964.

Skydsgaard, Kristen E. (ed.). *The Papal Council and the Gospel.* Minneapolis, 1961.

Sloyan, Gerald (ed.). *Shaping the Christian Message.* New York, 1958.

Smith, J. W., and Jamison, A. L. (eds.). *The Shaping of American Religion.* vol. I. Princeton, N.J., 1961.

Smith, Shelton H., Handy, Robert T., and Loetscher, Lefferts A. *American Christianity.* 2 vols. New York, 1960.

Sorensen, Theodore C. *Kennedy.* New York, 1965.

Spinka, Matthew. *The Quest for Church Unity.* New York, 1960.

Staff of *The Pope Speaks* (eds.). *The Encyclicals and Other Messages of John XXIII.* Washington, 1964.

Stahmer, Harold (ed.). *Religion and Contemporary Society.* New York, 1963.

Stokes, Anson Phelps. *Church and State in the United States.* 3 vols. New York, 1950.

Stuber, Stanley I. *How Protestants Differ from Roman Catholics.* New York, 1961.

———. *Primer on Roman Catholicism for Protestants.* New York, 1960.

Suhard, Emmanuel. *Growth or Decline?* Translated by James A. Corbett. South Bend, 1948.

Tavard, George. *The Catholic Approach to Protestantism.* New York, 1955.

*Therefore Choose Life.* Santa Barbara, 1965.

*To Live As Men: An Anatomy of Peace.* Santa Barbara, 1965.

Underwood, Kenneth W. *Protestant and Catholic: Religious and Social Interaction in an American Community.* Boston, 1957.

Vagaggini, Cipriano. *The Theological Dimensions of the Liturgy.* Translated by Leonard J. Doyle. Collegeville, Minn., 1959.

Van Dusen, Henry P. *One Great Ground of Hope.* Philadelphia, 1961.

Vawter, Bruce. *A Path Through Genesis.* New York, 1954.

Vidler, A. R. *A Century of Social Catholicism 1820–1920.* London, 1964.

Villain, Maurice. *L'Abbé Paul Couturier, apôtre de l'unité chrétienne.* Tournai, 1957.

Ward, Leo C. *Religion in All the Schools.* Notre Dame, Ind., 1960.

Weigel, Gustave. *A Catholic Primer on the Ecumenical Movement.* Westminster, Md., 1957.

Williams, Michael. *Catholicism and the Modern Mind.* New York, 1928.

———. *The Shadow of the Pope.* New York, 1932.

Yzermans, Vincent A. *A New Pentecost: Vatican Council II, Session I.* Westminster, Md., 1963.

*The following Protestant periodicals were systematically researched from 1958 through 1963.*

Baptist:              *Foundations* (Rochester, N.Y.)
                      *Missions* (Valley Forge, Pa.)
                      *Watchman-Examiner* (New York, N.Y.)

Southern Baptist:     *Baptist Program* (Nashville, Tenn.)
                      *Baptist Standard* (Dallas, Texas)
                      *Biblical Recorder* (Raleigh, N.C.)
                      *Journal of Church and State* (Waco, Texas)
                      *Southwestern Journal of Theology* (Ft. Worth, Texas)

Lutheran:             *Dialog* (Minneapolis, Minn.)
                      *Lutheran World* (Geneva, Switzerland)
                      *Lutheran Quarterly* (Gettysburg, Pa.)
                      *Lutheran Standard* (Minneapolis, Minn.)
                      *Lutheran* (Philadelphia, Pa.)
                      *Lutheran Witness* (St. Louis, Mo.).

Disciples:   *Christian* (St. Louis, Mo.)
*World Call* (Indianapolis, Ind.)

Presbyterian:   *Presbyterian Life* (Philadelphia, Pa.)
*Presbyterian Outlook* (Richmond, Va.)
*Presbyterian Survey* (Atlanta, Ga.)

United Church
of Christ:   *United Church Herald* (St. Louis, Mo.)

Methodist:   *Christian Advocate* (Park Ridge, Ill.)
*Motive* (Nashville, Tenn.)

Episcopal:   *Witness* (Dubuque, Iowa)
*Episcopalian* (Philadelphia, Pa.)
*Living Church* (Milwaukee, Wis.)
*Churchman* (St. Petersburg, Fla.)

Nondenomina-
tional:   *Union Seminary Quarterly Review* (New York, N.Y.)
*Religion in Life* (Nashville, Tenn.)
*Theology Today* (Princeton, N.J.)
*Christian Century* (Chicago, Ill.)
*Christianity and Crisis* (New York, N.Y.)
*Christianity Today* (Washington, D.C.)
*Christian Herald* (New York, N.Y.)
*Eternity* (Philadelphia, Pa.)
*United Evangelical Action* (Wheaton, Ill.)
*Moody Monthly* (Chicago, Ill.).

Protestant writings
in Catholic
journals:   *Cross Currents* (West Nyack, N.Y.)
*America* (New York, N.Y.)
*Commonweal* (New York, N.Y.)

# Index